Ec

& Galápagos

DREAM TRIP

ROBERT & DAISY KUNSTAETTER

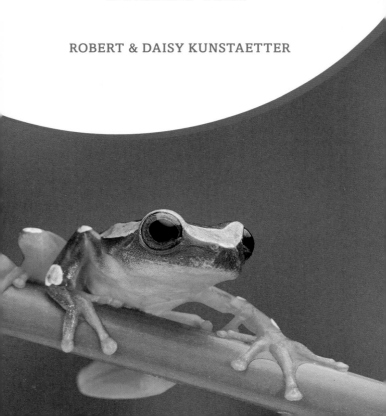

CONTENTS

THIS IS
ECUADOR

Ecuador is compact by South American standards, compact enough for you to have breakfast as you watch dawn break over the Amazon jungle canopy, lunch at the foot of a smoking snow-capped volcano and dinner amid the last rays of sunset over the Pacific Ocean. Within this small area, it boasts extraordinary diversity: geographical diversity ranging from an avenue of volcanoes straddling the equator, to rainforest, beaches and tropical islands; biological diversity, amongst the highest in the world, protected by 39 national parks and reserves; and cultural diversity, with 17 ethnically distinct indigenous groups.

With so much variety, Ecuador has something for everyone. Birdwatching, trekking, mountaineering, mountain biking, whitewater rafting, paragliding, and surfing are among the country's many privileged outdoor activities. Yet the draw is not only about hiking boots and adrenalin. Archaeology, art and local culture are also abundant and varied. The capital, Quito, and the southern highland city of Cuenca have two of the finest colonial districts in South America, an excellent selection of museums and a lively tourist scene.

Chimborazo

The smaller towns and villages of Ecuador offer the most authentic experience as well as the opportunity to share their traditions at fiestas and through community tourism. Indulge your senses at one of their many markets, with dizzying arrays of textiles, ceramics, carvings and other crafts, not to mention the plethora of domestic animals and cornucopia of fresh produce. They are all there for the local people but tourists are very welcome.

The Galápagos Islands, cradle and showcase of Darwin's theory of evolution, are the rich icing on the Ecuadorean cake. Fragile and expensive, the Galápagos are not for everyone, but if you are passionate about nature, they offer a once-in-a-lifetime experience worth saving for.

With so much to see and do throughout Ecuador, the two-week mainland routes described in this book are packed to the brim. If you can, we suggest you take additional time to enjoy the diversity of Ecuador at a more leisurely pace. You won't regret moving slower.

Ecuador is your dream trip and it is also our home. We are proud of its many wonders and concerned about their future. We warmly welcome you to share the sense of wonder that Ecuador can inspire and we ask you to please tread lightly here, so that the dream may continue.

Robert and Daisy

FIRST STEPS
PUTTING IT ALL TOGETHER

Ecuador is small enough to make travelling around easy, and varied enough to make almost any itinerary worthwhile.

Ecuador is small enough to make travelling around easy, and varied enough to make almost any itinerary worthwhile. Mix and match segments of the routes in this book to suit your pace, budget and taste. A visit to the Galápagos Islands is easily combined with any route but is not an indispensable part of a holiday in Ecuador.

Although there is ample domestic air service between main cities, road travel is the mainstay of transport. Buses are available on all routes but may not always be the most convenient option. For those with limited time, we recommend travelling some segments as part of a tour, arranging private transport with a tour agency, using shared taxis or vans, or hiring a car.

Quito is the point of arrival and departure for most visitors. Guayaquil, with good services and an airport closer to the city centre, is a sensible alternative if you prefer to avoid the altitude of the highlands or are heading directly to Galápagos. You can also arrive in Quito and depart from Guayaquil or vice versa. You could easily spend a week or more in Quito, enjoying sights, museums and nearby excursions. If, however, you are short on time or feel more comfortable in small towns and the countryside, then you can head out directly from Quito's new airport (opened in 2013) without ever entering the city.

Which regions of Ecuador you visit should depend on your interests. The northern and central Andes offer grand volcanic scenery, hiking, haciendas, highland indigenous culture and crafts. The Oriente jungle excels in mighty rivers, Amazon wildlife and adventure, providing a glimpse of its native people and their vanishing way of life. The Pacific Coast has good beaches, the opportunity to watch whales in season, and Isla de La Plata, which shares some marine creatures with Galápagos. The Galápagos Islands themselves are a UNESCO World Heritage Site, Ecuador's greatest treasure and one of the planet's foremost wildlife sanctuaries. Quito and Cuenca, also World Heritage Sites, have districts steeped in colonial art and architecture and, along with Guayaquil, offer a choice of museums, upmarket dining and accommodation.

It is not difficult to get off the tourist track in Ecuador, but you should speak some Spanish and have sufficient time and patience to accommodate unforeseen changes en route. You can head north to the Afro-Ecuadorean province of Esmeraldas; or south past Cuenca to Loja and the small towns of Vilcabamba, Zaruma and Zamora; or even set sail down the Río Napo bound for Peru and Brazil. Another way to get off the tourist track anywhere in Ecuador, is to take a sincere interest in Ecuadoreans. An evening spent chatting with the local family who runs your hotel or is vacationing there from Quito or Guayaquil, will provide more insights than keeping company with only fellow foreigners.

The Oriente jungle excels in mighty rivers, Amazon wildlife and adventure, providing a glimpse of its native people and their vanishing way of life.

→ DOING IT ALL

Quito → Otavalo → Mindo → Canoa → Bahía de Caráquez → Puerto López → Guayaquil → Galápagos → Guayaquil → Vilcabamba → Cuenca → Riobamba → Latacunga → Quilotoa → Chugchilán → Parque Nacional Cotopaxi → Quito → Papallacta → jungle lodge accessed from Lago Agrio or Coca → Tena → Misahuallí → Baños → Quito.

1 Capilla del Hombre **2** Fiesta in Cayambe **3** Rainforest **4** Black-breasted puffleg

DREAM TRIP 1
QUITO → NORTHERN HIGHLANDS → PACIFIC COAST

Best time to visit The highlands have spring-like temperatures all year, with warm days and cool nights. The rainy season in the mountains is October to May, but even then there are several hours of sunshine on most days. Along the coast, January to May is hottest and rainiest; From June to September it may be cool and misty in the morning. July and August are the months for whale watching. Ecuador is seldom crowded with foreign tourists but resort towns like Mindo and beaches such as Canoa fill with Ecuadoreans at weekends and on local holidays.

Quito (page 35), Ecuador's capital, sprawling at the foot of Volcán Pichincha and surrounded by snow-capped peaks, is sure to impress you. It has much to offer: colonial architecture, a variety of museums, beautiful panoramas, excellent cuisine, an active nightlife, traditional craft workshops and more. Many interesting excursions are within easy reach: the equator, nature reserves, hot springs, colonial haciendas, snow-capped volcanoes and Andean lakes. Allow three days for the city and to adjust to altitude, as it stands at 2850 m above sea level.

For the quintessential Andean experience, spend at least three days in the highlands north of Quito. Here there are beautiful mountains and lakes, colourful indigenous communities and an outstanding selection of crafts. Otavalo (page 58), best known for its markets, is a good base from which to explore this region. Take some time to meet the industrious people in one of the nearby

Allow three days for a taste of the city and to adjust to altitude, as it stands at 2850 m above sea level.

weavers' villages. Northwest of Otavalo, Cotacachi (page 63), centre for leather clothing and crafts, is the gateway to Laguna Cuicocha, a beautiful crater lake. Further north, outside the city of Ibarra (page 64) are San Antonio de Ibarra (page 65), where woodcarving is a fine art, and several other villages where beautiful embroidered tablecloths and blouses are made.

→GOING FURTHER

From Ibarra you can enjoy a short tourist train ride toward the coast, or continue further north to **Reserva Ecológica El Angel** where the velvet-leaved *frailejón* plants grow. → **page 66**

1 Church of San Francisco, Quito **2** Laguna Cuicocha **3** Blankets for sale in Otavalo **4** Statuesque *frailejones* in the Northern Highlands.

To the northwest of Quito lie the cloud forest-clad western slopes of Pichincha, a magnificent area of bird-rich nature reserves, pristine rivers and waterfalls. If travelling with private transport, make your way leisurely along the Ecoruta del Quinde (page 70), to one of the region's top-class lodges. If travelling by bus, head for Mindo (page 74), the main resort town in this area. You can easily spend three days here hiking to waterfalls, birdwatching, visiting a butterfly farm, tubing down a river, gliding along a zipline, or just relaxing and watching the birds fly by. Continuing west from Mindo to the lowlands, head for Pedernales on the coastal highway, via Santo Domingo de los Tsáchilas (page 79).

Ecuador's coastline, verdant in the north and gradually drier to the south, offers a wide range of options. Those with plenty of time are encouraged to explore it at leisure. In addition to lovely beaches, some with excellent surfing, there are life-rich mangroves, hills covered in dry tropical forest, archaeological sites and some of the country's best cuisine. For just a glimpse, our itinerary takes you along the central coast from Pedernales south to Guayaquil.

Ecuador's coastline, verdant in the north and gradually drier to the south, offers a wide range of options. Those with plenty of time are encouraged to explore it at leisure.

1 Sparkling violetear hummingbird **2** Mindo **3** Breaching humpback whale **4** Beach at Mompiche

→ **GOING FURTHER**

North of Pedernales lies the verdant province of **Esmeraldas**, home to the country's Afro-Ecuadorean population. Here are the lovely surfing beach of Mompiche, the party beach of Atacames and the endangered forests of the Chocó bioregion.
→ **page 80**

We suggest spending two nights at the seemingly endless beach of Canoa (page 78) or the nearby eco-city of Bahía de Caráquez (page 79), from where you can visit mangroves, frigate bird nesting grounds and the Chirije archaeological site. Continuing south, you go by the port city of Manta (from where you could fly back to Quito) and to the fishing town of Puerto López (page 82), the access to Parque Nacional Machalilla (page 83). If you have time for only one stop, especially if you are not going to Galápagos, you should allow two days for visiting Machalilla. The unsurpassed beauty of Los Frailes, a horseshoe-shaped beach surrounded by forest-covered promontories, the wildlife on and around Isla de la Plata and the opportunity to see humpback whales from June to September, make it the best park to visit on the coast of Ecuador.

Beyond Puerto López you continue along the scenic coastal road by several beach towns, including the popular surfing spot of Montañita (page 84), or along an inland route to Guayaquil (page 88), Ecuador's main port and largest and most vibrant city.

The unsurpassed beauty of Los Frailes, the wildlife on and around Isla de la Plata and the opportunity to see humpback whales from June to September, make Parque Nacional Machalilla the best park to visit on the coast of Ecuador.

Esmeraldas
Atacames
Chocó Bioregion

Reserva Ecológica El Angel ◆

Mompiche
Cojimíes

4 *Laguna Cuicocha*
Ibarra

Otavalo

3

Pedernales

6 Mindo

5

Ecoruta del Quinde

■ QUITO

1 **2**

Santo Domingo de los Tsáchilas

7
Canoa

Bahía de Caráquez

Manta

8
Isla de la Plata

Puerto López

9 ◆ *Parque Nacional Machalilla*

Montañita

10
Guayaquil

N

40 km
40 miles

1

1 Malecón 2000, Guayaquil **2** Quito viewed from El Panecillo

→ WISH LIST

1 Explore Quito's colonial heart on a walking tour. **2** For a grand overview of Quito, ride the Teleférico, head for the top of El Panecillo or Parque Itchimbía, or climb inside the Basílica's bell tower. **3** Be amazed at Otavalo's craft market and, if you are there on Saturday, don't miss the produce and animal markets. **4** Visit the beautiful crater lake of Cuicocha. **5** Get up early to enjoy the dawn chorus of birds along the Ecoruta del Quinde. **6** Visit at least one of the lovely waterfalls around Mindo and stop at a butterfly farm along the way. **7** Stroll along Canoa's long beach or, for a bird's eye view, go paragliding above it. **8** Visit Isla de La Plata, best June to September for whale watching, but worthwhile year round. **9** Visit the Salango Archaeological Museum near Puerto López. **10** Stroll along the breezy Malecón 2000, Guayaquil's popular riverfront promenade.

DREAM TRIP 2
QUITO → RIOBAMBA → CUENCA → VILCABAMBA

Best time to visit The weather in most of the highlands south of Quito is like that described for Dream Trip 1 (page 8). The best months for outdoor activities such as hiking and climbing are June to August and November to January. But each valley has its own microclimate. Baños is usually dry from November to April, and wet from May to October, when it can get quite chilly.

An impressive roll call of towering peaks lines the route south of Quito (page 35), appropriately named the Avenue of the Volcanoes by the 18th-century explorer Alexander von Humboldt. Given enough time, you could spend several days in this area: stay in a hacienda and learn about the life of the *chagra*, the Ecuadorean cowboy. You can also trek or go horse riding, climb a volcano or bike down its slopes.

After getting to know the capital, the first obligatory stop is spectacular Parque Nacional Cotopaxi (page 98); arrange a tour unless you are hiring a vehicle. Spend the night at one of the inns near Cotopaxi or in the colonial city of Latacunga (page 101). To the west of Latacunga is Laguna Quilotoa a magnificent turquoise-green crater lake. It is in Reserva Ecológica Los Ilinizas and part of the Quilotoa

1 Cotopaxi 2 Quilotoa 3 Bungee jumping near Baños

Circuit (page 102), a scenic loop of indigenous villages which could be explored at liesure in about four days. For just a glimpse, our itinerary allows for one night at one village: either Quilotoa or Chugchilán.

To warm from the chill of Cotopaxi and Quilotoa, head southeast to the resort town of Baños (page 107) and indulge yourself in the hot springs or a spa, followed by a good meal at one of the many restaurants and outdoor cafés. Don't miss Volcán Tungurahua, especially if it is active. If you are also feeling active, then you can hike, bike, go horse riding or take in some of the many adrenalin sports on offer. Baños merits at least two nights but some visitors stay for weeks.

Back on the Avenue of the Volcanoes, continue south to the market centre of Riobamba (page 110), at the foot of Chimborazo (page 112), Ecuador's highest summit at 6310 m. Riobamba is a good base from which to explore the Central Highlands, its beautiful mountains and indigenous communities. The city is also the hub of the Ecuadorean railway and the jumping-off point for the famous Devil's Nose train ride (page 112). If you catch the train out of Alausí (south of Riobamba) in the morning, then you can continue the same day to Ingapirca (page 123), the country's most important Inca site, en route to Cuenca. To do it more gradually, you can spend a night in Alausí and another in Igapirca, or visit Ingapirca as an excursion from Cuenca.

Cuenca (page 118) is Ecuador's third-largest and most congenial city. We suggest at least three days in Cuenca, but you could easily spend a week here between exploring its colonial centre and visiting nearby towns and Parque Nacional Cajas (page 124); longer if you also decide to stay for Spanish lessons, as many travellers do. If you don't have time to continue south, there are flights from Cuenca to Quito and Guayaquil.

1 Traditional dancing in Pujili, near Latacunga 2 Panama hats 3 Ingaparica 4 Devil's Nose train 5 Saraguro

South of Cuenca are Saraguro (page 125), home of the southern-most indigenous group in the highlands, the city of Loja (page 126) and Vilcabamba (page 127), the rainbow at the end of your dream trip. Vilcabamba is a delightful place to unwind, stroll, ride a horse or bicycle in the countryside, or just sit in a café by the main park and watch the world go by. Nearby is spectacular Parque Nacional Podocarpus (page 127). Like Baños, we recommend two nights in Vil-cabamba, but here some visitors stay forever.

Catamayo airport, two hours from Vil-cabamba, has flights to Quito and Guayaquil; there is also ample bus service from Loja.

We recommend two nights in Vilcabamba, but here some visitors stay forever.

→ **GOING FURTHER**

In the western foothills, five hours by bus from Loja, is the colonial gold-mining town of **Zaruma**, a true off-the-beaten-path gem. → **page 129**

QUITO

Reserva Ecológica
Los Ilinizas

1 ▲ Cotopaxi

Chugchilán
2 Laguna
Quilotoa

Latacunga

4

3

5 Baños

Chimborazo ▲

Tungurahua

Guaranda

Riobamba

6

Devil's Nose ⊙ Alausí

7

Parque
Nacional ♦
Cajas 9

Ingaparica

Cuenca

8

Saraguro

Zaruma

Parque
Nacional
♦ Podocarpus

Vilcabamba 10

N

50 km
50 miles

1 Visit the perfect cone of Cotopaxi, one of the highest active volcanoes in the world. **2** Walk down to the shore of beautiful Laguna Quilotoa. **3** Visit the Pailón del Diablo (Devil's Cauldron) waterfall from Baños. **4** Take in at least one indigenous market in or around Latacunga or Riobamba. **5** Go mountain biking on the slopes of Chimborazo. **6** Ride the rails over the Devil's Nose. **7** Don't miss Ingapirca, the finest Inca archaeological site in the Ecuador. **8** Stroll the streets of Cuenca's colonial centre and don't miss its immense blue-domed cathedral. **9** Visit some of the pristine lakes in Parque Nacional Cajas (there are more than 230 of them), only 29 km from Cuenca. **10** Go horse riding in the hills around Vilcabamba.

1 Ingapirca 2 Pailón del Diablo, near Baños 3 *Chagras* (Ecuadorean cowboys) near Cotopaxi 4 Cuenca Cathedral

DREAM TRIP 3
QUITO → ORIENTE → BAÑOS

Best time to visit As in
the rest of the Amazon
Basin, heavy rain can
fall at any time, but it is
usually wettest from March
to September. Likewise,
temperatures and humidity
are high year-round and
there are often biting
insects. Jungle lodges may
be more heavily booked
during the North American
and European holiday
seasons: July to September.

East of the Andes the hills fall away to the vast green carpet of
Amazonia. Some of this beautiful wilderness remains unspoiled and
sparsely populated, yet the Ecuadorean jungle has the advantage of
being easily accessible and tourist infrastructure here is well developed.
From Quito (page 35) you can fly in less than an hour to Lago Agrio or
Coca, gateways for the Cuyabeno Wildlife Reserve (page 140) and the
Lower Río Napo (page 140), respectively. These two areas have most
of the best-known jungle lodges in the country, surrounded by
tracts of primary rainforest teeming with life. Although not cheap,
this is Ecuadorean jungle tourism at its finest.

If you choose to travel overland instead of flying, then you can
also experience the spectacular transition from the Andes to the
Amazon. After visiting Quito head over the Eastern Cordillera to
Papallacta (page 136), the country's best developed thermal baths
in magnificent surroundings. This itinerary suggests spending the

1 Harpy eagle   2 Papallacta thermal baths   3 Río Napo

night here, but you could easily take several days to explore the area. Further east is Baeza (page 136), where the road divides; one branch leads northeast to Lago Agrio, the other south to Tena, with a branch going east to Coca. Those with extra time may wish to spend a couple of days in Baeza to hike or go kayaking. Regardless of your destination, don't miss Cascada San Rafael (page 137), Ecuador's highest waterfall, along the Lago Agrio road, and the active Volcán Reventador (page 137) nearby.

Regardless of your destination, don't miss Cascada San Rafael, Ecuador's highest waterfall.

→ GOING FURTHER

Sail through the jungle along the **lower Río Napo**, to the Peruvian border and beyond; it's a long, challenging and unforgettable journey.
→ page 139

DREAM TRIP 3
QUITO → ORIENTE → BAÑOS

Whether you reach them by air or road, it is the steamy oil towns of Lago Agrio (page 137) and Coca (page 140) which provide access to the jungle lodges. You can overnight at one of these towns, or arrive early in the morning to catch your tour and head straight for the jungle; this usually involves a long canoe ride. Most lodges offer excellent four-day all-inclusive packages but you can arrange to stay longer if you wish. There is also a live-aboard tourist vessel offering four-day cruises on the Río Napo. After your jungle tour, you could fly back to Quito or on to Guayaquil, but a good option is to travel to the jungle by air and return by road, or vice versa. Most roads linking the highlands and jungle are fully paved and bus services are frequent.

To continue overland from Coca or Lago Agrio, head for Tena via Parque Nacional Sumaco (page 140), with excellent birdwatching and a jungle-clad volcano to climb. Tena (page 141) is a small city, popular with travellers as a base for whitewater sports. There are also good opportunities for ethno-tourism in the area. If the big-name jungle lodges mentioned above do not suit your budget, then you can get a taste for the jungle from the laid-back riverside town of Puerto Misahuallí (page 143) or lodges on the Upper Río Napo (page 149), all reached from Tena. Although this is a pleasant area, it has seen more human impact and you cannot expect to see as much fauna as downriver. Count on at least two nights in this area.

To relax in a refreshingly cooler climate after the jungle, connect with Dream Trip 2 in Baños (page 107), from where you can return to Quito or go to Guayaquil for flights.

1 Whitewater rafting on Río Pastaza 2 Military macaw 3 Early morning on Río Napo

→ GOING FURTHER

Visit the less travelled Southern Oriente around **Macas** or **Zamora**. Here are the lowland sections of Parque Nacional Sangay and Parque Nacional Podocarpus, as well as the spectacular Alto Nangaritza Gorge and the excellent Kapawi Ecolodge and Reserve (accessed by air from Quito).
→ **page 150**

3

N

50 km
50 miles

Volcán Reventador

QUITO

Papallacta   Baeza

Cascada San Rafael

Parque Nacional Sumaco

Lago Agrio

Reserva Faunística Cuyabeno

Coca

Río Napo

Tena

Río Napo

Puerto Misahuallí

Baños

Puyo

Macas

To Zamora →

PERU

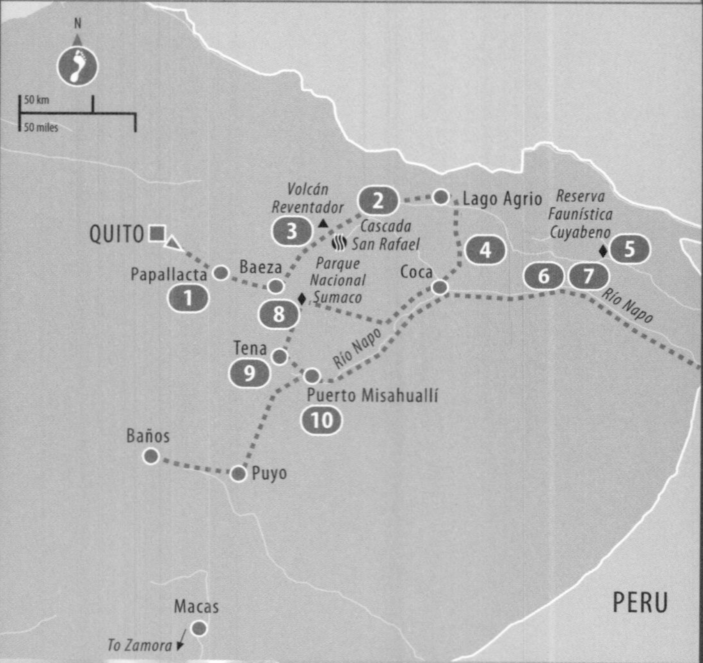

1 Volcán Reventador **2** Cascada San Rafael

1 Enjoy a sunset soak in Papallacta's thermal baths, within sight of snow-covered Volcán Antisana. **2** Visit Cascada San Rafael, Ecuador's highest waterfall at 145 m. **3** Hike to the base of Volcán Reventador, where you might catch a glimpse of its steaming lava flows. **4** Get a bird's eye view of the jungle from the canopy tower or walkway of your jungle lodge. **5** Paddle a canoe in Cuyabeno Wildlife Reserve. **6** Ask the boatman to turn off the engine and float down a small jungle stream **7** Experience a night-time visit to the jungle to get to know a completly different set of creatures. **8** Go birdwatching in Parque Nacional Sumaco. **9** Experience the thrill of whitewater rafting from Tena **10** Enjoy a laid-back visit to the 'near jungle' from Puerto Misahuallí.

2

DREAM TRIP
GALAPAGOS ISLANDS

Best time to visit The Galápagos are hot from December to May, when heavy but brief showers are possible. From June to November is the cooler misty *garúa* season, and evenings at sea can be chilly all year. The sea is cold from July to October; underwater visibility is best between January and March. Ocean temperatures are usually higher to the east and lower at the western end of the archipelago. Cruises are heavily booked in high season: June to September and December to January.

Galápagos is the main reason for many a visit to Ecuador. It is easily combined with any of the mainland Dream Trips described in this book. Access is only by air, from Quito or Guayaquil to either Baltra or San Cristóbal islands.

The Galápagos National Park and Marine Reserve include 97% of the islands' land area and 100% of the surrounding ocean. Within the park there are some 60 visitor sites, each with defined trails, so the impact of visitors to this fragile environment is minimized. These sites can only be visited with a national park guide, as part of a cruise or tour. Each visitor site has been carefully chosen to show the different flora and fauna and, due to the high level of endemism, nearly every trail has flora and fauna that can be seen nowhere else in the world.

The itineraries of tourist boats are strictly regulated in order to avoid crowding at the visitor sites and some sites are periodically closed by the park authorities in order to allow them to recover from the impact of tourism. Certain sites are only open to smaller

1 Sally Lightfoot crab 2 Pelican in the mangroves 3 South Plaza Island 4 Courtship dance of the blue-footed booby

boats and, additionally, limited to a maximum number of visits per month. The remaining 3% of Galápagos which is not national park is made up of towns and agricultural zones on four populated islands: Santa Cruz (page 170), San Cristóbal (page 171), Isabela (page 172) and Floreana (page 173). The populated parts of these islands are the only ones which may be visited independently, but there are also large restricted areas of national park land on these populated islands.

Due to the high level of endemism, nearly every trail has flora and fauna that can be seen nowhere else in the world.

DREAM TRIP
GALÁPAGOS ISLANDS

The animals have little instinctive fear of man, providing the most amazing photo opportunities.

There are various options for touring in Galápagos (page 160), but we recommend a seven-day live-aboard cruise as the very best way to make the most of this once-in-a-lifetime opportunity. Booking in advance is recommended, especially for the high season. Cruise vessels have capacities ranging from eight to 100 passengers and the type of experience varies accordingly. Larger boats take a longer time to disembark and re-embark people, while the smaller boats have a more lively motion, which is important if you are prone to seasickness. Many other factors come into play but the quality of most vessels is usually excellent. Almost all have Spanish- and English-speaking guides; you must make advance arrangements if you prefer guiding in another language.

While cruising, each day starts early and schedules are full. Your boat will probably have reached its destination before breakfast. After eating, you disembark for a morning on the island. Snorkelling is between the morning excursion and lunch. The midday meal is taken on board because no food is allowed on the islands. There might be a second visit to the same island after lunch or you'll move on to the next island for the afternoon excursion. After the day's activities, there is time to clean up, have a drink and relax before the briefing for the next day and supper.

1 Sea lion pup 2 Land iguana at sunset 3 A shoal of snapper

Whatever vessel you sail with, the islands' unique wildlife will be the focus of the voyage, often surpassing all expectations. You can snorkel with penguins, sea lions and marine iguanas, watch 200-kg tortoises lumbering through giant cactus forest, and enjoy the courtship display of the blue-footed booby and magnificent frigate bird, all in startling close-up. The animals have little instinctive fear of man, providing the most amazing photo opportunities. Underwater life is every bit as spectacular as the creatures on land and in the air, and Galápagos has some of the world's best dive sites (page 166).

Underwater life is every bit as spectacular as the creatures on land and in the air, and Galápagos has some of the world's best dive sites.

To Charles Darwin & Teodoro Wolf Islands ↑   Pinta

Marchena   Genovesa

Wolf ▲

Fernandina   Darwin ▲

La Cumbre ▲

Santiago   Bartolomé

Rábida   Sombrero Chino

Alcedo ▲   North Seymour
Baltra (South Sey

Isabela   Pinzón   Santa Rosa   Santa Cr

El Chato

Tortoise Reserve   Charles Darwin
Research Statio

Puerto Ayora

Sierra Negra ▲   Santo Tomás   Santa Fe

▲ Cerro Azul

Muro de las
Lágrimas   Puerto Villamil

Floreana

Puerto Velasco Ibarra ● ○ Asilo de la Paz

1 Waved albatross taking off   2 Galápagos tortoise   3 Parrotfish   4 Male frigate bird

1 The galápago's (giant tortoise's) smile. 2 The marine iguana squirting salt water as it clears its nostrils. 3 The land iguana munching on a cactus leaf. 4 The beach-master male sea lion patrolling its harem. 5 The wings of the flightless cormorant. 6 The tropicbird's tail. 7 The take-off and landing of the waved albatross. 8 The spectacle of boobies diving. 9 The male frigate bird's pouch. 10 The kaleidoscopic colours of the parrotfish.

Pacific Ocean

San Cristóbal
uerto ▲ Cerro Brujo
uerizo ▲ Cerro San Joaquín
oreno ⚓ El Progreso

N

20 km
20 miles

Española

Good Friday procession in Quito

DREAM TRIP 1
Quito→Northern Highlands→Pacific Coast 14 days

Quito 3 nights, page 35

Cochasquí en route, page 57
By road from Quito (1½ hrs)

Cayambe en route, page 58
By road from Quito (1½ hrs)

Otavalo 3 nights, page 58
Shared taxi or bus from Quito (2½ hrs) or
tour taking in attractions along the way

Cotacachi and Laguna Cuicocha
day trip, page 63
By road from Otavalo (25 mins)

Ibarra and around day trip, page 64
By road from Otavalo (40 mins)

Ecoruta del Quinde en route, page 70
By road from Quito (3 hrs) or Otavalo (5 hrs)

Mindo 3 nights, page 74
Bus from Otavalo (5 hrs; change in Quito),
tour or private transport

Santo Domingo de los Tsáchilas
en route, page 76
By road from Mindo (3½ hrs)

Pedernales en route, page 78
By road from Santo Domingo de los
Tsáchilas (3 hrs)

Canoa or Bahía de Caráquez 2 nights,
pages 78 and 79
Bus from Mindo (8½ hrs; change
in Santo Domingo and Pedernales;
from Pedernales to Canoa there are
also shared taxis) or private transport

Manta en route, page 81
By road from Canoa (3 hrs)

**Puerto López and Parque Nacional
Machalilla** 2 nights, page 82
Bus from Bahía de Caráquez
(6 hrs; change in Manta)

Montañita en route, page 84
By road from Puerto López (1 hr)

Guayaquil 1 night, page 88
Bus from Puerto López (4 hrs)

From Guayaquil there are 3 options:
bus/flight to Quito (8 hrs/45 mins);
flight to Galápagos (45 mins);
international flight home

GOING FURTHER

El Chota page 66
Train/bus from Ibarra (2 hrs with stops/
30 mins)

Reserva Ecológica El Angel page 66
Bus from Ibarra to El Angel (1½ hrs),
taxi to El Voladero (30 mins)

Esmeraldas page 80
Bus from the Mindo junction (4 hrs)
or Santo Domingo (3 hrs)

DREAM TRIP 1
Quito → Northern Highlands → Pacific Coast

From the colonial splendor of Ecuador's capital, through the indigenous craft towns of the northern Andes, the lush cloud forests of the western slopes and the lovely beaches of the central coast, to the bustling port city of Guayaquil, this route is a fine sampler. It starts in Quito, the world's first city to be named a UNESCO World Heritage Site, proud of its unmatched colonial district and lovely mountain setting. The route continues north with views of the magnificent snow-capped Volcán Cayambe to Otavalo, home to an industrious group of indigenous people and one of the largest and most colourful craft markets on the continent. Nearby are scenic lakes and countless villages, each specializing in its own particular craft.

The route then continues to the northwest of Quito, descending along the Ecoruta del Quinde (Route of the Hummingbird) to the resort-village of Mindo, an area with ample opportunities for hiking, birdwatching, whitewater and other adventure sports amid the lush cloud forest. Further west are the Pacific lowlands, covering a third of Ecuador's total area; they offer great natural beauty, diversity, a rich cultural heritage and excellent food. There are beaches for every taste along the coast. This itinerary takes in the popular beach resort of Canoa, the nearby city of Bahía de Caráquez and further south Puerto López, centre for humpback whale watching from June through September, and access to Parque Nacional Machalilla year-round. The park protects an important area of tropical dry forest, pre-Columbian ruins, coral reef and a wide variety of wildlife. Isla de la Plata, located in the park, is a more affordable alternative to Galápagos for seeing marine life. The route ends in Guayaquil, Ecuador's largest city and main port.

QUITO

Few cities have a setting to match that of Quito, the second highest capital in Latin America after La Paz. The city is set in a hollow at 2850 m, at the foot of the volcano Pichincha (4794 m). Quito's charm lies in its well preserved colonial centre – the Centro Histórico *as it's known, where pastel-coloured houses and ornate churches line a warren of steep and narrow cobbled streets, dipping to deep ravines. From the top of Cerro Panecillo, 183 m above the city level, there is a fine view of the city below and the encircling cones of volcanoes and other mountains.*

North of the colonial centre is modern Quito, the city's alter-ego, with tall buildings, traffic- and smog-filled avenues, parks and cosmopolitan dining. Here you'll find Quito's main tourist and business area: banks, tour agencies, airlines, language schools, smart shops, restaurants, bars, cafés, and a huge variety of hotels in the districts known a La Mariscal and La Carolina. Quito's working-class neighbourhoods stretch to the south of colonial Quito, while suburban sprawl fills the valleys to the east. In the far north and south are small industrial zones.

Quito is surrounded by scenic countryside well worth visiting on one-day or multi-day excursions. There are nature reserves, wonderful thermal baths, mountains to climb, quaint villages and – of course – the monument to the equator, all within easy reach of the city. The western slopes of Pichincha, also close at hand, are covered in beautiful cloud forest where nature lovers can indulge their taste for adventure.

Quito's spectacular location and the wonderful revival of its colonial centre are matched only by the complex charm of the capital's people, the 'Chullas Quiteños' as they call themselves; the term defies translation but is akin to 'real Quitonians'. These are not the colourfully dressed inhabitants of highland villages, tending crops and haggling with tourists to sell their crafts. They are young professionals, office workers and government bureaucrats, conservatively attired and courteous to a fault, and they form the backbone of a very urban society. You will see them going out for lunch with colleagues during the week, making even a cheap almuerzo seem like a formal occasion. You will also find them in the city's bars and clubs at weekends, letting their hair down with such gusto that they seem like entirely different people.

→ ARRIVING IN QUITO

GETTING THERE

Air Mariscal Sucre airport, opened in 2013, is in Tababela, about 30 km northeast of the city, off Highway E-35 (T02-395 4200, www.quiport.com). The tourist information office (Arrivals level, T02-281 8363, open 24 hours), will assist with hotel bookings. Set taxi rates to different zones of the city are posted by Arrivals (US$24.50 to La Mariscal, US$26 to colonial Quito); taxi rates from the city to the airport are about 12% cheaper. **Aero Servicios** express bus, T02-604 3500, runs every 30 minutes, 24 hours per day, between the new airport and the old airport in northern Quito, US$8; taking a taxi from the old airport to your hotel is recommended. Regional buses with limited stops, run every 15 minutes, 0500-2230, between the airport and Terminal Quitumbe in the south and Terminal Río Coca in the north, US$2. **Trans-Rabbit** (T02-290 2690) or **Achupallas** (T02-330 1493) van services are good value for groups (to La Mariscal: US$30 for one to three passengers, US$5 per additional person; to colonial Quito: US$35 for one to three passengers). Note there is only one access road from the city to the airport and traffic is congested. It may take as much as two hours to reach the airport, allow enough time. Additional access roads are under construction in 2013. If going to the airport from other cities, take a bus that bypasses Quito along highway E-35 (available from Baños, Ambato and Ibarra), get off at the airport roundabout and take the regional bus 4.5 km from there. If coming from the east (Papallacta, Baeza or Oriente), go as far as Pifo and transfer to the regional bus there.

Bus Long-distance terminals are at the extreme north and south edges of the city, see Getting around, below.

MOVING ON
Two alternative roads lead from Quito to **Otavalo** (page 60), two hours north of the capital; if you are driving or taking a tour, we suggest going via Cochasquí (page 57) and returning via Cayambe (page 58) or viceversa. Buses to Otavalo leave from Terminal Carcelén and **Taxis Lagos** (T02-256599) offer shared taxi service on this route. **Mindo** (page 74), two hours northwest of Quito, is reached either via the Ecoruta Paseo del Quinde (page 70) or via the new route (Calacalí–La Independencia, page 71). Buses to Mindo take the latter route and leave from Estación La Ofelia in northern Quito. The Ecoruta Paseo del Quinde requires private transport: either hiring a car or taking a tour or transfer from one of the lodges in this area or from a tour operator.

On Dream Trip 2, **Latacunga** (see page 101) is two hours south of Quito. In order to visit Cotopaxi (see page 98) along the way, you must take a tour or drive. Buses to Latacunga leave from Terminal Quitumbe; **Servicio Express** offers shared taxi service. There is also a tourist train Thursday-Sunday (see www.ecuadorbytrain.com).

On Dream Trip 3, **Papallacta** (page 136), two hours from the city to the east, is also best reached with a tour or driving. The **Termas de Papallacta Resort** also offers private van service, convenient for groups. Buses bound for Tena or Lago Agrio, which depart from Terminal Quitumbe, and buses to Baeza, which depart from La Marín, near the colonial city, pass near the village of Papallacta, from where you can take a taxi.

ORIENTATION
Quito is a long, narrow city, stretching from north to south for almost 47 km, and east to west for only 3-5 km. The best way to get oriented is to look for Pichincha, the mountain which lies to the west of the city. El Panecillo hill is a landmark at the south end of colonial Quito. The street numbering system is based on N (Norte), E (Este), S (Sur), Oe (Oeste), plus a number for each street and a number for each building, however, an older system of street numbers is also still in use. Note that, because of Quito's altitude and notorious air pollution, visitors may feel some discomfort: slow your pace for the first 48 hours.

The areas of most interest to visitors are the colonial city, with its many churches, historical monuments, museums and some hotels and restaurants; La Mariscal or Mariscal Sucre district, east from Avenida 10 de Agosto to Avenida 12 de Octubre, and north from Avenida Patria to Avenida Orellana, where you'll find many hotels, restaurants, bars, clubs, tour operators and some banks; and the environs of Parque La Carolina, north of La Mariscal as far as Avenida Naciones Unidas and from Avenida 10 de Agosto east to Avenida Eloy Alfaro, where the newer hotels, restaurants, main banking district, airline offices and a number of shopping malls are located.

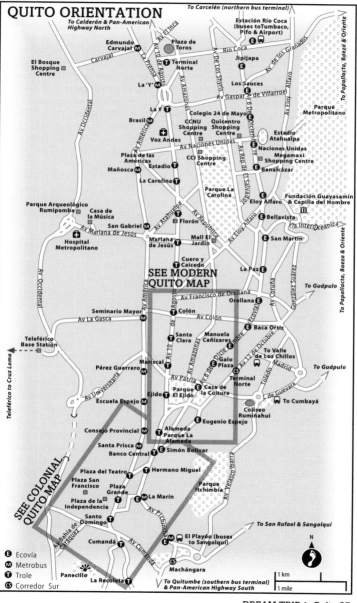

QUITO ORIENTATION

To Carcelén (northern bus terminal)

To Calderón & Pan-American Highway North

Estación Río Coca (buses to Tumbaco, Pifo & Airport)

Edmundo Carvajal Ⓜ

Plaza de Toros

Río Coca

El Bosque Shopping Centre

Jipijapa

Terminal Norte Ⓣ

La 'Y' Ⓜ

Los Sauces

Av Gaspar de Villarroel

La Y Ⓣ

Colegio 24 de Mayo Ⓔ

Parque Metropolitano

Brasil Ⓜ

CCNU Shopping Centre

Quicentro Shopping Centre

Voz Andes

Av Naciones Unidas

Estadio Atahualpa

Naciones Unidas Ⓔ

Plaza de las Américas

CCI Shopping Centre

Megamaxi Shopping Centre

Mañosca Ⓜ

Estadio Ⓣ

Benalcázar Ⓔ

La Carolina Ⓣ

Parque La Carolina

Fundación Guayasamín & Capilla del Hombre

Parque Arqueológico Rumipamba

Casa de la Música

Eloy Alfaro Ⓔ

San Gabriel

El Florón Ⓣ

Bellavista Ⓔ

Av Mariana de Jesús

Hospital Metropolitano

Mariana de Jesús Ⓣ

Mall El Jardín

Via Interoceánica

San Martín Ⓔ

Cuero y Caicedo

SEE MODERN QUITO MAP

La Paz Ⓔ

To Guápulo

Teleférico Base Station

Seminario Mayor Ⓜ

Av Francisco de Orellana

Orellana Ⓔ

Av La Gasca

Colón Ⓣ

Av Colón

Baca Ortiz Ⓔ

Teleférico to Cruz Loma

Santa Clara Ⓣ

Manuela Cañizares

To Valle de Los Chillos

Mariscal Ⓣ

Galo Plaza Ⓖ

Madrid

To Guápulo

Pérez Guerrero

Av Patria

Terminal Norte

Ejido Ⓣ

Parque El Ejido

Casa de la Cultura

To Cumbayá

Escuela Espejo

Coliseo Rumiñahui

Consejo Provincial Ⓜ

Alameda Ⓔ Parque La Alameda

Eugenio Espejo Ⓔ

Santa Prisca

Banco Central Ⓣ

Simón Bolívar Ⓣ

Plaza del Teatro Ⓣ

Hermano Miguel Ⓣ

Parque Itchimbía

Plaza San Francisco

Plaza Grande

La Marín Ⓜ Ⓣ

SEE COLONIAL QUITO MAP

Plaza de la Independencia

Santo Domingo Ⓣ

To San Rafael & Sangolquí

Cumandá Ⓣ

El Playón (buses to Sangolquí) Ⓜ Ⓔ

Machángara

N

Ⓔ Ecovía
Ⓜ Metrobus
Ⓣ Trole
Ⓖ Corredor Sur

Panecillo

La Recoleta Ⓣ

To Quitumbe (southern bus terminal) & Pan-American Highway South

1 km

1 mile

GETTING AROUND

Both colonial Quito and La Mariscal in modern Quito can be explored on foot, but getting between the two requires some form of public transport.

Taxi Using taxis is the best option; it is convenient and cheap, starting at US$1. Authorized taxis display a unit number on the windshield, the driver's photograph and have a working meter. They are safer and cheaper than unauthorized taxis. Expect to pay US$1-2 more at night when the meter may not be used. At night it is safer to use a radio taxi; these have black markings in front, for example **Taxi Americano**, T02-222 2333 or **City Taxi**, T02-263 3333. Make sure they give you the taxi number so that you get the correct vehicle, some radio taxis are unmarked. To hire a taxi by the hour costs from US$8 in the city, more out of town. For trips outside Quito, agree the fare beforehand, about US$70-85 a day. Outside luxury hotels cooperative taxi drivers have a list of agreed excursion prices.

Bus **Local** Quito has four parallel mass transit lines running from north to south on exclusive lanes, covering almost the length of the city: Trole, Ecovía, Metrobus and Corredor Sur. There are several transfer stations where you can switch from one line to another without cost. Feeder bus lines (*alimentadores*) go from the terminals to outer suburbs. Within the city the fare is US$0.25; the combined fare to some suburbs is US$0.40. There are also regular city buses. Public transit is not designed for carrying heavy luggage and is often crowded. Outer suburbs are served by green *Interparroquial* buses; those running east to the airport leave from the Estación Río Coca. Regional destinations have their own bus stations.

Long distance Quito has two main bus terminals: **Terminal Quitumbe** in the southwest of the city (T02-398 8200), serves destinations south, the coast via Santo Domingo, Oriente and Tulcán (in the north). It is served by the Trole (line 4: El Ejido–Quitumbe, best taken at El Ejido) and the Corredor Sur, however it is advisable to take a taxi, about US$6, 30-45 minutes to the colonial city, US$8-10, 45 minutes-one hour to La Mariscal. Arrivals and tourist information are on the ground floor. Ticket counters (destinations grouped and colour coded by region) and departures in the upper level. Left luggage (US$0.90 per day) and food stalls are at the adjoining shopping area. The terminal is large; allow extra time to reach your bus. Watch your belongings at all times. On holiday weekends it is advisable to reserve the day before. The smaller **Terminal Carcelén** (Avenida Eloy Alfaro, where it meets the Panamericana Norte, T02-3961600) serves destinations to the north (including Otavalo) and the coast via the Calacalí–La Independencia road. It is served by feeder bus lines from the northern terminals of the Trole, Ecovía and Metrobus; a taxi from Carcelén to La Mariscal costs about US$5, 30-45 minutes, to colonial Quito, US$7, 45 minutes-one hour. Ticket counters are organized by destination. Express buses connect the two terminals, with an intermediate stop by Parque El Ejido. Several companies run better quality coaches on the longer routes and some have private terminals in modern Quito. In addition to frequent bus services to all regions of Ecuador, there are international buses to Peru, Colombia and Venezuela.

Shared taxis and vans For intercity travel, shared taxis and vans are a good alternative to long-distance buses. They offer door-to-door service and you avoid the hassle of reaching Quito's bus terminals. From the capital there is service north to Otavalo and Ibarra and south to Latacunga, Ambato, Baños and Riobamba. Reserve at least two days ahead.

ON THE ROAD
Choosing a hotel in Quito

There are over 350 hotels in Quito. With so much accommodation being offered, you can find a good place to stay regardless of your taste or budget, but the large selection can be bewildering.

Narrow your search by reading up on the city and its neighbourhoods, before you arrive. Colonial Quito boasts several posh hotels in beautifully refurbished colonial mansions by the old city's main plazas. This area also has more economical and even cheap accommodation. The old city at night with its churches lit up is very beautiful.

Modern Quito has the greatest number of hotels. Many are concentrated in La Mariscal, Quito's tourist neighbourhood par excellence, the place for those who want to be in the heart of the action. Here you will be surrounded by restaurants, bars, nightlife, tour agencies, craft shops, cybercafés, Spanish schools, and even laundromats. Many budget hotels are in this area. With so much going on, it is not surprising that parts of La Mariscal are noisy, nor that this is where thieves and drug dealers can find the highest concentration of tourists.

Around Parque La Alameda and Parque El Ejido, the area between Colonial and modern Quito, are ageing residential neighbourhoods with neither the charm of the old city, nor the vibrant tourist scene of La Mariscal. The sector is nonetheless convenient to all areas and home to some good-value accommodation.

La Floresta and other neighbourhoods to the east of La Mariscal, as well as La Carolina to the north, offer a variety of good accommodation in more relaxed residential surroundings. This is also where a number of international hotels are located, and international chains are well represented in the city. In the western suburbs, along the flanks of Pichincha, are a couple stylish hotels in a rural setting not far from the city. In the suburbs to the east, such as Puembo, Pifo and Tababela, are weekend resorts convenient for the airport; book ahead as these are often full.

The following websites have hotel lists: www.in-quito.com, www.hotelesecuador.com, www.infohotel.ec, www.ecuadorboutiquehotels.com and www.guiahotelesecuador.com.

Driving Quito's main arteries run the length of the city and traffic congestion along them is a serious problem. Avenida Occidental is a somewhat more expedite road to the west of the city. The Corredor Periférico Oriental is a bypass to the east of the city running 44 km between Santa Rosa in the south and Calderón in the north. Roads through the eastern suburbs in the Valle de los Chillos and Tumbaco can be taken to avoid the city proper. **Note** There are vehicular restrictions on weekdays 0700-0930 and 1600-1930, based on the last digit of the licence plate. Colonial Quito is closed to vehicles Sunday 0900-1600 and main avenues across the city are turned into a bicycle route, the *ciclopaseo* (see page 46), on Sunday 0800-1400.

TOURIST INFORMATION
Empresa Metropolitana Quito Turismo/Quito Visitors' Bureau ① *T02-299 3300, www.quito.com.ec*, has information offices with English-speaking personnel, brochures and maps, and an excellent website. They also run walking tours of the colonial city, see Paseos Culturales, page 45. **Airport** ① *Arrivals, T02-281 8363, open 24 hrs.* **Bus station** ① *Terminal Quitumbe, T02-382 4815, daily 0900-1730.* **Train station** ① *T02-261 7661, Mon-Fri 0800-1630.* **Colonial Quito** ① *El Quinde craft shop at Palacio Municipal, Venezuela*

y Espejo, Plaza de la Independencia, T02-257 2445, Mon-Fri 0900-1800, Sat 0900-2000, Sun 0900-1700. **Modern Quito**, **Galería Ecuador** ① *Reina Victoria N24-263 y García, La Mariscal, T02-223 9469, Mon-Sat 0900-2100, Sun 1000-2000,* inside gourmet shop and café; **República del Cacao** ① *Reina Victoria 258 y Pinto, Plaza Foch, Mon-Sat 0900-1900, Sun 1000-1800;* inside chocolate shop, also sell tickets for the double decker bus tours, see page 45.

The **Ministerio de Turismo** ① *El Telégrafo E7-58 y Los Shyris, T02-399 9333 or T1-800-887476, www.ecuador.travel, Mon-Fri 0830-1730,* has an information counter with brochures, some staff speak English. **South American Explorers** ① *Jorge Washington 311 y Leonidas Plaza, T02-222 5228, quitoclub@saexplorers.org, Mon-Fri 0930-1700, Sat 0900-1200,* is a resource centre with a wide range of services for members. General information about Quito can be found at www.in-quito.com.

SAFETY

Quito has important public safety issues. In colonial Quito, Plaza de la Independencia and La Ronda are patrolled by officers from the **Policía Metropolitana** who speak some English and are very helpful. El Panecillo is patrolled by neighbourhood brigades (see page 42). In modern Quito, La Carolina and La Mariscal districts call for vigilance at all hours. Plaza Foch or El Quinde (Calle Foch y Reina Victoria) in La Mariscal is also patrolled, but do not stray outside its perimeter at night. Do not walk through any city parks in the evening or even in daylight at quiet times. There have been reports of scams on long-distance buses leaving Quito, especially to Baños; do not give your hand luggage to anyone and always keep your things on your lap, not in the overhead storage rack or on the floor. The **Policía de Turismo** ① *HQ at Reina Victoria N21-208 y Roca, T02-254 3983, open 0800-1800 for information, 24 hrs for emergencies, offices at Plaza de la Independencia, Pasaje Arzobispal, Chile Oe4-66 y García Moreno, T02-295 5785, 0800-2200,* and at the *airport*, offers information and is one place to obtain a police report in case of theft.

→ BACKGROUND

Archaeological studies suggest that the valley of Quito and the surrounding areas have been occupied for some 10,000 years. The remains of ancient Palaeoindian peoples, nomadic hunters who used obsidian to make stone tools, have been found at various sites around town. During the subsequent Formative era (4500-500 BC), pre-Ecuadorean peoples began to settle in villages, till fields and make ceramics. One of the best-known formative sites of highland Ecuador is located in northwest Quito, in Cotocollao. Dwellings of the Regional Development period (500 BC-AD 500) can be seen in Rumipamba, also in the northwest of the city.

Quito is named after the Quitus, a kingdom of the Integration period (AD 500-1500) which was inhabited in pre-Inca times. Quitu remains have been found along the lower flanks of Pichincha from El Placer in the south to La Florida in the north. By the end of the 15th century, the Northern Highlands of Ecuador were conquered by the Incas and Quito became the capital of the northern half of the empire under the rule of Huayna Capac and later his son Atahualpa. As the Spanish conquest approached, Rumiñahui, Atahualpa's general, razed the city, to prevent it from falling into the invaders' hands.

The colonial city of Quito was founded by Sebastián de Benalcázar, Pizarro's lieutenant, on 6 December 1534. It was built at the foot of El Panecillo on the ruins of the ancient city, using the rubble as construction material and today you can still find examples of

Inca stonework in the façades and floors of some colonial buildings, such as the cathedral and the church of San Francisco. Following the conquest, Quito became the seat of government of the Real Audiencia de Quito, the crown colony, which governed current-day Ecuador as well as parts of southern Colombia and northern Peru.

The city changed gradually over time. The Government Palace, for example, was built in the 17th century as the seat of government of the Real Audiencia, yet changes were introduced at the end of the colonial period and during the republican era in the 19th and 20th centuries. The 20th century saw Quito's expansion both to the north and south, first with the development of residential neighbourhoods and later with a transfer of the commercial and banking heart north of the colonial centre. In 1978, Quito was the first city to be declared a UNESCO World Heritage Site; its colonial heart has been wonderfully revitalized since then. In the 1980s and 1990s the number of high-rise buildings increased, the suburban valleys of Los Chillos and Tumbaco to the east of town were incorporated into a new Distrito Metropolitano, and a number of new poor neighbourhoods sprawled in the far north and south. The growth spurt continues; Quito stretches for almost 50 km from north to south and it is expected to grow vertically in the future, now that the airport has been relocated away from the city.

→ COLONIAL QUITO

Quito's historical district, among the largest and best restored in the Americas, is a pleasant place to stroll and admire the colonial architecture, monuments and art. At night, the illuminated plazas and churches are very beautiful. You could spend days exploring its narrow streets, churches and museums, but if your time is limited, a walking tour (see Paseos Culturales, page 45) is a very good option.

PLAZA DE LA INDEPENDENCIA AND AROUND
The heart of the old city is Plaza de la Independencia or **Plaza Grande**, whose pink-flowered arupo trees bloom in September. It is dominated by a somewhat grim **cathedral** ⓘ *entry through museum, Venezuela N3-117, T02-257 0371, Tue-Sun 0930-1600, no visits during Mass 0600-0900, US$2 for the museum, night visits to church and cupolas on request*, built 1550-1562, with grey stone porticoes and green-tile cupolas. The portal and tower were only completed in the 20th century. On its outer walls are plaques listing the names of the founding fathers of Quito. Inside, in a small chapel are the tomb of independence hero Antonio José de Sucre and other historical personalities, as well as a famous *Descent from the Cross* by the indigenous painter Caspicara. There are many other 17th- and 18th-century paintings and some fine examples of the Quito School of Art. The interior decoration, especially the ceiling, shows Moorish influence. Facing the cathedral is the **Palacio Arzobispal**, part of which now houses shops around stone courtyards. Next to it, in the northwest corner, is the **Hotel Plaza Grande** (1930), with a baroque façade, the first building in the old city with more than two storeys. On the northeast side is the concrete **Municipio**, which fits in quite well. The low colonial **Palacio de Gobierno** or **Palacio de Carondelet** ⓘ *T02-382 7118, visitors can take tours Mon 1500-1900, Tue-Fri 0900-1900, Sat 0900-1200, 1300-2200, Sun 0900-1200, 1300-1600, take passport*, silhouetted against the flank of Pichincha, is on the northwest side of the plaza. It was built in the 17th century and remodelled in neoclassical style by Carondelet, president of the Crown Colony and later by presidents Flores and Ponce Enríquez. On the first floor are a large mosaic mural

of Orellana navigating the Amazon and a painting by contemporary artist Oswaldo Guayasamín depicting milestones in Latin American history. The ironwork of the balconies looking over the plaza are from the Tuilleries in Paris. On Mondays at 1100 you can see the changing of the presidential guard in colonial uniform.

From Plaza de la Independencia two main streets, Venezuela and García Moreno, lead straight towards the Panecillo. Parallel with Venezuela is Calle Guayaquil, the main shopping street. These streets all run south from the main plaza to meet Calle Morales, better known as **La Ronda**, one of the oldest streets in the city. This narrow cobbled pedestrian way and its colonial homes with wrought-iron balconies have been refurbished and house restaurants, hotels, bars, cultural centres and shops. It is a quaint corner of the city growing in popularity for a night out or an afternoon stroll. On García Moreno N3-94 is the beautiful **El Sagrario Chapel** ① *T02-228 4398, Mon-Fri 1000-1600, Sat-Sun 1000-1400, no entry during Mass, free*, with impressive baroque columns and gilded inner doors. The **Centro Cultural Metropolitano** is at the corner of Espejo, housing the municipal library, a museum for the visually impaired, temporary art exhibits and the **Museo Alberto Mena Caamaño** ① *entry on C Espejo, T02-258 4362 ext 135, www.centrocultural-quito.com, Tue-Sun 0900-1700, US$2*. This wax museum, well worth a visit, depicts scenes of Ecuadorean colonial history. The scene of the execution of the revolutionaries of 1809 in the original cell is particularly vivid. The fine Jesuit church of **La Compañía** ① *García Moreno N3-117 y Sucre, T02-258 4175, Mon-Fri 0930-1700, Sat and holidays 0930-1630, Sun 1300-1600, US$3, students US$1.50*, has the most ornate and richly sculptured façade and interior. Many of its most valuable treasures, including a painting of the Virgen Dolorosa, framed in emeralds and gold, are in vaults at the Banco Central and appear only at special festivals. Replicas of the impressive paintings of hell and the final judgement by Miguel de Santiago, the colonial *mestizo* painter, can be seen at the entrance. If you only have time to visit one church, it should be this one. Diagonally opposite is the **Casa Museo María Augusta Urrutia** ① *García Moreno N2-60 y Sucre, T02-258 0103, Tue-Sat 1000-1800, Sun 1000-1700, US$3.00*, the lovely home of a Quiteña who devoted her life to charity, showing the lifestyle and traditions of 20th-century aristocracy. The guiding and explanations are good.

On **El Panecillo** ① *Mon-Thu 0900-1700, Fri-Sun 0900-2100, US$1 per vehicle or US$0.25 pp if walking, contribution for the neighbourhood brigade; entry to the interior of the monument US$2*, there is a statue of the Virgen de Quito and a good view from the observation platform. Although the neighbourhood patrols the area, it is safer to take a taxi (US$6 return from the colonial city, US$10 from La Mariscal, with a short wait). To the west of El Panecillo, is the museum of the monastery of **San Diego** ① *Calicuchima 117 y Farfán (by the cemetery of the same name, just west of El Panecillo), entrance to the right of the church, T02-295 2516, Tue-Sun 1000-1300, 1500-1730, US$2*, guided tours (Spanish only) take you around four colonial patios where sculpture and painting are shown. Of special interest are the gilded pulpit by Juan Bautista Menacho and the *Last Supper* painting in the refectory, in which a *cuy* and *humitas* have taken the place of the paschal lamb. To the southeast of El Panecillo is the neighbourhood of Chimbacalle, where Quito's train station is located. Here you'll find the excellent **Museo Interactivo de Ciencia** ① *Tababela Oe1-60, west of Maldonado, T02-264 7834, ext 132, Wed-Fri 1000-1700, Sat-Sun 1000-1400, US$3, children US$1*. Housed in La Industrial textile factory (1935-1990), it is an interactive science museum for kids and children at heart; a must if travelling with children and teachers will love it too.

PLAZA DE SAN FRANCISCO AND AROUND

Southwest of Plaza de la Independencia is Plaza de San Francisco or **Plaza Bolívar**, the scene of many of the city's political rallies. Here stand the great church and monastery of the patron saint of Quito, **San Francisco** ⓘ *daily 0800-1200, 1500-1800*. Built in 1553 on the site

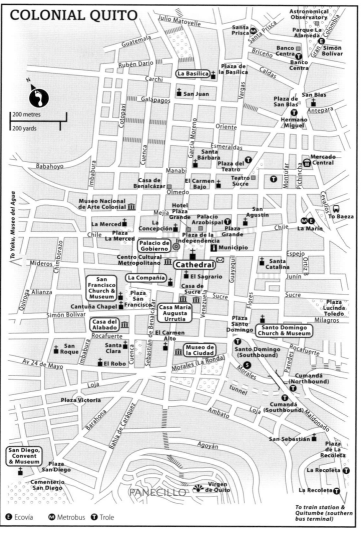

COLONIAL QUITO

ⒺEcovía ⓂMetrobus ⓉTrole

of Inca Huayna Capac's palace, this is Quito's first and largest colonial church. It is here that the famous Quito School of Art was founded. The two towers were felled by an earthquake in 1868 and later rebuilt. A modest statue of the founder, Fray Jodoco Ricke, the Flemish Franciscan who sowed the first wheat in Ecuador, stands nearby. See the fine woodcarvings in the choir, a high altar of gold and an exquisite carved ceiling. There are some paintings in the aisles by Miguel de Santiago. The **Museo Franciscano Fray Pedro Gocial** ① *in the church cloisters to the right of the main entrance, T02-295 2911, Tue-Sat 0900-1800, Sun 0900-1200, US$2*, has a fine collection of religious art. Also adjoining San Francisco, the small **Cantuña Chapel** ① *Cuenca y Bolívar, T02-295 2911, daily 0800-1200, 1500-1800, free*, with fine sculptures, is popular among locals. Not far to the south along Calle Cuenca is the excellent archaeological museum, **Museo Casa del Alabado** ① *Cuenca N1-41 y Rocafuerte, T02-228 0940, Tue-Sat 0900-1730, Sun-Mon 1000-1600, US$4, for English-speaking guide call ahead (tip appreciated)*. Housed in a beautifully restored building, it presents the most impressive display of pre-Columbian art from all regions of Ecuador. North of San Francisco is the early 17th-century church of **La Merced** ① *Chile y Cuenca, 0630-1200, 1300-1800, free*, built in many splendidly elaborate styles to commemorate Pichincha's eruptions which threatened to destroy the city. Nearby is the **Museo de Arte Colonial** ① *Cuenca N6-15 y Mejía, T02-228 2297, Tue-Sat 0900-1230, 1400-1630, US$2*, housed in a lovely 17th-century mansion, it features a well displayed collection of colonial sculpture and painting.

In El Placer, to the west of Plaza de San Francisco, is **Yaku Museo del Agua** ① *El Placer Oe11-271, best accessed by taxi, T02-251 1100, www.yakumuseoagua.gob.ec, Tue-Sun 0900-1730, US$3, call ahead if you need an English-speaking guide*, one of Quito's old waterworks converted to an interactive museum. The main themes are water and nature, society and heritage; great for children. The views of the city are excellent and there is also a self-guided *eco-ruta* with native plants.

PLAZA DE SANTO DOMINGO AND AROUND

In Plaza de Santo Domingo (or Plaza Sucre), to the southeast of Plaza de la Independencia, stands a statue of Mariscal Sucre pointing to the slopes of Pichincha, where he won the decisive battle for the independence of Ecuador. Here, the 17th-century church and monastery of **Santo Domingo** ① *daily 0700-1800*, has a carved Moorish ceiling over its large central nave and rich woodcarvings. In the main altar is an impressive silver throne, El Trono de la Virgen, weighing several hundred pounds. To the right of the main altar is the remarkable **Capilla del Rosario** (visit included in musem tours), built on top of the arch of the same name. In the monastery is the **Museo Dominicano Fray Pedro Bedón** ① *T02-228 2695, daily 1300-1700, US$1*, with another fine collection of religious art. It is named after the friar and painter who created the first brotherhood of indigenous painters. On the south side of the plaza is the colonial **Arco de la Capilla del Rosario**. Going through the arch you enter La Mama Cuchara (the 'great big spoon'), a street which ends at a roundabout in the authentic residential neighbourhood of La Loma Grande.

A few blocks north of Santo Domingo is the **Museo Casa de Sucre** ① *Venezuela 573 y Sucre, T02-295 2860, Tue-Sun 0900-1700 US$1*, in the beautiful, restored house of Sucre, with a museum about life in the 19th century and Sucre's role in Ecuador's independence. To the northeast, the **Museo Monacal Santa Catalina** ① *Espejo 779 y Flores, T02-228 4000, Mon-Fri 0900-1700, Sat 0900-1230, US$1.50*, said to have been built on the ruins of the Inca House of the Virgins, depicts the history of cloistered life. Many of the heroes of Ecuador's struggle for independence are buried in the 16th-century monastery of **San Agustín** ⓘ *Chile y Guayaquil, daily 0700-1200, 1300-1800*, which has beautiful cloisters on three sides and where the first act of independence from Spain was signed on 10 August 1809. Here is the **Museo Miguel de Santiago** ⓘ *Chile 924 y Guayaquil, T02-295 5525, www.migueldesantiago. com, Mon-Fri 0900-1230, 1430-1700, Sat 0900-1300, US$2*, with a fine religious art collection.

Housed in the fine restored, 16th-century Hospital San Juan de Dios, is the **Museo de la Ciudad** ⓘ *García Moreno 572 y Rocafuerte, T02-228 3879, www.museociudadquito.gob.ec, Tue-Sun 0930-1730, US$2, foreign-language guide service US$6 per group (request ahead)*. It takes you through Quito's history from pre-Hispanic times to the 19th century, with imaginative displays and a lovely café in the patio. Nearby is La Ronda, see page 42.

NORTH OF PLAZA DE LA INDEPENDENCIA

To the northeast of Plaza de la Independencia is **Plaza del Teatro**, where open-air cultural events are held. Here stand the neoclassical 19th-century **Teatro Nacional Sucre** ⓘ *Manabí N8-131 y Guayaquil, www.teatrosucre.com*, a lovely theatre and Quito's main cultural centre, and the smaller **Teatro Variedades Ernesto Albán**, both beautifully restored. Nearby is the **Museo Camilo Egas** ⓘ *Venezuela N9-02 y Esmeraldas, T02-257 2012, Mon-Fri 0900-1245, free*, a small gem housed in a restored 18th-century home. It exhibits the work of the Ecuadorean artist Camilo Egas (1889-1962); it is interesting to see the evolution of style over time, the life of the Ecuadorean *indígena* in the 1920s and life in New York during the Great Depression.

Further north is the large **Basílica del Voto Nacional** ⓘ *on Plaza de la Basílica, Carchi 122 y Venezuela, T02-228 9428, daily 0900-1700, US$3*, which has many gargoyles (some in the shape of Ecuadorean fauna), stained-glass windows and fine, bas relief bronze doors. Begun in 1926, some final details still remain unfinished due to lack of funding. Be sure to climb above the coffee shop to the top of the clock tower for stunning views. In the neighbourhood of San Juan, north of the Basílica, the **Centro de Arte Contemporáneo**, also called **Centro Cultural Bicentenario** ⓘ *Luis Dávila y Venezuela, San Juan, T02-398 8800, Tue-Sun 0900-1730, free*, in the beautifully restored Antiguo Hospital Militar, was built in the early 1900s and has rotating art exhibits.

CITY TOURS

There are a number of ways of exploring Quito. Whichever one you choose, be sure to visit at least one of the sites which afford views of the city and surrounding mountains; these include: El Panecillo (page 42), Parque Itchimbía (page 46), the Basílica (above) and the Teleférico (page 50). To get to know the colonial centre, stroll around or take a tour. **Paseos Culturales** ⓘ *Plaza de la Independencia tourist information office, Venezuela y Espejo, T02-257 2445*, are walking tours of the colonial city led by English- or French-speaking officers of the Policía Metropolitana. Several options are on offer: a two-hour historic buildings tour (daily 0900-1600, also at 1800 with previous arrangement, US$5); a religious art route or a Quito daily life route, with stops at three museums (daily departures at 0900, 1000, and 1400, 2½ hours, US$15, children and seniors US$7.50, includes museum entrance fees, Monday is not a good day because many museums are closed); and Quito heritage routes, which include visits to traditional neighbourhoods and craft workshops (these heritage tours require prior arrangement, 2½ hours, US$4).

Tours on double-decker buses are offered by **Quito Tour Bus** ⓘ *T02-245 8010, www.quitotourbus.com, hourly departures 0900-1600, 3-hr ride, US$12, children and seniors US$6; night tour US$10*. The bus stops at 12 places of interest (10 on Sunday) both in colonial Quito and the modern city, starting and ending by Parque La Carolina on Avenida Naciones Unidas. There are several ticket sales points. You can alight at any site and continue later on another bus; the ticket is valid all day.

Should you be in Quito on a Sunday, you can explore town by bike. The city organizes a **ciclopaseo**, a cycle day, every Sunday from 0800 to 1400. Key avenues are closed to vehicular traffic and thousands of cyclists cross the city in 29 km from north to south. This and other cycle events are run by **Fundación Ciclópolis** ① *Equinoccio N17-171 y Queseras del Medio, T02-322 6502, www.ciclopolis.ec; they also hire bikes US$5.60 per ciclopaseo, must book Mon-Fri, US$11.20 per day on other days*; rentals are also available from **La Casa del Ciclista** ① *Eloy Alfaro 1138 y República, near the ciclopaseo route, T02-254 0339, US$3 per hr, US$12 per day*. Quito has a few bike paths including one around the perimeter of Parque La Carolina, another at Parque Bicentenario (old airport) in the north, one in Quitumbe, in the south, and one along a disused railway line in the Tumbaco Valley. If staying a long time in the city, sign up with BiciQ, to use their bikes stationed throughout town. **Biciacción** (www.biciaccion.org), has information about routes in the city and organizes trips outside Quito.

→ MODERN QUITO

LA ALAMEDA TO EL EJIDO

Dating from 1873, **Parque La Alameda** has South America's oldest **astronomical observatory** ① *T02-257 0765, museum: Wed-Sun 1000-1300, 1400-1700, US$2, observation on clear nights: Thu-Fri 1830-2030*. There is also a splendid monument to Simón Bolívar, lakes, and in the northwest corner a spiral lookout tower with a good view. East of La Alameda is **Parque Itchimbía** ① *JM Aguirre N4-108 y Concepción, T02-228 2017*; a natural lookout over the city with walking and cycle trails and a cultural centre housed in a 19th-century 'crystal palace' which came from Europe and once housed the Santa Clara market. There are restaurants nearby with lovely views.

A short distance north of La Alameda is **Parque El Ejido**, popular with local families at the weekend. There are craft stalls and along the Avenida Patria edge, artists sell their paintings at the weekend. Opposite El Ejido along Avenida 6 de Diciembre is **Parque El Arbolito**, its northern end occupied by the large Casa de la Cultura complex, housing a library, several theatres, exhibit halls and museums. Within the complex are the Museo Nacional (see below) and the **Casa de la Cultura museums** ① *T02-222 1007, ext 321, Tue-Sat 0900-1300, 1400-1630, US$2*. Museums belonging to the Casa de la Cultura include: **Museo de Arte Moderno**, paintings and sculpture since 1830, and rotating exhibits; **Colección Etnográfica**, traditional dress and adornments of indigenous groups; **Museo de Instrumentos Musicales**, an impressive collection of musical instruments, said to be the second in importance in the world.

If you have time to visit only one museum in Quito, it should be the **Museo Nacional** ① *Patria y 6 de Diciembre, T02-222 3258, www.museos-ecuador.gob.ec, Tue-Fri 0900-1700, Sat-Sun 1000-1600, free, guided tours in English or French by appointment*, also housed in the Casa de la Cultura. It is the most comprehensive museum in the country. Of its five sections, the **Sala de Arqueología** is particularly impressive with beautiful pre-Columbian ceramics. The **Sala de Oro** has a nice collection of pre-Hispanic gold objects. The remaining three halls house art collections. Near the Casa de la Cultura, in the **Catholic University's cultural centre** ① *12 de Octubre y Roca, T02-299 1700, Mon-Fri 0800-1600*, are the **Museo Jijón y Caamaño**,

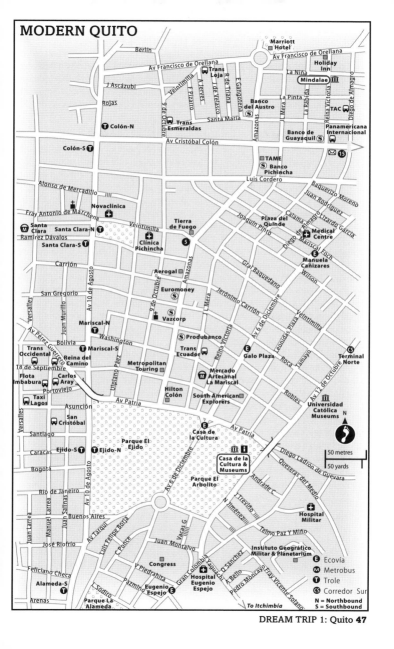

with a private collection of archaeological objects, historical documents and art, very well displayed (closed for relocation in 2013); the **Museo Weilbauer**, with archaeological and photo collections; and temporary exhibits. At the Politécnica Salesiana, north of Universidad Católica, the Centro Cultural Abya Yala runs the **Museo Etnográfico Culturas Amazónicas** ① *12 de Octubre N23-116 y Wilson, T02-223 6175, Tue-Sun 0900-1700, US$3, Spanish guides only*, with interesting displays of Amazonian flora and fauna, tribal culture and the impact of oil exploration and drilling. There is also a bookstore (mostly books in Spanish).

LA MARISCAL

The district of La Mariscal, extending north of Parque El Ejido, is the heart of Quito's nightlife, with a multitude of restaurants, bars and clubs. It is also the most important tourist area with many hotels and tour operators. A focal point in La Mariscal, at the intersection of Reina Victoria and Foch, is the small **Plaza El Quinde** (the hummingbird), also known as **Plaza Foch**, a popular meeting place throughout the week, surrounded by cafés and restaurants. Nearby, at the intersection of Amazonas y Washington, is **Plaza de los Presidentes**, with a 24-hour café, some restaurants and live music on Friday and Saturday night.

At the corner of Reina Victoria and La Niña, known as **Plaza Yuyu**, another area with cafés, restaurants and bars, is the excellent **Museo Mindalae** ① *T02-223 0609, www.sinchisacha.org, Mon-Sat 0930-1800, Sun 1030-1630, US$3, 1st Sun of each month free*, which exhibits Ecuadorean crafts and places them in their historical and cultural context, as well as temporary exhibits, a good fair-trade, non-profit shop and restaurant. To the southeast is **Folklore** ① *Colón E10-53 y Caamaño, T02-254 1315, www.olgafisch.com, Mon-Fri 0900-1900, Sat 1000-1800, donations welcome,* another fine handicrafts shop with a small museum. The private collection is of the late Olga Fisch, an immigrant who for five decades worked side by side with Ecuadorean artisans to encourage them to excel and rescue native designs and techniques.

To the east of La Mariscal is the residential neighbourhood of **La Floresta** dating to the mid-20th century. Some of the homes here have been converted to restaurants and lodgings, a good option for those looking for a quiet location. Here **Casa Cultural Trude Sojka** ① *Toledo N24-569 y Coruña, entrance from Pasaje Moeller, T02-222 4072, www.trude-sojka.com, Mon-Sat 1000-2000*, exhibits the works of Trude Sojka (1909-2006), a Czech-born painter and sculptor, and has a small Holocaust memorial. The area has a number of universities and towards the south is the **Coliseo Rumiñahui**, a sports facility where many popular concerts are also held. North of La Floresta are more modern neighbourhoods such as **La Paz** and **González Suárez**, with rows of high-rise apartment buildings dominating Quito's eastern skyline. The views from here to Guápulo and the valleys to the east are lovely. There are a few hotels in this area and many upmarket restaurants.

LA CAROLINA

North of La Mariscal is the large **Parque La Carolina**, a favourite recreational spot at weekends. Around it is the banking district, several shopping malls, hotels and restaurants. In the park is the **Jardín Botánico** ① *T02-333 2516, Mon-Fri 0800-1700, Sat-Sun 0900-1700, US$3.50, www.jardinbotanicoquito.com*, which has an excellent cross section of Andean flora and is a good place for birdwatching. Also the **Vivarium** ① *T02-227 1820, Tue-Sun 0930-1730, US$3*, dedicated to protect endangered snakes, reptiles and amphibians, and the **Museo de Ciencias Naturales** ① *T02-244 9824, Mon-Fri 0830-1630, US$2*, with dusty

ON THE ROAD
Dining out in Quito

Quito offers excellent, varied, cosmopolitan and upmarket dining, which is nonetheless reasonable by international standards. The majority of restaurants are in modern Quito, where almost any type of cuisine can be found. At Plaza El Quinde, in La Mariscal, are various restaurants, bars and cafés. Many upscale restaurants are found in La Floresta neighbourhood, east of La Mariscal, near Swissôtel and also east of Parque La Carolina, around Avenida República de El Salvador corner Portugal and along the upper part of Avenida Eloy Alfaro. The international hotels also have good speciality restaurants. Colonial Quito does not lag behind; here too are some very elegant expensive establishments serving international and Ecuadorean food.

If you are on a tight budget, fear not, for not all Quito dining is highbrow. There are a great many simple little places throughout the city serving cheap and adequate set meals, *almuerzos* (at midday) and *meriendas* (in the evening), from US$2.50 to US$5. Look around, they are everywhere and you are sure to find one close by. Let the locals guide you, if a place is full then in all likelihood *la cocinera tiene buena cuchara* – literally 'the cook has a good spoon', meaning the food is tasty. Note that many places serving set lunches close in the evening and some of those serving *meriendas* might close as early as 1900. There are also a number of reasonable restaurants in the food courts of shopping malls.

Many restaurants throughout the city close on Sunday evenings. Those with stickers indicating acceptance of credit cards do not necessarily do so; ask first. In many of the more expensive restaurants 12% tax and 10% service is added to the bill.

¡Buen provecho!

specimens. The northern border of Parque La Carolina, along Avenida Naciones Unidas, is a promenade used for exhibits, known as **El Bulevar;** here is the main stop of the **Quito Tour Bus**, see page 45. Just to the east, at Naciones Unidas and 6 de Diciembre is **Estadio Atahualpa**, the city's main soccer stadium. To the east of Parque La Carolina are a number of upmarket hotels and restaurants.

Parque Metropolitano, east of the stadium, is good for walking, running or biking through the forest; it has some picnic areas with grills. North of La Carolina, occupying part of the old airport grounds, is **Parque Bicentenario**, with cycling and jogging paths.

→ QUITO SUBURBS

EAST

To the east of Quito lie the valleys of the Machángara, San Pedro, Pita and Huambi rivers. Formerly Quito's market garden, the area is rapidly filling with suburbs and the towns are now part of the city's metropolitan area. With a milder climate, the valleys and their thermal pools attract inner city dwellers at weekends. Fine colonial haciendas remain here, some of which have opened their doors to visitors and today are exclusive inns.

The beautiful district of **Guápulo**, a colonial town, is perched on the edge of a ravine on the eastern fringe of Quito, overlooking the Río Machángara. It is popular with Quito's bohemian community and a worthwhile place to visit. The **Santuario de Guápulo** ① *Mass*

Mon-Fri 1900, Sat 0700, Sun 0700-1200, 1600-1700, built by indigenous slaves in 1693, is well worth seeing for its many paintings, gilded altars, stone carvings and the marvellously carved pulpit by Juan Bautista Menacho. Next to the Santuario, the **Museo Fray Antonio Rodríguez** ① *Av de los Conquistadores N27-138, T02-256 5652, Tue-Sun 0900-1700, US$2*, has religious art and furniture, from the 16th to the 20th centuries. Guided tours (Spanish only) include a visit to the beautiful Santuario.

Overlooking the city from the northeast is the grandiose **Capilla del Hombre** ① *Lorenzo Chávez E18-143 y Mariano Calvache, Bellavista, take a taxi, T02-244 8492, www.capilladelhombre.com, Tue-Sun 1000-1700, US$6 (for both Guayasamín museums), tour of both sites takes 1¾ hrs*, a monument to Latin America conceived by the famous Ecuadorean artist Oswaldo Guayasamín (1919-1999) and completed after his death. The fate of people in this continent is presented through the artist's murals and paintings; an eternal flame represents the ongoing fight for human rights. A few blocks away is the fine **Museo Fundación Guayasamín** ① *Bosmediano E15-68, T02-245 2938*, displaying the artist's work and pre-Columbian and contemporary collections; all highly recommended. You can also buy works of art and jewellery with pre-Hispanic designs.

The **Valle de los Chillos** lies southeast of the centre of Quito. It is accessed via the Autopista General Rumiñahui, which starts at El Trébol, east of the colonial city. The first suburb you reach is San Rafael, where you find the lovely **Casa de Kingman Museo** ① *Portoviejo 111 y Dávila, 1 block from the main park, T02-286 1065, Thu-Fri 1000-1600, Sat-Sun 1000-1700, US$3, free art classes offered*. This is a collection of the renowned artist's work, in his home, alongside other colonial, republican and 20th-century art. Take a taxi or a **Vingala** bus from Isabel La Católica y Mena Caamaño, behind Universidad Católica.

The largest town in Los Chillos is **Sangolquí**, with a pleasant park and a nice church. It has a busy Sunday market (and a smaller one on Thursday) and few tourists. On two roundabouts east of town are lovely mosaic sculptures by the well known 20th-century artist Gonzalo Endara Crow: an ear of corn, the main crop of the valley, and a hummingbird. Beyond Sangolquí is the **Río Pita**. Its ice-cold water, fed by the snow melt from Cotopaxi, runs through a scenic rocky canyon surrounded by remnants of Andean forest; there are 18 waterfalls along its course.

To the north of Los Chillos is the extinct volcano Ilaló, which can be climbed, and north of it the **Valle de Tumbaco**. Here are the suburbs of Cumbayá, Cunuyacu, Tumbaco, Puembo and Pifo, accessed through the Vía Interoceánica, the road leading east from Quito to Papallacta and the Northern Oriente. Near Pifo are Tababela and Quito's airport.

WEST
Several Quito neighbourhoods climb along Pichincha's steep slopes, which afford good views of the city and surrounding mountains. Above these is Bosque Protector Pichincha, a belt of eucalyptus forest. A couple of haciendas in this area offer accommodation. For spectacular views ride the **Teleférico** ① *Av Occidental above La Gasca, T02-222 1320, daily 0800-1930, US$8.50, children and seniors US$6.50; take a Trans Alfa bus bound for Comuna Obrero Independiente from the Seminario Mayor, América y Colón, or a taxi from the same place (US$1.50)*. The cable car is part of a complex with an amusement park, shops and food courts. It climbs to 4050 m on the flanks of Pichincha, where there are walking trails, including one to the summit of Rucu Pichincha, and horse riding just past the fence.

North of the teleférico, **Parque Arqueológico y Ecológico Rumipamba** ① *east side of Av Occidental just north of Mariana de Jesús, T02-295 7576, Wed-Sun 0830-1630, free, some English-speaking guides*, is a 32-ha park, where vestiges have been found of human occupation of several pre-Inca periods, dating from 1500 BC to AD 1500. There are walking trails in some pockets of native vegetation. Northwest of Rumipamba, in the neighbourhood of San Vicente de la Florida is the **Museo de Sitio La Florida** ① *C Antonio Costas y Villacrés, T09-9923 4351, Wed-Sun 0800-1600, free, some English-speaking guides*, at the north end of the Marín–San Vicente bus line. At this necropolis of the Quitus people, 10 burial chambers, dating to AD 220-640, have been excavated, each 17 m deep. The elaborate dress and jewellery found in the tombs suggests most were prominent citizens.

→ AROUND QUITO

Despite Quito's bustling big city atmosphere, it is surrounded by pretty and surprisingly tranquil countryside, with many opportunities for day excursions as well as longer trips. A combination of city and interparroquial buses and pickup trucks will get you to most destinations. Excursions are also offered by Quito tour operators. The monument on the equator, the country's best-known tourist site, is just a few minutes away; there are nature reserves, craft-producing towns, excellent thermal swimming pools, walking and climbing routes and a scenic train ride. Otavalo (page 60), Mindo (page 74), Cotopaxi (page 98) and Papallacta (page 136), described as part of the different Dream Trips, can all be visited as day trips from the city. See www.pichincha.gob.ec (click on 'turismo') for attractions near Quito.

MITAD DEL MUNDO AND AROUND

The location of the equatorial line here, 23 km north of central Quito, was determined by Charles-Marie de la Condamine and his French expedition in 1736, and agrees to within 150 m with modern GPS measurements. The monument forms the focal point of **Ciudad Mitad del Mundo** ① *T02-239 4806, www.mitaddelmundotour.com, daily 0900-1800 (crowded on Sun), entry US$3*, a leisure park built as a typical colonial town, with restaurants, gift shops, post office and tour operator. There are free live music and dance performances at weekends from 1200 to 1800. It is all rather touristy but the monument itself has a very interesting **Museo Etnográfico** ① *additional US$3*, inside. A lift takes you to the top, then you walk down with the museum laid out all around with exhibits of different indigenous cultures every few steps. There is also an interesting **model of colonial Quito**, about 10 m square, with artificial day and night. **Museo Inti-Ñan** ① *200 m north of the monument, T02-239 5122, www.museointinan.com.ec, daily 0900-1700, US$3*, eclectic, very interesting, educational and with lots of fun activities, gives Equator certificates for visitors. Research about the equator and its importance to prehistoric cultures is carried out near Cayambe by an organization called **Quitsa-to** (www.quitsato.org). To reach the monument, take the Metrobus to La Ofelia station and a 'Mitad del Mundo' feeder bus from there (transfer ticket US$0.15). Some buses continue to the turn-off for Pululahua or Calacalí beyond. A taxi from La Mariscal costs about US$15; US$25 with one-hour wait; US$30 to include Pululahua.

Four kilometres beyond Mitad del Mundo, off the road to Calacalí, is the **Pululahua crater**, which is well worth visiting. Go in the morning as there is often cloud later. On the edge of the rim is the Mirador, a lookout with wonderful views of the crater floor.

In the crater, with its own warm microclimate, is the hamlet of Pululahua, surrounded by agricultural land and, to the west of it, the **Reserva Pululahua**. The crater is breached northwest; the climate gets warmer and the vegetation more lush as you descend. There are two access points to the crater. From the Mirador, a track leads down into the crater, a half-hour walk down to the agricultural zone and one hour back up. A second much longer road allows you to drive into the crater, go through the reserve and then reach the village and agricultural zone.

PASOCHOA

Refugio de Vida Silvestre Pasochoa ① *45 mins southeast of Quito by car, free, very busy at weekends*, is a natural park set in a remnant of humid Andean forest, between 2700 m and 4200 m. The reserve has more than 120 species of bird (unfortunately some of the fauna has been frightened away by the noise of visitors) and 50 species of tree. This is a suitable place for a family picnic or an acclimatization hike close to Quito. There are good walks of 30 minutes to eight hours. There is a refuge (US$6-10 per person per night, with hot shower and cooking facilities) but take food, water and a sleeping bag; camping is US$4 per person. From Quito buses run from El Playón to Amaguaña US$0.50 (ask the driver to let you off at the 'Ejido de Amaguaña'); from there follow the signs. It's an 8-km walk, with little traffic, except at weekends, or book a pick-up from Amaguaña (Cooperativa Pacheco Jr, T02-287 7047, for about US$6).

TRAIN RIDES

Tourist trains run from Quito south through a lush agricultural area surrounded by magnificent volcanoes, including Cotopaxi and Los Ilinizas. Tours start with a visit to the Quito railway museum, followed by a folklore show in Machachi and a visit to Area Nacional de Recreación El Boliche, a reserve abutting on Parque Nacional Cotopaxi. Two kilometres south of colonial Quito is the lovely refurbished train station, **Estación Eloy Alfaro** or **Chimbacalle** ① *Maldonado y Sincholagua, T1-800-873637, T02-265 6142, www.trenecuador.com, Mon-Fri 0800-1630; purchase tickets in advance by phone, or at the station or El Quinde craft shop, Palacio Municipal, Venezuela y Espejo (you need each passenger's passport number and age to purchase tickets)*. Trains run Thursday to Sunday and holidays from Quito to Machachi (0815, US$15-20), El Boliche (0815, US$20-25) and Latacunga (motorized rail car at 0800, US$10); you cannot purchase tickets to board at Latacunga.

QUITO LISTINGS

WHERE TO STAY

Colonial Quito

$$$$ Casa Gangotena, Bolívar y Cuenca, T02-400 8000, www.casagangotena.com. Superb location by Plaza San Francisco, luxury accommodation in beautifully refurbished classic family home, rooms and suites, includes breakfast, fine restaurant.

$$$$ La Casona de la Ronda, Morales Oe1-160 y Guayaquil, T02-228-7503, www.lacasonadelaronda.com. Beautiful restored colonial house in an excellent location. Bright ample common areas, 22 superbly decorated rooms and suites, includes buffet breakfast, restaurant.

$$$$ Mansión del Angel, Los Ríos N13-134 y Pasaje Gándara, T02-254 0293, www.mansiondelangel.com.ec. Luxurious hotel decorated with antiques in a beautifully renovated mansion, 15 ample rooms and a palatial suite, includes breakfast, dinner available, nice gardens, lovely atmosphere.

$$$$ Plaza Grande, García Moreno N5-16, Plaza de la Independencia, T02-251 0777, www.plazagrandequito.com. Exclusive top-of-the-line hotel with an exceptional location, 15 suites (including a presidential suite), jacuzzi in all rooms, climate control and 3 restaurants, including **La Belle Epoque** (gourmet French cuisine) and a wine cellar, mini-spa, 110/220V outlets.

$$$ Relicario del Carmen, Venezuela 1041 y Olmedo, T02-228 9120, www.hotelrelicariodelcarmen.com. Beautifully refurbished colonial house, includes breakfast, good restaurant, cafeteria, pleasant rooms and service, no smoking.

$$ Catedral Internacional, Mejía Oe6-36 y Cuenca, T02-295 5438. Attractively restored colonial house with 15 carpeted rooms, heaters, small patio with fountain, includes breakfast, popular restaurant, spa.

$$ San Francisco de Quito, Sucre Oe3-17 y Guayaquil, T02-295 1241, www.sanfranciscodequito.com.ec.

Nicely converted colonial building, includes breakfast in attractive patio or underground cloisters, restaurant, sauna, jacuzzi, suites are particularly good value, well run by owners, street-side rooms can be noisy.

$ Flores, Flores N3-51 y Sucre, T02-228 0435. Well refurbished and decorated, private bath, hot water, laundry facilities, patio, good value.

$ L'Auberge Inn, Colombia N15-200 y Yaguachi, just north of the old city, T02-255 2912, www.auberge-inn-hostal.com. Spacious rooms, duvets, private or shared bath, excellent hot water, restaurant, spa, cooking facilities, parking, lovely garden, terrace and communal area, tour operator, helpful, good atmosphere.

Modern Quito

$$$$ Casa Aliso, Salazar E12-137 y Toledo, La Floresta, T02-252 8062, www.casaliso.com. Lovely refurbished family house with 10 tastefully decorated spacious rooms, sitting room with fireplace, restaurant, buffet breakfast is extra, pleasant garden.

$$$$ Le Parc, República de El Salvador N34-349 e Irlanda, T02-227 6800, www.leparc.com.ec. Modern hotel with 30 executive suites, full luxury facilities and service, restaurant, spa, gym.

$$$$ Nü House, Foch E6-12 y Reina Victoria, T02-255 7845, www.nuhouse hotels.com. Modern luxury hotel with minimalist decor, includes breakfast, restaurant, some suites with jacuzzi, all furnishings and works of art are for sale.

$$$ City Art Hotel Silberstein, Wilson E5-29 y JL Mera, T02-254 3898, www.galextur.com. 10 comfortable rooms in an attractively refurbished house, includes buffet breakfast.

$$$ Hostal de la Rábida, La Rábida 227 y Santa María, T02-222 2169, www.hostalrabida.com. Lovely converted home, bright comfortable rooms, good restaurant, parking, British/Italian-run.

$$$ La Cartuja, Plaza 170 y 18 de Septiembre, T02-252 3577, www.hotela cartuja.com. In the former British Embassy, beautifully decorated, spacious comfortable rooms, includes breakfast, cafeteria, parking, lovely garden, very helpful and hospitable.

$$$ La Casa Sol, Calama 127 y 6 de Diciembre, T02-223 0798, www.lacasasol. com. Charming small hotel with courtyard, includes breakfast, 24-hr cafeteria, very helpful, English and French spoken.

$$$ Sierra Madre, Veintimilla E9-33 y Tamayo, T02-250 5687, www.hotel sierramadre.com. Fully renovated villa, comfortable, restaurant, nice sun roof, English spoken.

$$$ Villa Nancy, Muros N27-94 y 12 de Octubre, T02-256 2483, www.hotelvilla nancy.com. Quaint hotel in quiet residential area, includes buffet breakfast, homely and comfortable, sauna, helpful staff.

$$ Queen's Hostel/Hostal de la Reina, Reina Victoria N23-70 y Wilson, T02-255 1844, www.hostaldelareina.com. Nice small hotel, popular among travellers and Ecuadoreans, cafeteria, cooking facilities, sitting room with fireplace.

$$-$ Casa Helbling, Veintimilla E8-152 y 6 de Diciembre, T02-222 6013, www. casahelbling.de. Very good, popular hostel, spotless, breakfast available, private or shared bath, laundry and cooking facilities, English, French and German spoken, family atmosphere, good information, tours.

$$-$ Posada del Maple, Rodríguez E8-49 y 6 de Diciembre, T02-254 4507, www.posadadelmaple.com. Popular hostel, includes breakfast, private or shared bath, also dorms, cooking facilities, warm atmosphere. Many others in the same street.

$$-$ Travellers Inn, La Pinta E4-435 y Amazonas, T02-255 6985, www.travellers ecuador.com. Hostel in converted home, includes good breakfast, private or shared bath, parking, nice common area and garden, bike rentals.

$ Casona de Mario, Andalucía 213 y Galicia, La Floresta, T02-254 4036, www.casonademario.com. Popular hostel, shared bath, hot water, laundry facilities, well equipped kitchen, sitting room, nice garden.

Quito suburbs

$$$$ Hacienda Rumiloma, Obispo Díaz de La Madrid, T02-254 8206, www.haciendarumiloma.com. Luxurious hotel in a 40-ha hacienda on the slopes of Pichincha. Sumptuous suites with lots of attention to detail, lounges with antiques, includes breakfast, good restaurant, nice views, personalized attention from owners, ideal for someone looking for a luxurious escape not far from the city.

$$$ Hostería San José, Manuel Burbano s/n, Barrio San José, Puembo, 20 mins from the airport, T02-239 0276, T1-800-180180, www.hosteriasanjose.com. 18th-century hacienda with 4-ha grounds, modern rooms, restaurant, includes breakfast, pool and spa; airport transfers US$8 pp.

$$$ Hostal Su Merced, Julio Tobar Donoso, Puembo, 20 mins from the airport, T09-8536 0545, www.sumerced. com. Attractively refurbished 18th-century hacienda house, well appointed rooms with bathtubs, includes restaurant, sauna and gardens; airport transfers US$8 per vehicle.

$$ Hostería San Carlos, Justo Cuello y Maldonado, Tababela, 10 km from the airport, T02-359 9057, www.hosteriasan carlostababela.com. Hacienda-style inn with ample grounds, restaurant, includes breakfast, pool, jacuzzi, rooms with bath and dorms, airport transfers.

$$-$ El Vergel, E-35 Km 27, at the airport roundabout, 4.5 km from the terminal, T02-239 1550, info.elvergel@ gmail.com. Small rooms in a complex with pools and spa, breakfast available daily, restaurant at weekends.

RESTAURANTS

Colonial Quito

$$$ El Ventanal, Carchi y Nicaragua, west of the Basílica, in Parque San Juan, take a taxi to the parking area and a staff member will accompany you along a footpath to the restaurant, T02-257 2232, www.elventanal. ec. Tue-Sat 1200-1500, 1800-2200, Sun 1200-1700. International nouvelle cuisine with a varied menu including a number of seafood dishes, fantastic views over the city.

$$$ Theatrum, Plaza del Teatro, above Teatro Sucre, T02-228 9669, www.theatrum. com.ec. Mon-Fri 1230-1600, 1930-2330, Sat and Sun 1900-2300. Excellent creative gourmet cuisine in the city's most important theatre, wide selection of fruit desserts which come with an explanatory card.

$$ Vista Hermosa, Mejía 453 y García Moreno. Mon-Sat 1400-2400, Sun 1200-2100. Good meals, drinks, pizza, live music at weekends, lovely terrace-top views of the colonial centre.

$$-$ San Ignacio, García Moreno N2-60 y Sucre. Sun-Mon 0800-1530, Tue-Sat 0800-1930. Breakfast, good economical set lunches with small salad bar, also international and Ecuadorean food à la carte.

Modern Quito

$$$ Carmine, Catalina Aldaz N34-208 y Portugal, T02-333 2829, www.carmine ristorante.com. Mon-Sat 1200-1530, 1900-2230, Sun 1200-1800. Creative international and Italian cuisine.

$$$ San Telmo, Portugal 440 y Casanova, T02-225 6946. Mon-Sat 1200-2300, Sun until 2200. Good Argentine grill, seafood, pasta, pleasant atmosphere, great service.

$$$ Zazu, Mariano Aguilera 331 y La Pradera, T02-254 3559, www.zazuquito. com. Mon-Fri 1230-1500, 1900-2230, Sat 1900-2230. Very elegant and exclusive dining. International and Peruvian specialities, extensive wine list, attentive service, reservations required.

$$$-$$ La Briciola, Toledo 1255 y Salazar, T02-254 7138, www.labriciola.com.ec. Daily 1200-2400. Extensive Italian menu, excellent food, homey atmosphere, very good personal service.

$$ Chez Alain, Baquedano E5-26 y JL Mera. Mon-Fri 1200-1530. Choice of good 4-course set lunches, pleasant relaxed atmosphere.

$$ Mama Clorinda, Reina Victoria N24-150 y Calama. Daily 1100-2300. Ecuadorean cuisine à la carte and set meals, filling, popular, good value.

$$ Paléo, Cordero E5-36 y JL Mera. Mon-Sat 1200-1500 1830-2200. Authentic Swiss specialities such as rösti and raclette. Also good economical set lunch, pleasant ambiance. Recommended.

$ Sakti, Carrión E4-144 y Amazonas. Mon-Fri 0830-1830. Good quality and value vegetarian food, breakfast, set lunches and à la carte, fruit juices, great desserts (also a few rooms, **$**).

Coffee Tree/Garden, Reina Victoria y Foch, also at Amazonas y Washington, and La Niña y Reina Victoria. Open 24 hrs. Popular cafés serving a variety of snacks, pasta, burgers, coffee, Wi-Fi.

WHAT TO DO

Language schools

Quito has over 80 Spanish schools; many offer study-travel programmes. The following have received favourable reports:
Amazonas, www.eduamazonas.com.
Andean Global Studies, www.andeanglobalstudies.org.

Beraca, www.beraca.net.
Bipo & Toni's, www.bipo.net.
Colón, www.colonspanishschool.com.
Equinox, www.ecuadorspanish.com.
La Lengua, www.la-lengua.com.
Mitad del Mundo, www.mitadmundo.com.ec.

Sintaxis, www.sintaxis.net.
South American,
www.southamerican.edu.ec.
Superior, www.instituto-superior.net.
Universidad Católica, T02-299 1700
ext 1388, mejaramillo@puce.edu.ec.
Vida Verde, www.vidaverde.com.

Tour operators
Biking Dutchman, Foch E4-283 y
Amazonas, T02-256 8323, after hours T09-
9420 5349, www.biking-dutchman.com.
One- and several-day biking tours, great
fun, good food, very well organized, English,
German and Dutch spoken, pioneers in
mountain biking in Ecuador.
Climbing Tours, Ecotourism &
Adventure, Amazonas N21-221 y Roca,
T02-254 4358, www.climbingtour.com.
Climbing, trekking and other adventure
sports, market tours, tailor-made itineraries;
also sell Galápagos and jungle trips.
Ecuador Galápagos Travels, Veintimilla
E10-78 y 12 de Octubre, Edif El Girón, Torre E,
of 104, T02-254 7286, www.ecuador
galapagostravels.ec. Wide range of traditional
and adventure tours throughout Ecuador
including Galápagos; tailor-made itineraries.
Ecuador Treasure, JL Mera N24-82 y Foch,
T02-254 4198, www.ecuadortreasure.
com. Adventure and standard trips; tailor-
made tours and private transport. They
sell Galápagos and jungle trips and run
Chuquirahua Lodge, near Los Ilinizas.
Enchanted Expeditions, de las Alondras
N45-102 y de los Lirios, T02-334 0525,
www.enchantedexpeditions.com. Operate
the *Cachalote* and *Beluga* Galápagos vessels
and a wide range of highland tours, set or
custom-made itineraries and jungle trips
to Cuyabeno. Very experienced.
Equateur Voyages Passion, in
L'Auberge Inn, Gran Colombia N15-200 y
Yaguachi, T02-322 7605, www.equateur-
voyages.com. Full range of adventure and
standard tours in highlands, coast and
jungle; set and custom-made itineraries;
also last-minute Galápagos specials.

Happy Gringo, Foch E6-11 y Reina
Victoria, T02-222 0031, www.happygringo.
com. Operate tours to Otavalo, Quito and
surroundings, Quilotoa area; custom-made
trips to all regions, Galápagos and jungle.
Good service.
Jean Brown, T09-9419 4417, justgo2
ecuador@yahoo.com. Very experienced
guide and travel planner arranges
unusual and exclusive personalized
itineraries throughout Ecuador for
small groups, families or individuals.
Highly recommended.
Original Ecuador, T09-9554 5821, www.
originalecuador.com. Run 4- and 7-day
highland tours which involve walking several
hours daily, also custom-made itineraries.
Safari Tours, Reina Victoria N25-33 y
Colón, p 11, of 1101, T02-255 2505, www.
safari.com.ec. Adventure and cultural tours,
specialized itineraries and Galápagos tours.
A good source of travel information.
Tierra de Fuego, Amazonas N23-23 y
Veintimilla, T02-250 1418, www.ecuador
tierradefuego.com. Provide transport and
tours throughout the country, flight tickets,
also sell Galápagos tours.
Tropic Journeys in Nature, Pasaje Sánchez
Melo Oe1-37 y 10 de Agosto, T02-240 8741,
www.tropiceco.com. Environmental and
cultural jungle tours; also highlands, coast
and Galápagos land-based tours.
Wasinku, T02-246 6746, www.wasinku.
com. Custom-designed luxury tours.
Yacu Amu Experiences, Los Shyris
N34-40 y República de El Salvador, of 104,
T02-246 1511, www.yacuamu.com. Tailor-
made adventure, nature and cultural trips
throughout Ecuador for active couples,
families and small groups.
Zenith Travel, JL Mera N24-264 y
Cordero, T02-252 9993, www.zenith
ecuador.com. Galápagos cruises and
land-based tours and a wide range
of tours in Ecuador and Peru. Tailor-
made itineraries. Multilingual service,
knowledgeable helpful staff, good value.

NORTHERN HIGHLANDS

The area north of Quito to the Colombian border is very beautiful. The landscape is mountainous, with views of the Cotacachi, Imbabura and Chiles volcanoes, as well as glacier-covered Cayambe, interspersed with lakes. The region is also renowned for its artesanía. Countless villages specialize in their own particular craft, be it textiles, hats, woodcarvings, bread figures or leather goods. And, of course, there is Otavalo, with its outstanding market, a must on everyone's itinerary. North of Otavalo is Cotacachi, centre for leather crafts, and beyond, the provincial capitals of Ibarra and Tulcán.

To the west of the Andean peaks lie subtropical valleys surrounded by cloud forest-clad slopes and Reserva Ecológica Cotacachi-Cayapas. To the east is the wild country of Reserva Ecológica Cayambe-Coca. At the heart of this protected area and dominating the scene is Volcán Cayambe, Ecuador's third highest peak.

In addition to natural beauty, the Northern Highlands offer a rich cultural experience. The Cayambi people in their colourful dress, the industrious Otavalo nation and the Afro-Ecuadorean people of the Chota region, form part of the cultural mosaic of the northern Andes. A number of community tourism projects are on offer, opening the door to cultural exchange.

→ QUITO TO OTAVALO

On the way from the capital to the main tourist centre in northern Ecuador, the landscape is dominated by the Cayambe volcano. There is a choice of two scenic roads to take, so it is a good idea to go north along one and return on the other.

At **Calderón**, 32 km north of the centre of Quito and 5 km from the periphery, you can see the famous bread figurines being made, though not on Sunday. Especially attractive is the Nativity collection; prices are lower than in Quito. On 1-2 November, the graves in the cemetery are decorated with bread figures, flowers, drinks and food for the dead. The Corpus Christi processions are also very colourful. Take a bus at La Ofelia Metrobus terminal. From Calderón, the Pan-American Highway goes to **Guayllabamba**, home of the Quito zoo (www.quitozoo.org), where it branches, one road going through Cayambe and the second through Tabacundo before rejoining at Cajas, before Otavalo,

COCHASQUI

Ten kilometres past Guayllabamba on the road to Tabacundo, just north of the toll booth, a cobbled road to the left (signed Pirámides de Cochasquí) leads to Tocachi and further on to the archaeological site of **Tolas de Cochasquí** ① *T02-254 1818, 0830-1600, www.pichincha. gob.ec/turismo/cochasqui.html, US$3, entry only with a 1½-hr guided tour.* The protected area contains 15 truncated clay pyramids, nine with long ramps, built between AD 950 and 1550 by the Cara or Cayambi-Caranqui people. Festivals with dancing are celebrated at the equinoxes and solstices. There is a site museum and views from the pyramids, south to Quito, are marvellous. From Terminal Carcelén, be sure to take a bus that goes on the Tabacundo road and ask to be let off at the turn-off. From there it's a pleasant 8-km walk. A taxi from Tabacundo to Cochasquí costs US$12 or US$20 round trip with 1½-hour wait; from Cayambe it's US$15, US$25 round trip.

On the other road, 8 km before Cayambe, a globe carved out of rock by the Pan-American Highway is at the spot where the French expedition marked the Equator (small shop sells drinks and snacks). A few metres north is **Quitsato** ① *T02-236 3042, www.quitsato.org*, where studies about the equator and its importance to ancient cultures are carried out. There is a sun dial, 54 m in diameter, and the **Museo de la Cultura Solar** with information about indigenous cultures and archaeological sites along the equator, they have special events for the solstices and equinoxes.

CAYAMBE

Cayambe, on the eastern (right-hand) branch of the highway, 25 km northeast of Guayllabamba, is overshadowed by the snow-capped volcano of the same name. The surrounding countryside consists of a few dairy farms and many flower plantations. The area is noted for its *bizcochos* (biscuits) served with *queso de hoja* (string cheese). At the Centro Cultural Espinoza-Jarrín is the **Museo de la Ciudad** ① *Rocafuerte y Bolívar, Wed-Sun 0800-1700, free*, with displays about the Cayambi culture and ceramics found at **Puntiachil**, an important but poorly preserved archaeological site at the edge of town. There is a fiesta in March for the equinox with plenty of local music; also Inti Raymi solstice and San Pedro celebrations in June. Market day is Sunday.

VOLCAN CAYAMBE

Cayambe, Ecuador's third highest peak, lies within the **Reserva Ecológica Cayambe-Coca**. It is the highest point in the world to lie so close to the equator (3.75 km north). The equator goes over the mountain's flanks. About 1 km south of Cayambe is an unmarked cobbled road heading east via Juan Montalvo, leading 26 km to the Ruales-Oleas-Berge refuge at 4600 m. The *refugio* costs US$24.40 per person per night, can sleep 37 in bunks; bring a sleeping bag, it is very cold. There is a kitchen, fireplace, hot water and electric light. The climb to the summit is technical and requires experience. The standard route, from the west, uses the refuge as a base. There is a crevasse near the summit which can be very difficult to cross if there isn't enough snow, ask the refuge keeper about conditions. There are nice acclimatization hikes around the refuge. Otavalo and Quito operators offer tours here.

→ OTAVALO AND AROUND

Otavalo, only a short distance from the capital, is a must on any tourist itinerary in Ecuador. The Tabacundo and Cayambe roads join at Cajas, then cross the *páramo* and suddenly descend into the land of the *Otavaleños*, a thriving, prosperous group, famous for their prodigious production of woollens. The town itself, consisting of rather functional modern buildings, is one of South America's most important centres of ethno-tourism and its enormous Saturday market, featuring a dazzling array of textiles and crafts, is second to none and not to be missed. Men here wear their hair long and plaited under a broad-brimmed hat; they wear white, calf-length trousers and blue ponchos. The women's costumes consist of embroidered blouses, shoulder wraps and many coloured beads. Indigenous families speak Quichua at home, although it is losing some ground to Spanish with the younger generation. Otavalo is set in beautiful countryside, with mountains, lakes and small villages nearby. The area is worth exploring for three or four days.

ARRIVING IN OTAVALO

Getting there Tour operators offer tours or private transfer service from Quito to Otavalo which allow you to stop at places of interest along the way. For direct transport, a good

ON THE ROAD
The Otavaleños

The Otavaleños are a proud and prosperous people who have made their name not only as successful weavers and international business people, but also as unsurpassed symbols of cultural fortitude. Today, they make up the economic elite of their town and its surroundings and provide an example which other groups have followed. The Otavalo dialect of Quichua, the highland native tongue, has been adopted as the national standard.

There is considerable debate over the origin of the Otavaleños. In present-day Imbabura, pre-Inca people were Caranquis, or Imbaya, and in Otavalo, the Cayambi. They were subjugated by the Caras who expanded into the highlands from the Manabí coast. The Caras resisted the Incas for 17 years, but the conquering Incas eventually moved the local population away to replace them with *mitmaq* – vassals from Peru and Bolivia. One theory is that the Otavaleños are descended from these forced migrants and also Chibcha salt traders from Colombia, while some current-day Otavaleños prefer to stress their local pre-Inca roots.

Otavalo men wear their hair long and plaited under a white trophy hat. They wear white, calf-length trousers and blue ponchos. The women's colourful costumes consist of embroidered blouses, shoulder wraps, a plethora of gold-coloured necklace beads and red bead bracelets. Their ankle-length skirts, known as *anacos*, are fastened with an intricately woven cloth belt or *faja*. Traditional footwear for both genders is the *alpargata*, a sandal whose sole was originally made of coiled hemp rope, but today has been replaced by rubber.

Perhaps the most outstanding feature of the Otavaleños, however, is their profound sense of pride and self-assurance. This is aided not only by the group's economic success, but also by achievements in academic and cultural realms. In the words of one local elder: "My grandfather was illiterate, my father completed primary school and I finished high school in Quito. My son has a PhD and has served as a cabinet minister!"

option is to take a shared taxi with **Taxis Lagos** ① *in Quito, Asunción Oe2-146 y Versalles, T02-256 5992; in Otavalo, Av Los Sarances y Panamericana, T06-292 3203*. They run a door-to-door service to/from modern Quito only and will divert to resorts just off the highway. If staying in Colonial Quito, take a taxi to their office. They have hourly departures Monday to Saturday from 0715 to 1500 and five departures on Sunday (1½ hours, US$9.50 per person, buy ticket at least one day before); they also serve Ibarra. A private taxi costs US$50 one way, US$80 return with three hours wait. The Otavalo bus terminal is at Atahualpa y Ordóñez, at the north end of town. From Terminal Carcelén in Quito, **Coop Otavalo** and **Coop Lagos** go via Tabacundo to Otavalo (two hours, US$2, every 10 minutes); buses bound for Ibarra or Tulcán drop you off at the highway, this is not recommended.

The **Ciclovía** is a bicycle path which runs along the old rail line 21 km between Eugenio Espejo de Cajas to the north and Otavalo. Because of the slope it is best to start in Cajas. You can take a tour or hire a bike and take a bus bound for Quito to the start of the bike path.

Moving on To continue from Otavalo to **Mindo** (page 74) by public transport, you must first return to Quito (two hours). From Terminal Carcelén take a taxi to Estación La Ofelia (15 minutes) from where buses leave for Mindo (two hours). Both terminals are in the north of Quito. If travelling with private transport, the most expeditious route to Mindo is also through Quito (see Moving on from Quito to Mindo, page 36). If you have the time and interest to explore some back roads, or if you are taking a tour, it is possible to reach Mindo via the beautiful and off-the-beaten-path Intag region, to the west of Otavalo or take a shortcut via San José de Minas.

Getting around The centre is quite small, Calle Sucre the main street has wide sidewalks and is a pleasant place to stroll. You can walk between the craft market at Plaza de Ponchos and the produce market at Plaza 24 de Mayo. The livestock market is more of a hike. There is a frequent bus service from the bus terminal and from Plaza Copacabana (Atahualpa y Montalvo) to Peguche, villages around Lago San Pablo and other nearby towns. From the terminal there is also a frequent service to Cotacachi, Ibarra and Cayambe. Taxis are also plentiful.

Tourist information Contact iTur ① *corner of Plaza de Ponchos, Jaramillo y Quiroga, T06-292 7230, Mon-Fri 0800-1230, 1400-1800, Sat 0800-1600,* for local and regional information. **Cámara de Turismo** ① *Sucre y Quiroga, p2, T06-292 1994, Mon-Fri 0900-1300,* has information and pamphlets.

PLACES IN OTAVALO
While most visitors come to Otavalo to meet its native people and buy their crafts, you cannot escape the influence of the outside world here, a product of the city's very success in trade and tourism. The streets are lined not only with small kiosks selling homespun wares, but also with wholesale warehouses and international freight forwarders, as well as numerous hotels, cafés and restaurants catering to decidedly foreign tastes.

The **Saturday market** comprises four different markets in various parts of the town with the central streets filled with vendors. The *artesanías* market is held from 0700 to 1800, based around the Plaza de Ponchos (Plaza Centenario). The livestock section begins at 0500 and continue until 1000, outside town; go west on Colón from the town centre beyond the highway. The produce market lasts from 0700 till 1400, in Plaza 24 de Mayo. The *artesanías* industry is so big that the Plaza de Ponchos is filled with vendors every day of the week. The selection is better on Saturday but prices are a little higher than other days when the atmosphere is more relaxed. Wednesday is also an important market day with more movement than other weekdays. Polite bargaining is appropriate in the market and shops; reciprocity and courtesy are important Andean norms. Otavaleños not only sell goods they weave and sew themselves, but they bring crafts from throughout Ecuador and from Peru and Bolivia. Indigenous people in the market respond better to photography if you buy something first, then ask politely. **Note** The produce market will be relocated to where the stadium is and the animal market might transfer to the road to Peguche. The **Museo Etnográfico Otavalango** ① *Vía a Selva Alegre Km 1, antigua Fábrica San Pedro, T09-8726 9827, call ahead, US$5,* has displays on all cultural aspects of Otavaleño life; they put on live presentations of local traditions for groups. The **Museo Arqueológico** ① *Parque San Sebastián in the north of town, T09-9428 4976, Mon-Fri 0830-1200, 1430-1700, Sat 0900-1500, free,* has an extensive collection from all over Ecuador. The **Museo de Tejidos El Obraje** ① *Sucre 6-08 y Olmedo, T06-292 0261, US$2, call ahead,* shows the process of traditional Otavalo weaving from shearing to final products. There are good views of town from the **Centro de Exposiciones El Colibrí** ① *C Morales past the railway line.*

PEGUCHE AND OTHER WEAVERS' VILLAGES

Otavalo weavers come from dozens of communities, but it is easiest to visit the nearby towns of Peguche, Ilumán, Carabuela and Agato which are only 15 to 30 minutes away and all have a good bus service. There are also tours going to these villages. Many families weave and visitors should shop around as the less known weavers often have better prices and some of the most famous ones only sell from their homes. In **Peguche**, a few kilometres northeast of Otavalo, are various weaving workshops and stores around the plaza. Nice tapestries are also sold behind the church. You can also find musical instruments and traditional food. Near the village is the **Cascada de Peguche**, a lovely waterfall, a site for ritual purification for the Otavalo people, now also used by mestizos and foreigners. From Peguche's plaza, facing the church, head right and continue straight until the road forks. Take the lower fork to the right, but not the road that heads downhill. There is a small information centre (contributions are appreciated). The patch of eucalyptus forest near the base of the falls is a popular spot for weekend outings and picnics and can get crowded; camping is possible. From the top of the falls (left side, excellent views) you can continue the walk to Lago San Pablo. The **Pawkar Raimi** festival is held in Peguche during carnival.

OTAVALO

In **Ilumán**, east of the Panamericana, north of the turn-off for Cotacachi, you can get backstrap loom weaving demonstrations at **Artesanías Inti Chumbi**. There are also many felt hat-makers in town who will make hats to order and *yachacs* or shamans who do *limpias* (ritual spiritual cleansing), mostly north of the plaza – look for signs. In **Agato**, northeast of Otavalo, there are weaving demonstrations at **Tahuantinsuyo Workshop**. In **Carabuela**, west of the Panamericana, just south of the road to Cotacachi, many homes sell crafts including hand-knitted wool sweaters. This is also a centre for *alpargata* (local footwear) production.

LAGO SAN PABLO

To the southeast of Otavalo, at the foot of Cerro Imbabura and just off the Panamericana is the scenic Lago San Pablo, the largest natural lake in the country. A secondary road circumnavigates the lake. Along it are several native villages and a number of upmarket *hosterías* (inns). San Pablo is a popular weekend destination for wealthier Ecuadoreans looking for water sports, good food, or just a place to get away. In the park at **San Rafael**, along the Panamericana, there is an exhibition of crafts made with *totora* reeds from the lake.

There is a network of old roads and trails between Otavalo and the Lago San Pablo area, none of which takes more than an hour or two to explore. It is worth walking either to or from the lake for the views. Going in a group is recommended for safety. The walk via **El Lechero**, a lookout by a large tree considered sacred among indigenous people, is recommended. The trail starts at the south end of Calle Morales in Otavalo (the road to drive to El Lechero starts from Calle Piedrahita). The walk back to Otavalo via the outlet stream from the lake, staying on the right-hand side of the gorge, takes two to three hours, and is also recommended. For a shorter walk, take a bus to the town of San Pablo and walk towards the lake. The views of Imbabura are wonderful. Various sights can be combined into a day hike or mountain-biking trip: starting in Otavalo go to Peguche, the waterfall, Lago San Pablo, Pucará Alto (see Parque Cóndor, below), El Lechero and back to Otavalo. To explore the lake itself, boats can be hired at **Parque Acuático El Totoral**, below the community of Araque, or at **Cabañas del Lago** and **Puerto Lago** hotels).

On a hill called Curiloma, near the community of Pucará Alto between Otavalo and Lago San Pablo, is **Parque Cóndor** ① *T06-292 4429, www.parquecondor.org, Tue-Sun 0930-1700, raptor flight demonstrations at 1100 and 1600, US$4, crowded at weekends*, a 17-ha reserve created to rescue and rehabilitate birds of prey, including condors; some 15 species of bird can be seen. Environmental education for the community is one of the park's goals; they also have a recreational park. It is 4 km from the Panamericana, you can also walk there in 30 minutes from the Cascada de Peguche or 45 minutes from Otavalo; there are a couple of buses daily from Otavalo to Pucará Alto; a taxi from Otavalo costs US$3.

From San Pablo del Lago it is possible to climb **Cerro Imbabura**, a dormant volcano at 4630 m and often under cloud; allow at least six hours to reach the summit and four hours for the descent. Navigation is tricky and the final ascent requires technical rock-climbing equipment and skills. An alternative access, preferred by many, is from La Esperanza or San Clemente, south of Ibarra (see page 65). Easier, and no less impressive, is the nearby **Cerro Huarmi Imbabura**, 3845 m.

LAGUNAS DE MOJANDA

Southwest of Otavalo are the impressive Lagunas de Mojanda, accessed by cobbled roads from Otavalo or Tabacundo or by a path from Cochasquí. Caricocha (or Laguna

Grande de Mojanda), a crater lake, is the largest of the Mojanda lakes. It is 18 km away from and 1200 m higher than Otavalo. About 25 minutes' walk above Caricocha is Laguna Huarmicocha and a further 25 minutes is Laguna Yanacocha. The views on the descent are excellent. There are no services by the lakes. Take warm clothing and waterproofs. For safety, the area is best visited with a tour.

From Caricocha a trail continues south about 5 km before dividing: the left-hand path leads to Tocachi, the right-hand to Cochasquí (see page 57). Both are about 20 km from Caricocha and offer beautiful views of Quito and Cotopaxi. You can climb Fuya Fuya (4263 m) and Yanaurco (4259 m).

→ COTACACHI AND AROUND

West of the highway between Otavalo and Ibarra is Cotacachi, home to a growing expatriate community. Leather goods are made and sold here. There is also access along a secondary road from Otavalo through Quiroga. The **Casa de las Culturas** ① *Bolívar 1334 y 9 de Octubre, T06-291 5140*, a beautifully refurbished 19th-century building is a monument to peace. It houses a café and temporary exhibits. The **Museo de las Culturas** ① *García Moreno 13-41, due to re-open in late 2013*, off the main plaza, is housed in a nicely refurbished old building with a patio and fountain. It has good displays of Ecuadorean history including maps for different periods, regional crafts (ceramics, basketry, textiles, sisal, silver and leather), regional festivals and traditions, and musical instruments.

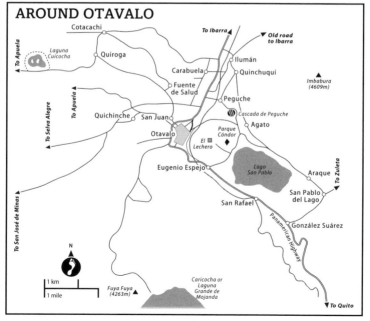

To promote rural and ethno-cultural tourism, the municipality has set up the **Runa Tupari** ① *www.runatupari.com*, or 'meet the natives' programme, which is based in a series of country inns in five nearby villages. Visitors experience life with a native family by taking part in daily activities. The comfortable inns have space for three, fireplace, bathroom and hot shower (US$30 per person including breakfast and dinner and transport from Otavalo). Arrange with Runa Tupari Native Travel or other operators in Otavalo.

Tourist information and a city map are found at www cotacachi.gob.ec. Local festivals include Inti Raymi/San Juan in June and Jora during the September equinox.

Laguna Cuicocha, 15 km from Cotacachi, is part of the **Reserva Ecológica Cotacachi-Cayapas**, which extends from Cotacachi volcano to the tropical lowlands on the Río Cayapas in Esmeraldas. It is a beautiful crater lake with two islands, which are closed to the public for biological studies. There is a well-marked, 8-km path around the lake, which takes four to five hours and provides spectacular views of the Cotacachi, Imbabura and, occasionally, Cayambe volcanos. The best views are in the morning, when condors can sometimes be seen. There is a lookout at 3 km, two hours from the start. Take water and a waterproof jacket. There is a shorter trail which takes 40 minutes. The visitor centre has good natural history and cultural displays. **Note** Enquire locally about safety before heading out and don't take valuables. Do not eat the berries which grow near the lake, as some are poisonous. The path around the lake is not for vertigo sufferers.

Motor boat rides around the islands cost US$2.75 per person for minimum six persons (easier at weekends). Hostería Cuicocha (www.cuicocha.org), at the lake shore, offers tours to a nearby community which raises alpacas. A couple of days' advanced booking is required.

→ IBARRA AND AROUND

Ibarra, the provincial capital, is the main commercial centre and transport hub of the Northern Highlands. The city has an interesting ethnic mix, with black inhabitants from the Chota valley and Esmeraldas alongside Otavaleños and other highland *indígenas*, mestizos and Colombian immigrants. For information, contact **Dirección de Turismo de Imbabura** ① *Bolívar y Oviedo, T06-295 5832, www.imbaburaturismo.gob.ec, Mon-Fri 0800-1300, 1500-1800,* and the municipal tourist office, i-**Tur** ① *Sucre y Oviedo, T06-260 8489, www.touribarra.gob.ec, free Wi-Fi.*

On **Parque Pedro Moncayo** stand the cathedral, the Municipio and Gobernación. One block away, at Flores y Olmedo, is the smaller Parque 9 de Octubre (or **Parque de la Merced**, after its church). Beyond the railway station, to the south and west of the centre, is a busy commercial area with several markets, beyond which is the bus terminal. The **Museo Regional Sierra Norte** ① *Sucre 7-21 y Oviedo, T06-260 2093, Mon-Fri 0830-1700, Sat 1000-1300, 1400-1600,* has interesting displays about cultures from northern Ecuador. **Bosque Protector Guayabillas** ① *Urb La Victoria, on the eastern outskirts of town, www.guayabillas. com, daily 0900-1730,* is a 54-ha park on a hill overlooking the city. There are trails, animals, volunteer opportunities, and accommodation. Virgen del Carmen festival is on 16 July and Fiesta de los Lagos is in the last weekend of September.

Off the main road between Otavalo and Ibarra is **San Antonio de Ibarra**, well known for its wood carvings. It is worth seeing the range of styles and techniques and shopping around in the galleries and workshops. About 8 km from Ibarra on the road to Olmedo is **La Esperanza**, a pretty village in beautiful surroundings. Some 15 km further along, by Angochagua, is the community of **Zuleta** with a fine hacienda (www.haciendazuleta.com). The region is known for its embroidery. West of La Esperanza, along a road that starts at Avenida Atahualpa, and also 8 km from Ibarra, is the community of **San Clemente** (www. sclemente.com), which has a very good grassroots tourism project, **Pukyu Pamba**. From either La Esperanza or San Clemente you can climb **Cubilche** volcano and **Cerro Imbabura** more easily than from San Pablo del Lago (see page 62). From the top you can walk down to Lago San Pablo. *Guías nativos* are available for these climbs.

GOING FURTHER

Warm valleys and cold páramos

To the north of Ibarra is a land of striking contrasts. Deep eroded canyons and warm subtropical valleys stand side by side with windswept moorlands and potato fields.

El Chota

The lush, sugar cane-growing valleys of the Chota and Mira rivers, surrounded by arid hills, lie to the north of Ibarra, at an altitude around 1700 m. They are home to 38 Afro-Ecuadorean communities and many tourist complexes, popular with vacationing Colombians and Ecuadoreans who descend from the highlands for the warmer temperatures and *sabor tropical*. Expressions of Afro-Ecuadorean culture can be experienced during festivities such as Carnaval Coangue, when the local bands play the rhythmical *bomba*. For a taste of this area, ride the **tourist train** ① *www.ecuadorbytrain.com*, from Ibarra to Salinas, 29 km away. Here you'll find the **Museo de la Sal**, an ethnographic cultural centre and eateries offering local cuisine. You can continue by bus from Salinas to San Lorenzo on the coast. The train runs Wednesday to Sunday and holidays at 1030, the ride takes two hours and costs US$10-15 one way, US$15-20 return. At weekends, there is also *autoferro* service at 0830, for US$6.50, which does not include a tour. Purchase tickets in advance at any train station or through T1-800-873637 or info@trenecuador.com; you need each passenger's passport number and date of birth to purchase tickets. **Estación Ibarra** ① *Espejo y Colón, T06-295 5050, open daily 0800-1630*.

Reserva Ecológica El Angel

North of El Chota, near the Colombian border, is **Reserva Ecológica El Angel** ① *T06-297 7597, office in El Angel near the Municipio; best time to visit is May to Aug*. It protects 15,715 ha of *páramo* ranging in altitude from 3400 to 4768 m. The *páramo* is a high Andean moorland which acts like a sponge, gradually releasing water to the valleys. It is composed of a blend of grasses, mosses, club mosses, sedges, cushion plants, ferns, horsetails, lichens and a variety of herbs and shrubs – all adapted to harsh winds and cold temperatures. The sunflower family is the most diverse of flowering plants here, and especially characteristic are the statuesque composite espeletias, known as *frailejón*. Large stands of this elegant, velvet-leafed perennial are found in the reserve. Also common are the spiny *achupallas*, a terrestrial bromeliad with giant compound flowers. The fauna includes condors, *curiquingues* (caracara), deer and foxes. There are also many beautiful little lakes. The closest place to see the *frailejones* is **El Voladero**, 16 km north of the town of El Angel. From the ranger station/shelter, a self-guided trail climbs over a low ridge (30 minutes' walk) to two crystal-clear lakes. They are also found in the centre of the park, reached along the road from El Angel to La Libertad, Socabones and Morán. Before Socabones is **Polylepis Lodge** (T09-9403 1467), with rustic cabins surrounded by forest, and in the village of Morán, **Las Orquídeas** (T09-8641 6936), a simple shelter. The latter is the start of a nice three-day walk through cloud forest to Las Juntas, a warm area off the Ibarra–San Lorenzo road.

NORTHERN HIGHLANDS LISTINGS

WHERE TO STAY

Otavalo

$$$ Posada del Quinde, Quito y Miguel Egas, T06-292 0750, www.posadaquinde. com. Nicely decorated, lovely garden, comfortable rooms and an apartment, includes breakfast, good restaurant, parking.

$$ Acoma, Salinas 07-57 y 31 de Octubre, T06-292 6570, www.hotelacoma.com. Lovely colonial-style house, includes breakfast, cafeteria, nice comfortable rooms, private or shared bath, also suites.

$$ Doña Esther, Montalvo 4-44 y Bolívar, T06-292 0739, www.otavalohotel.com. Colourfully restored colonial house, good restaurant, nice wooden floors.

$$-$ Rincón del Viajero, Roca 11-07 y Quiroga, T06-292 1741, www.hostalrincon delviajero.com. Very pleasant hostel, simple but attractively decorated rooms, includes a choice of good breakfasts, private or shared bath, rooftop hammocks, sitting room with fireplace, camping. Good value.

Around Otavalo

$$$$ Ali Shungu Mountaintop Lodge, 5 km west of Otavalo by Yambiro, T09-8950 9945, www.alishungumountaintoplodge. com. Country inn on a 16-ha private reserve. 4 comfortable guesthouses for 6, with woodstove and kitchenette. Includes breakfast and dinner (vegetarian available).

$$$$ Casa Mojanda, Vía a Mojanda Km 3.5, T09-9972 0890, www.casamojanda. com. Comfortable cabins on a beautiful hillside. Includes breakfast, tasty dinner and short guided hike to waterfall. Each room is decorated with its own elegant touch, outdoor hot tub with great views, quiet.

$$$ Hacienda Cusín, by the village of San Pablo del Lago to the southeast of the lake, T06-291 8013, www.haciendacusin. com. Converted 17th-century hacienda with lovely courtyard and garden, includes

breakfast, fine expensive restaurant, rooms with fireplace, sports facilities, library. Book in advance, British-run.

$$$ La Casa Sol, near the Cascada de Peguche, T06-269 0500. Comfortable rustic hotel on a hillside. Rooms and suites with balcony, some with fireplace, lovely attention to detail, price includes breakfast and dinner, restaurant.

$$-$ Aya Huma, on the railway line in Peguche, T06-269 0164, www.ayahuma. com. In a country setting between the unused rail tracks and the river. Restaurant, quiet, pleasant atmosphere, live music Sat night, Dutch/Ecuadorean-run, popular.

Cotacachi and Laguna Cuicocha

$$$$ La Mirage, 500 m west of town, T06-291 5237, www.mirage.com.ec. Luxurious hacienda with elegant suites and common areas, includes breakfast and dinner, excellent restaurant, pool, gym and spa, beautiful gardens, tours arranged.

$$$ Hostería Cuicocha, Laguna Cuicocha, by the pier, T06-264 8040, www.cuicocha.org. Modern comfortable rooms overlooking the lake, includes breakfast and dinner, restaurant, tours.

$$ Land of Sun, García Moreno 1376 y Sucre, T06-291 6009, www.hoteltierradel sollandofsun.amawebs.com. Refurbished colonial house in the heart of town, includes breakfast, restaurant in lovely patio, sauna, parking.

$$ Runa Tupari, a system of homestays in nearby villages, see page 64.

Ibarra

$$$$ La Estelita, Km 5 Vía a Yuracrucito, T09-9811 6058, www.laestelita.com.ec. On a hill overlooking town. Rooms and suites with lovely views, includes breakfast, good restaurant, pool, spa, paragliding.

RESTAURANTS

Otavalo

$$-$ Buena Vista, Salinas entre Sucre y Jaramillo, p2, www.buenavistaotavalo.com. Open 1200-2200, Sat from 0800, closed Tue. Bistro with balcony overlooking Plaza de Ponchos. Good international food, sandwiches, salads, vegetarian options, trout, good coffee, Wi-Fi.

$$-$ Deli, Quiroga 12-18 y Bolívar. Sun-Thu 1100-2000, Fri 1100-2200, Sat 0800-2200. Mexican and international food, also pizza, tasty desserts, good value.

$ Aly Allpa, Salinas 509 at Plaza de Ponchos. Good-value set meals, breakfast and à la carte including trout, vegetarian and meat.

$ D'Angelos, Sucre y Quito. Daily 1000-2200. Very good pizza and lasagna, good service.

La Casa de Intag, Colón 465 y Sucre. Mon-Sat 0800-2000, Sun 0900-2000. Fair-trade cafeteria/shop run by Intag coffee growers and artisans associations. Good organic coffee, breakfast, pancakes, salads, sandwiches, sisal crafts, fruit pulp and more.

Around Otavalo

Inns around Lago San Pablo, including **Puerto Lago** and **Cabañas del Lago** welcome non-guests to their restaurants.

Cotacachi and Laguna Cuicocha

A local speciality is *carne colorada* (spiced pork).

$$ D'Anita, 10 de Agosto, y Moncayo. Daily 0800-2100. Good set meal of the day, local and international dishes à la carte, popular.

$$-$ La Marqueza, 10 de Agosto y Bolívar. Daily 0730-2130. Set lunches and à la carte.

$ Bhakti, 10 de Agosto y Tarqui, www.bhaktivegan.blogspot.com. Closed Mon. Good vegan breakfast, set lunches and à la carte dishes.

Café Río Intag, Imbabura y Rocafuerte. Mon-Fri 0800-2000, Sat 1000-2200, Sun 1030-1500. The best coffee, snacks, meeting place.

Ibarra

$$ El Argentino, Sucre y P Moncayo, at Plazoleta Francisco Calderón. Tue-Sun. Good mixed grill and salads, small, pleasant, outdoor seating.

Heladería Rosalía Suárez, Oviedo y Olmedo. Excellent home-made *helados de paila* (fruit sorbets made in large copper basins), an Ibarra tradition since 1896.

WHAT TO DO

Otavalo

Most common tours are to indigenous communities, Cuicocha and Mojanda, US$20-30 pp.

All about EQ, Los Corazas 433 y Albarracín, at the north end of town, T06-292 3633, www.all-about-ecuador.com. Interesting set itineraries or tailor-made routes in all regions of Ecuador, outdoor activities; also transport. English and French spoken.

Ecomontes, Sucre y Morales, T06-292 6244, www.ecomontestour.com. A branch of a Quito operator organizing trekking, climbing and rafting. They also sell tours to Cuyabeno and Galápagos.

Leyton's Tours, Quito y Jaramillo, T06-292 2388. Horseriding and bike tours.

Runa Tupari, Sucre y Quiroga, p3, Plaza de Ponchos, T06-292 5985, www.runatupari.com. Indigenous homestays in the Cotacachi area as well as tours, trekking, horse riding and cycling trips; also transport.

Ibarra

EcuaHorizons, Bolívar 4-67, T06-295 9904. Regional tours, bilingual guides.

Intipungo, Rocafuerte 6-08 y Flores, T06-295 7766. Regional tours.

WESTERN SLOPES

Despite their proximity to the capital, the western slopes of Pichincha and surroundings are surprisingly wild, offering nature lovers and outdoor enthusiasts plenty to explore. A very scenic region with beautiful cloud forests, clear rivers and waterfalls, covers a great range of altitudes and is therefore a biodiversity hotspot, protected by many nature reserves. These provide ample opportunities for walking, water and adventure sports and especially birdwatching. Some 450 species of bird have been identified in this area. Walking trails include portions of pre-Inca roads known as Caminos de los Yumbos, some leading to archaeological sites.

The area to the northwest of Quito is known as El Noroccidente and the main resort town here is Mindo, a popular holiday spot for city folk from the capital. Its mild climate is a welcome change after several days exploring the highlands and it is a fine place to relax or take in some of the activities on offer. To the west of Mindo is a warm subtropical area with more rivers and waterfalls and a growing number of tourist developments.

→ NOROCCIDENTE NATURE RESERVES

With increased awareness of the need to conserve the cloud forests of the northwest slopes of Pichincha and of their potential for tourism, the number of reserves here is steadily growing. Keen birdwatchers are no longer the only visitors, and the region has much to offer all nature lovers. Infrastructure at reserves varies considerably. Some have comfortable upmarket lodges offering accommodation, meals, guides and transport. Others may require taking your own camping gear, food, and obtaining a permit.

The reserves listed below are along or reached from the two roads (Ecoruta Paseo del Quinde and Main Route); others are mentioned in the Mindo section (see pages 74-76).

ARRIVING IN THE NOROCCIDENTE

From Quito, two roads lead to the Noroccidente. The main road, fully paved, starts at El Condado roundabout along Avenida Occidental, Quito's western ring road, and goes to the Mitad del Mundo monument, Calacalí, Nanegalito, the turn-off for Mindo, San Miguel de los Bancos, Pedro Vicente Maldonado and Puerto Quito, before joining the Santo Domingo–Esmeraldas road at La Independencia in the lowlands. Parallel to this road is the much older and somewhat rougher, but very scenic, Quito–Nono–Mindo road, famous for its excellent birdwatching. This road begins towards the northern end off Avenida Occidental at the intersection with Calle Machala and is paved as far as Nono. There are several connections between the Calacalí–La Independencia road and the Nono–Mindo road, so it is possible to drive on the main road most of the way even if your destination is one of the lodges on the Nono–Mindo road. If you are not continuing to the coast, we recommend taking one road in one direction and returning along the other; both are very scenic. Two additional roads lead from Quito to the western lowlands, through the southwestern slopes.

Getting there There is a frequent bus service along the main Calacalí–La Independencia road which departs from La Ofelia bus station in Quito; hourly **Trans Esmeraldas** buses, bound for Esmeraldas, also leave from their private station at Santa María 870 y 9 de Octubre in La Mariscal. Buses to Nono depart from Plaza de Cotocollao in northern Quito, but these do not continue west. To travel the older route you require a tour or private transport.

ECORUTA PASEO DEL QUINDE

ⓘ *www.ecorutadelquinde.org.*

The older Nono–Mindo road is famed for its birds, among them over 50 species of hummingbird. Efforts to conserve nature in this special area have led to the creation of the Ecoruta Paseo del Quinde or the **Route of the Hummingbird**, a trail conceived by the **Mindo Cloud Forest Foundation** and involving the local communities. There are a number of private reserves and lodges along the way, which provide a good alternative for visitors looking to have nature close at hand.

The route is 62 km long and has information centres at the villages and lookouts along the way. **Nono,** the first and largest village reached, is just 17 km from Quito, but seems like another world; a forgotten little town surrounded by lush pastures. Cascada Guagrapamba is 5 km from town. From Nono a side road goes to Calacalí. At Km 43 is the hamlet of **Tandayapa,** around which many reserves are clustered; nearby is Cascada Los Yumbos, another waterfall. From Tandayapa, a side road goes to the main Calacalí–La Independencia road, joining it at Km 52, east of Nanegalito. The old road continues to **San Tadeo,** another hamlet with a visitor centre at Km 62, and then on to the main road, joining it at Km 72, before the intersection for Mindo. Visit the Ecoruta website for more details on this route and see below for information on some of the reserves in this area.

Allpalluta ⓘ *T02-249 0567 (Quito), www.allpalluta.com,* is a 260-ha reserve near San Tadeo, with bird- and epiphyte-rich primary and secondary forest between 2000 m and 2230 m. It has a lodge (**$$$**) with cabins with private bath, restaurant, camping area and playground. Price includes breakfast and one guided hike or horse ride. Full-board packages are available.

Bellavista ⓘ *T02-211 6232 (Bellavista), in Quito at Washington E7-25, T02-290 1536, www.bellavistacloudforest.com, at the top of the Tandayapa Valley,* is part of a mosaic of private protected areas dedicated to the conservation of one of the richest accessible areas of west-slope cloud forest. At 2200 m the 700-ha Bellavista Reserve is the highest of these, and the easiest place to see the incredible plate-billed mountain-toucan. Over 300 species of bird have been seen in the Tandayapa Valley, including large numbers of hummingbirds drawn to the many feeders at the lodge. The area is also rich in orchids and other cloud forest plants. There are 20 km of trails ranging from easy to suicidal. A dramatic dome-shaped lodge (**$$$$-$$$**) is perched in beautiful cloud forest, it includes full board (good

food, vegetarian on request), suites and private rooms; simple dormitory accommodation (**$$** per person) is available in the research area and cottage; camping is US$7 per person. Package tours including guide and transport from Quito are available; book in advance. There are several access routes, the fastest is to take the main road to Km 52, from where it is 12 km uphill to Bellavista. A taxi from Nanegalito costs about US$15. Recommended.

El Quinde ① *T02-225 7016 (Quito), www.profafor.com, 2 km east of Tandayapa on the Nono–Mindo road*, is a 2200-ha reserve run by **Fundación Bosques para la Conservación**. About half the area is primary forest and has walking trails.

San Jorge ① *T02-339 0403 (Quito), www.eco-lodgesanjorge.com*, runs a series of reserves in bird-rich areas. Just west of northern Quito, 4 km along the Ecoruta is the 80-ha **Reserva Ecológica San Jorge**, a remnant of high-altitude native vegetation at 3100 m. It has a lodge (**$$$**) in a converted hacienda, a good pricey restaurant, heating, pool, sauna and jacuzzi. **San Jorge de Tandayapa** is a 40-ha cloud forest reserve at 1500 m, just below Tandayapa, along the Nono–Mindo road; it has good trails and a lodge. **San Jorge de Milpe** is a 55-ha upper lowland forest reserve at 900 m, to the north of the Calacalí–La Independencia road at Km 91. It has nice trails, waterfalls, and a lodge. They also run a reserve to the east of Quito in the Cosanga area.

Tandayapa Lodge ① *T02-224 1038 (Quito), on the Ecoruta, up hill from Tandayapa, www. tandayapa.com*, is owned by dedicated birders who strive to keep track of all rarities on the property; they can reliably show you practically any of 318 species, even such rare birds as the white-faced nunbird or the lyre-tailed nightjar; recommended for serious birders. The lodge (**$$$$**) includes full board, 12 very comfortable rooms with private bath and hot water, some rooms have a canopy platform for observation and there's a large common area. Packages are available including guide and transport from Quito; book well in advance. Access is faster via the Calacali–La Independencia road: take the signed turn-off to Tandayapa at Km 52; it is 6 km from there. At the intersection with the Ecoruta turn right; pickup from Nanegalito US$7.

Verdecocha ① *T02-255 1508 (Quito), www.verdecocha.com, 2.6 km from the Ecoruta, along a secondary road which branches off at La Sierra, 8.6 km west of Nono*, is a 750-ha reserve at 2200-3480 m, run by **Fundación Nube Sierra**. They offer horse riding, cycling, llama trekking and volunteer opportunities.

Yanacocha ① *www.fjocotoco.org, 10 km from the Ecoruta along a secondary road which branches off at Km 8.7*, is a 964-ha reserve run by the **Jocotoco Foundation**. It was created to protect a remnant of elfin polylepis forest at 3500 m. It is the home of the black-breasted pufflegg, Quito's emblematic hummingbird, an endangered species.

MAIN ROUTE

From the Mitad del Mundo monument the road goes past the turn-off for Pululahua crater (page 51) and by **Calacalí**, whose plaza has an older monument to the equator. Beyond Calacalí is a toll where a road turns south to Nono and north to Yunguilla. Another road at Km 52 goes to Tandayapa. The main road, with heavy traffic at weekends, continues to to

Nanegalito (Km 56), Miraflores (Km 62), the turn-offs to the Ecoruta (Km 72) and to Mindo (Km 79), and beyond to San Miguel de los Bancos, Pedro Vicente Maldonado, Puerto Quito and La Independencia.

In **Nanegalito**, a small supply centre and important transport hub for the region, the **tourist information office** ① *on the highway, next to the police station, T02-211 6222, daily 0900-1700*, has a crafts and local produce shop, an orchid shop and offers guiding services. A road due north of Nanegalito goes to the hamlet of **Nanegal**, the access to the Maquipucuna and Santa Lucía reserves (see below).

At Armenia (Km 60), a few kilometres beyond Nanegalito, a road heads northwest through Santa Clara, with a handicrafts market on Sunday, to the village and archaeological site of **Tulipe** (14 km; 1450 m). The site consists of several man-made 'pools' linked by water channels. A path leads beside the Río Tulipe in about 15 minutes to a circular pool surrounded by trees. The site **museum** ① *T02-285 0635, www.museodesitiotulipe.com, US$3, Wed-Sun 0900-1600, guided tours (arrange ahead for English)*, has exhibits in Spanish on the Yumbos culture and the *colonos* (contemporary settlers). There is also an orchid garden. The Yumbos were traders who linked the Quitus with coastal and jungle peoples between AD 800 and 1600. Their trails are called *culuncos*, 1 m wide and 3 m deep, covered in vegetation for coolness. Several treks in the area follow them. Also to be seen are *tolas*, raised earth platforms; there are some 1500 around Tulipe.

There are lodging options in Tulipe (including www.hosteriasumakpakari.com) and in the community of Las Tolas, 6 km away. For reserves and tours in the area see www.tulipecloudforest.org and www.cloudforestecuador.com.

To the northwest of Tulipe are **Gualea** and **Pacto**, beyond which are **Sahuangal**, on the Río Guayllabamba to the north, and to the northwest **Mashpi** with a reserve and lodge (www.mashpilodge.com).

Maquipucuna ① *T02-250 7200, 09-9237 1945, www.maqui.org, entry US$10, guide US$25 (Spanish) US$100 (English) per day for group of 9*, has 6000 ha surrounded by an additional 14,000 ha of protected forest. The cloud forest at 1200-2800 m contains a tremendous diversity of flora and fauna, including over 325 species of bird. Especially noteworthy are the colourful tanager flocks, mountain toucans, parrots and quetzals. The reserve has 40 km of trails ranging in duration from 15 minutes to all day. The comfortable rustic lodge (**$$$$-$$$**) includes full board with good meals using ingredients from their own organic garden (vegetarian and vegan available); rooms have private or shared bath with hot water and electricity. The campsite is 20 minutes' walk from the main lodge. There is also a research station, experimental organic garden, organic coffee orchard and reforestation project. To get there, turn right at Nanegalito, follow the road to Nanegal for 12 km and turn right again (before Nanegal). Pass through the village of Marianitas and it's another 4 km to the reserve. Past the turn-off for Nanegal the road is poor, especially in the January-May wet season; 4WD vehicles are recommended; transport is offered from the Quito office.

Milpe and Río Silanche ① *www.mindocloudforest.org, entry US$5*. The **Mindo Cloudforest Foundation** owns several bird-rich reserves which protect the habitat of important Chocó-endemic species. **Santuario de Aves Milpe**, 700 m north of the main road (turn-off at Km 91), is a 62-ha reserve (1020-1150 m) with basic facilities for four researchers. **Santuario de Aves Río Silanche**, 7 km from the main road (turn-off at Km 127) below Pedro Vicente Maldonado, is an 80-ha reserve in the low foothills (300-350 m); it has a canopy tower and walking trails.

Pachijal ⓘ *T09-9955 4560, T02-255 4627 (Quito), www.pachijalreserve.com*, is a 120-ha reserve, 3 km north of the main road at Km 72. The bird-rich forest at 1600 m has 30 km of trails and the small six-room lodge (**$$$**) includes breakfast, restaurant for guests only and rooftop terrace with views. Horse riding is available.

Reserva Orquideológica El Pahuma ⓘ *T09-9520 3497, www.ceiba.org, day visits 0700-1700, US$4, guide US$1 pp*, at Km 43 on the main road, is a 600-ha cloud forest reserve, less than one hour from Quito, with easy access. It is an interesting collaboration between a local landowner and the **Ceiba Foundation for Tropical Conservation**. It features an orchid garden and an orchid propagation programme. Trails start at 1900 m and go to 2800 m. A five-hour walk takes you to the Ecoruta del Quinde road, following for 4 km the pre-Inca Camino de los Yumbos (guide compulsory, US$20). Birds, such as mountain toucans, torrent ducks and tanagers, are present, and spectacled bears have been seen. On the south side of the road are a visitor centre and hostel (**$**) with shared bath, hot water and kitchen facilities. On the north side is a restaurant. To get there, take any bus for Nanegalito or points west.

Santa Lucía ⓘ *office in Nanegal, 02-215 7242, www.santaluciaecuador.com*, is a successful community-based conservation and ecotourism project. It protects a beautiful 730-ha tract of cloud forest, between 1900 and 2500 m, to the east of Maquipucuna. The area is very rich in birds (including the cock-of-the-rock lek) and other wildlife. There are waterfalls and walking trails, including the ancient Camino de los Yumbos. The lodge (**$$$**) with panoramic views is a 1½-hour walk from the access to the reserve. The price includes full board with good food and guiding. There are cabins with private bath, rooms with shared bath and hot showers and dormitories (**$** per person including food but not guiding). The British organization **Rainforest Concern** is involved with this reserve and offers volunteer programmes here. Access to the reserve is 30 minutes by car from Nanegal, next to Maquipucuna (see page 72). Day tours combining Pululahua, Yunguilla and Santa Lucía and four-day walking tours from Yunguilla to Santa Lucía are available.

Tucanopy ⓘ *by the community of Miraflores, 2 km north of the main road, turn-off at Km 63.5, www.tucanopy.com, 0900-1600, closed Wed*, is a 100-ha reserve at 1700 m, with trails including a Camino de los Yumbos, 2150 m of canopy ziplines and accommodation. They are involved with conservation projects and offer volunteer opportunities.

Mindo is a small town surrounded by dairy farms, rivers and lush cloud forest that climbs the western slopes of Pichincha. It is an excellent base for many outdoor activities: walking, horse riding, bathing in waterfalls, tubing (floating down the river in inner tubes), canyoning, canopy ziplining (a Tyrolean traverse from treetop to treetop or treetop to the ground), birdwatching and more. In and around town you can see many birds, including a variety of hummingbirds attracted to feeders. The access road into town is particularly good for birdwatching, as is the private 'Yellow House Trail' (Hacienda San Vicente, see Where to stay, page 77). There are orchid gardens and butterfly and frog farms. Mindo is a popular destination among Quiteños, who are attracted by the mild climate and outdoor activities; it gets busy at weekends and even more so during holidays. **Note** There is only one ATM, so take cash.

ARRIVING IN MINDO

The most direct access from Quito is along the Calacalí–La Independencia road; at Km 79 is the turn-off for Mindo to the south, from where it is 8 km down a side road to the town. It can also be reached via the Ecoruta Paseo del Quinde.

Getting there From Quito's Estación La Ofelia, **Flor del Valle** buses (T02-236 4393) depart Monday to Friday at 0800, 0900 and 1600; Saturday at 0740, 0820, 0920 and 1600; Sunday at 0740, 0820, 0920, 1400 and 1700 (US$2.50, two hours); weekend buses fill quickly, buy ahead. From Estación La Ofelia, you can also take any bus bound for San Miguel de los Bancos or from **Trans Esmeraldas'** private station in La Mariscal (Santa María 870 y Amazonas, T02-250 9517, hourly departures), take a bus bound for Esmeraldas, and get off at the turn-off for Mindo from where there are taxis until 1930 (US$0.50 per person or US$3 without sharing).

Moving on To continue to the coast by bus, **Cooperativa Kennedy** has six daily departures to Santo Domingo (US$4, 3½ hours, see page 76). From Santo Domingo, buses depart every 15 minutes to Pedernales (US$4, three hours, see page 78). From Pedernales, **Coactur** buses run about every hour to Canoa (US$2.50, two hours, see page 78), some continue to Bahía de Caráquez (see page 79); there are also vans along this route.

If driving, you can either take the main road to La Independencia and go south from there to Santo Domingo; alternatively, at San Miguel de los Bancos, 8 km beyond the Mindo turn-off, take a secondary paved road to Santo Domingo via Alluriquín.

To return to Quito from Mindo, buses depart at least three times a day.

Getting around Mindo is a small town. Pickup taxis are available to reach attractions outside town; if you are up to walking longer distances, strolling to the different sites can be very pleasant. There are several private information offices along Avenida Quito, the main street.

PLACES IN MINDO

Mindo, is the main access for the 19,500-ha **Bosque Protector Mindo-Nambillo**. The reserve, which ranges in altitude from 1400 to 4780 m, features beautiful flora (many orchids and bromeliads), fauna (butterflies, birds including the cock-of-the-rock, golden-headed quetzal and toucan-barbet) and spectacular cloud forest and waterfalls. Access to the reserve proper is restricted to scientists, but there is a buffer zone of private reserves which offers many opportunities for exploring. The region's rich diversity is threatened by proposed mining in the area. **Amigos de la Naturaleza de Mindo** ① *1½ blocks from the Parque Central, T02-217 0086, US$1, guide US$30 for group of 12*, runs the **Centro de Educación Ambiental** (CEA), 4 km from town, within a 17-ha buffer zone, capacity for 25-30 people. Lodging **$** per person full board; or use of kitchen US$1.50). Arrangements have to be made in advance. During the rainy season, access to the reserve can be rough. **Acción por la Vida** runs **Refugio Centro de Rescate La Esperanza** ① *contact César Fiallo, T09-9466 5732*, a 2000-ha reserve, part of a conservation and sustainable development project which also takes in confiscated animals; volunteers are welcome. **El Monte** ① *www.ecuadorcloudforest.com*, **Estación Científica, Hacienda San Vicente** ① *www.yellowhousetrails.com*, **Sachatamia** ① *www.sachatamia.com*, and **Séptimo Paraíso** ① *www.septimoparaiso.com*, are all private reserves with fine lodges; they run tours on their properties.

Some of the area's diversity can be admired at orchid gardens and butterfly farms where the stages of metamorphosis are displayed and explained, 250 species of butterfly have been identified around Mindo. **Mariposas de Mindo** ① *3 km from town on the road to CEA, T02-217 0193, www.mariposasdemindo.com, US$3*, is a nice butterfly farm with restaurant and lodging. **Nathaly** ① *100 m from the main park, US$2*, is a small simple butterfly farm and orchid garden. A fine collection of the region's orchids can be seen at **Jardín de Orquídeas** ① *2 blocks from the church, by the stadium, T02-217 0131, www.birdingmindo.com, US$2*, which also has cabins and a restaurant. **Mindo Lago** ① *300 m from town on the road to Quito, T02-217 0201, US$1 day visit, frog concert at 1830, US$3*, has trails and cabins around a pretty pond surrounded by vegetation, where you can listen to frogs around sunset.

Several waterfalls can be visited, all on private land. Since the owners cut and maintain access trails, they all charge an entrance fee (US$3-5). On the Río Nambillo is the **Cascada de Nambillo**, a four-hour return walk. Just nearby is **Santuario de Cascadas**, a series of falls on a tributary of the Nambillo, with the added attraction of a 530-m-long *tarabita* (cable car) to cross the river; if you do not want to use the *tarabita*, you can still cross the river on a bridge; tickets and transport are available from Café Mindo on the main street. **La Isla** ① *office on the main street, T02-217 0181, www.laislamindo.com, camping US$5 pp, 5-6 hrs return walking*, is a small forest reserve on the Río Saguambi, with a shelter and camping area. Here are three scenic waterfalls, one used for rapelling (guide compulsory). Canopy ziplines, are available on the way to Santuario de Cascadas; the price varies according to the length and steepness of the run. **Mindo Canopy** ① *T09-9453 0624, www.mindocanopy.com*, with 3500 m of lines, is reported as good. **Mindo Ropes & Canopy** ① *T02-217 0131*, has 2650 m of lines. **Tucanopy**, see page 73, in a reserve near Nanegalito, has 2150 m of lines.

A very popular activity in the Mindo area is **regattas**, the local name for inner-tubing – floating down a river on a raft made of several inner tubes tied together. The number of tubes that can run together depends on the water level. Several local agencies and hotels offer this activity for US$3-5. It is usually done on the Río Mindo, but experts also run the Río Blanco, where competitions are held during local holidays.

WEST OF MINDO

The main road continues west beyond the turn-off to Mindo, descending to the subtropical zone north of Santo Domingo de los Tsáchilas. The entire area is good for birdwatching, swimming in rivers and natural pools, walking, kayaking or simply relaxing in natural surroundings. There are many reserves, resorts, lodgings and places to visit along the route. **San Miguel de los Bancos**, perched on a ridge above the Río Blanco, is a market town with a pleasant climate. A road goes south from here and shortly splits: one branch, paved, goes to Alluriquín, on the Quito–Santo Domingo highway; the second one leads to Santo Domingo via Valle Hermoso.

Further west, **Pedro Vicente Maldonado** is a small supply town in a subtropical cattle-ranching area. A secondary road goes from here northwest to the Río Guayllabamba. The main road bypasses town to the south. About 8 km west of PV Maldonado, at Km 124 along the main road, is **Finca San Carlos**. Within the farm, it's a 15-minute walk to **Laguna Azu**, a lovely pool at the base of a striking 35-m waterfall on the Río Negro. On the shores of the lovely Río Caoni is **Puerto Quito**, a small town which was once intended to be the capital's port. The main road bypasses the centre of town to the south. The Calacalí road meets the Santo Domingo–Esmeraldas road 28 km southwest of Puerto Quito. Just south of the junction, on the way to Santo Domingo, is the village of La Independencia and 5 km further south the town of La Concordia.

Santo Domingo de los Tsáchilas, 129 km from Quito, is an important commercial centre, transport hub and provincial capital. The city is noisy and dangerous; caution is recommended at all times in the market areas, including the pedestrian walkway along 3 de Julio. Sunday is market day; shops and banks close on Monday instead. In the past, it was known as 'Santo Domingo de los Colorados', a reference to the traditional red hair dye, made with *achiote* (annatto) and worn by the indigenous Tsáchila men. Today the Tsáchila only wear their indigenous dress on special occasions. There are less than 2000 Tsáchilas left, living in eight communities off the roads leading from Santo Domingo towards the coast. Visitors interested in their culture are welcome at the **Complejo Turístico Huapilú**, in the **Comunidad Chigüilpe**, where there is a small but interesting museum (contributions expected). Access is via the turn-off east at Km 7 on the road to Quevedo, from where it is 4 km. Tours are run by agencies in town. The Santo Domingo area also offers opportunities for nature trips and sports such as rafting. There is a **Cámara de Turismo ①** *Río Mulaute y Av Quito, T02-275 2146, Mon-Fri 0830-1300, 1430-1800, English spoken.*

From Santo Domingo, several roads lead to the coast. One goes north past La Independencia, where it intersects with the road from Mindo and Calacalí, and continues to the port of Esmeraldas. Another road goes west to El Carmen, where it divides: one branch goes northwest to Pedernales; the second branch goes to Chone where it divides again, with one branch leading west to Bahía de Caráquez and the second one to Portoviejo and Manta. The suggested route for this trip is to take the branch that goes to Pedernales, in order to go south along the scenic coastal road. Another important road goes southwest from Santo Domingo to Quevedo, Babahoyo and Guayaquil.

WESTERN SLOPES LISTINGS

WHERE TO STAY

Mindo

$$$$ El Monte, 2 km form town on road to CEA, then opposite Mariposas de Mindo, cross river on *tarabita* (rustic cable car), T02-217 0102, Quito T02-255 8881, www.ecuadorcloudforest.com. Beautifully constructed lodge in 44-ha property, newer cabins are spacious and very comfortable, includes 3 meals, some (but not all) excursions with a *guía nativo* and tubing; other adventure sports and horse riding are extra, no electricity, reserve in advance.

$$ Hacienda San Vicente (Yellow House), 500 m south of the plaza, T02-217 0124, Quito T02-223 6275. Family-run lodge set in 200 ha of very rich forest, includes excellent breakfast and dinner, pleasant rooms, good walking trails open to non-guests for US$5, reservations required, good value. Highly recommended for nature lovers.

$$-$ El Descanso, 300 m from main street, take 1st right after bridge, T02-217 0213, www.eldescanso.net. Nice house with comfortable rooms, includes breakfast, cheaper in loft with shared bath, parking.

$$-$ Jardín de los Pájaros, 2 blocks from the main street, 1st right after bridge, T02-217 0159. Family-run hostel, includes good breakfast, small pool, parking, large covered terrace, good value.

West of Mindo

$$$$ Arashá, 4 km west of PV Maldonado, Km 121, T02-390 0007, Quito T02-244 9881 for reservations, www.arasharesort.com. Well-run resort and spa with pools, waterfalls (artificial and natural) and hiking trails. Comfortable thatched cabins, price includes all meals (world-class chef), use of the facilities (spa extra) and tours. Can arrange transport from Quito, attentive staff, popular with families, elegant and very upmarket.

$$$ Selva Virgen, at Km 132, east of Puerto Quito, T02-390 1317, www.selvavirgen.com.ec. Nice *hostería* in a 100-ha property owned by the Universidad Técnica Equinoccial (UTE). Staffed by students. Includes breakfast, restaurant, spacious comfortable cabins with a/c, fridge, jacuzzi and nice porch, cheaper in rooms with ceiling fan, pool, lovely grounds.

$ Mirador Río Blanco, San Miguel de los Bancos, main road, at the east end of town, T02-277 0307. Popular hotel/restaurant serving tropical dishes, small rooms, parking, terrace with bird feeders (many hummingbirds and tanagers) and magnificent views of the river.

RESTAURANTS

Mindo

$$ Fuera de Babilonia, Las Buganvillas, 1 block from the park. Daily 0730-2300. Pleasant restaurant, set meals and à la carte, pasta, vegetarian available.

$ Panadería Pizzería Don Pan, Av Quito, 1 block from the park. Daily 0600-2200. Great pizza, good bread and sweets, drinks, pavement seating.

WHAT TO DO

Mindo

Mindo Bird, Sector Saguambi, just out of town on the road to CEA, T02-217 0188, www.mindobird.com. Birdwatching, regattas, cycling, hiking, waterfalls, English spoken, very helpful.

Vinicio Pérez, T09-947 6867, www.bird watchershouse.com. A recommended birding guide who speaks some English.

PACIFIC COAST

The Pacific Lowlands comprise a third of mainland Ecuador. This vast tract of land covers everything west of the Andes and north of the Guayas delta. Though popular with Quiteños and Guayaquileños, who come here for weekends and holidays, this region receives relatively few foreign visitors, which is surprising given the natural beauty, diversity and rich cultural heritage of the coast. Here you can surf, watch whales, visit archaeological sites, or just relax and enjoy some of the best food this country has to offer.

The village of Canoa boasts some of the finest beaches in Ecuador. To the south, on the other side of the Río Chone estuary, is Bahía de Caráquez, a relaxed resort town and a pleasant place to spend a few days. Passing by more great beaches, good roads run south from Bahía to Manta, Ecuador's largest seaport and the main city north of Guayaquil, and continue south along the shore past various beaches to Puerto López and Parque Nacional Machalilla. One of the finest coastal national parks, it protects an important area of primary tropical dry forest, pre-Columbian ruins, coral reef and a wide variety of wildlife. This is also the best place for whale watching (June to September). More beaches line the route south of Puerto López for 100 km to the Santa Elena Peninsula, seaside playground of Guayaquil.

Getting there For details of the route from Mindo to Canoa via Santo Domingo de los Tsáchilas and Pedernales, see Moving on, page 74.

Moving on There are frequent local buses from Canoa to Bahía de Caráquez via San Vicente, 15 minutes. From Bahía, long-distance buses run to Manta, US$3, three hours. Change in Manta (see page 81) for a bus to Puerto López (bus every two hours, US$3, three hours; see page 82). There are several beaches along the way and sufficient public transport to allow you to get off the bus and later catch another vehicle headed south, but you may not get a seat. Exploring the coast at your leisure is easier with a private vehicle.

→ CANOA AND BAHIA DE CARAQUEZ

PEDERNALES TO CANOA

Pedernales is a market town and crossroads; the church has a nice mosaic mural and stained-glass windows. It the closest bathing beach to Quito but the shore is not particularly clean or attractive in town. However, to the north is a beautiful long beach that stretches as far as the village of Cojimíes. South of Pedernales the road crosses the equator and goes by the **Reserva de Bosque Seco Lalo Loor** ① *www.ceiba.org*, a dry tropical forest reserve with walking trails and a simple cabin. Further south are **Punta Prieta** and 1 km beyond, at the next headland, **Punta Blanca**; the black and white promontories, respectively. This area has a handful of interesting and very tranquil upmarket places to stay (see www.hotelpuntablanca.com, www.samvara-ecolodge.com and www.puntaprieta.com). Next is the small market centre of **Jama**, home to another of Ecuador's expatriate enclaves, where the road turns inland to emerge again by the shore at Canoa.

CANOA

Once a quiet fishing village with a splendid 200-m-wide beach. Canoa has grown rapidly and is increasingly popular with Ecuadorean and foreign tourists. It has lost some of its charm along the way, but it is still pleasant on weekdays, crowded, noisy and dirty at weekends and especially holidays. The choice of accommodation and restaurants is very good. The beautiful beach between Canoa and San Vicente, 17 km south, is great for walking, horse or bike riding. Horses and bicycles can be hired through several hotels. Surfing is good, particularly during the wet season, December to April. In the dry season there is good wind for windsurfing. Canoa is also a good place for hang-gliding and paragliding. Tents for shade and chairs are rented at the beach for US$3 a day. About 10 km north of Canoa, the **Río Muchacho organic farm** (www.riomuchacho.com) accepts visitors and volunteers; it's an eye-opener to rural coastal (*montubio*) culture and to organic farming.

BAHÍA DE CARAQUEZ AND AROUND

Set on the southern shore at the seaward end of the Chone estuary, Bahía has an attractive riverfront laid out with parks along the Malecón which goes right around the point to the ocean side. The beaches in town are nothing special, but there are excellent beaches nearby between San Vicente and Canoa and at Punta Bellaca to the south. Town is busiest July and August when highlanders have school holidays. Bahía has declared itself an 'eco-city', with recycling projects, organic gardens and ecoclubs. Tricycle rickshaws called 'eco-taxis' are a popular form of local transport. Information about the eco-city concept can be obtained from **Río Muchacho organic farm** in Canoa (see above) and the **Planet Drum Foundation**, www. planetdrum.org. There's a **Ministerio de Turismo** and **Dirección Municipal** ① *T05-269 1124 and T05-269 1044, www.bahiadecaraquez.com, both at Bolívar y Padre Laennen, Mon-Fri 0830-1300, 1430-1730, Sat 0800-1300.* The **Museo Bahía de Caráquez** ① *Malecón Alberto Santos y Aguilera, T05-269 2285, Tue-Sat 0830-1630, free,* has an interesting collection of archaeological artefacts from pre-Hispanic coastal cultures, a life-size balsa raft and modern sculpture. Bahía is a port for international yachts, with good service at **Puerto Amistad** (T05-269 3112).

Saiananda ① *5 km from Bahía along the bay, T05-239 8331, owner Alfredo Harmsen, biologist, entry US$2,* is a private park with extensive areas of reforestation and a large collection of animals, a cactus garden and spiritual centre. It can be reached by taxi or any bus heading out of town. They also offer first-class accommodation (**$$** including breakfast) and vegetarian meals served in an exquisite dining area over the water.

The Río Chone estuary has several islands with mangrove forest. The area is rich in birdlife, and dolphins may also be seen. **Isla Corazón** has a boardwalk through an area of protected mangrove forest and there are bird colonies at the end of the island which can only be accessed by boat. The village of **Puerto Portovelo** is involved in mangrove reforestation and runs an eco-tourism project (tour with *guía nativo*, T09-9750 0203). You can visit independently, taking a Chone-bound bus from San Vicente, or with an agency. Visits here are tide-sensitive, so check for the best time to visit. Inland near Chone is **La Segua** wetland, which is also very rich in birds; Bahía hotels can arrange tours.

Chirije (www.chirije.com) is an archaeological site, 45-minutes by car south of Bahía. It was a seaport of the Bahía culture (500 BC to AD 500), which traded as far north as Mexico and south to Chile. There is an on-site museum, as well as cabins (**$$$**) and a restaurant. It is surrounded by dry tropical forest, good beaches, walking and birdwatching possibilities. Access is along a seasonal road (not suitable after rain) or along the beach. On the way to Chirije is the scenic Punta Bellaca; near it is the Cerro Viejo or Cerro de las Orquídeas hill, with dry tropical forest, which is worth exploring. **Bahía Dolphin Tours** (www.bahiadolphintours. com) offers tours to Chirije.

GOING FURTHER
Esmeraldas

A mixture of palm-lined beaches (some with good surfing), mangroves (where they have not destroyed for shrimp production), tropical rainforest, Afro-Ecuadorean and Cayapa indigenous communities characterize the northernmost part of Ecuador's Pacific Lowlands, located in the province of Esmeraldas.

Mompiche
North of Pedernales the coastal highway veers northeast, going slightly inland, then crosses into the province of Esmeraldas near the authentic little village of **Chamanga**. Some 31 km north of Chamanga and 7 km from the main road along a side road is **Mompiche** with a lovely beach and one of Ecuador's best surfing spots. There is an international resort complex nearby but the beach by the village retains much of its original charm and there are a couple of good places to stay such as **$$-$ Iruña** (T09-9497 5846) and **$ Gabeal** (T09-9969 6543).

Playa Escondida, Súa, Same and Atacames
Following the coast road north, 25 km past El Salto (turn-off for the somewhat faded beach at Muisne), the next crossroad is the fishing village of **Tonchigüe**. South of it, a paved road goes west and follows the shore to **Punta Galera**. Along the way is the secluded beach of **Playa Escondida**, a charming hideaway with good birdwatching set in 100 ha with a 500-m beach stretching back to dry tropical forest. Run by Canadian Judith Barett on an ecologically sound basis, it has rustic cabins overlooking a lovely little bay and an excellent restaurant (**$$$** with full board).

Three kilometres northeast of Tonchigüe, Playa de **Same** is a beautiful, long, clean, grey sandy beach, safe for swimming. The accommodation here is mostly upmarket, intended for wealthy Quiteños, but it is wonderfully quiet in the low season. There is good birdwatching in the lagoon behind the beach and some of the hotels offer whale-watching tours in season. Ten kilometres east of Same is **Súa**, a friendly little beach resort, set in a beautiful bay. It gets noisy at weekends and during the high season (July-September), but is otherwise tranquil. Four kilometres east of Same is **Atacames**, one of the main resorts on the Ecuadorean coast, a real 24-hour party town during the high season (July-September), at weekends and national holidays.

Esmeraldas and north to Colombia
Thirty kilometers northeast of Atacames is Esmeraldas, the provincial capital. Neither safe nor salubrious (mosquitoes and malaria are a serious problem from here north, especially in the rainy season, January-May), it is nonetheless a good place to learn about Afro-Ecuadorean culture. Some visitors enjoy its very relaxed swinging atmosphere. Marimba groups can be seen practising in town; enquire about schedules at the **tourist office** ① *Bolívar y Ricaurte, Edif Cámara de Turismo, p3, T06-271 1370, Mon-Fri 0900-1200, 1500-1700.*

Further northeast en route to the Colombian border, far off the beaten path, are a few beaches and mangroves, as well as the last remnants of Ecuador's unique Chocó rainforest and authentic Afro-Ecuadorean and Cayapa villages.

BAHIA DE CARAQUEZ TO MANTA

About 30 km south of Bahía de Caráquez are **San Clemente** and, 3 km further south, **San Jacinto**. The ocean is magnificent but be wary of the strong undertow. Both places get crowded during the holiday season and have a selection of cabañas and hotels. Some 3 km north of San Clemente is **Punta Charapotó**, a high promontory clad in dry tropical forest, above a lovely beach. Here are some nice out-of-the way accommodations and an out-of-place upmarket property development.

A rapidly growing resort, 12 km south of San Jacinto and 45 minutes by road from Manta, **Crucita** is busy at weekends and holidays when people flock here to enjoy ideal conditions for paragliding, hang-gliding and kite-surfing. The best season for flights is July to December. There is also an abundance of seabirds in the area. There are many restaurants serving fish and seafood along the seafront. A good one is **Motumbo**; try their *viche*. They also offer interesting tours and rent bikes.

MANTA AND AROUND

Ecuador's second port after Guayaquil is a busy town that sweeps round a bay filled with all sorts of boats. A constant sea breeze tempers the intense sun and makes the city's *malecones* pleasant places to stroll. At the gentrified west end of town is Playa Murciélago, a popular beach with wild surf (flags indicate whether it is safe to bathe) and good surfing from December to April. Here, the Malecón Escénico has a cluster of bars and seafood restaurants. It is a lively place especially at weekends, when there is good music, free beach aerobics and lots of action. The **Museo Centro Cultural Manta** ⓘ *Malecón y C 19, T05-262 6998, Mon-Fri 0900-1630, Sat-Sun 1000-1500, free*, has a small but excellent collection of archaeological pieces from seven different civilizations which flourished on the coast of Manabí between 3500 BC and AD 1530. Three bridges join the main town with its seedy neighbour, **Tarqui**. For tourist information there's a **Ministerio de Turismo** ⓘ *Paseo José María Egas 1034 (Av 3) y C 11, T05-262 2944, Mon-Fri 0900-1230, 1400-1700*; **Dirección Municipal de Turismo** ⓘ *C9 y Av 4, T05-261 0171, Mon-Fri 0800-1700*; and **Oficina de Información ULEAM** ⓘ *Malecón Escénico, T05-262 4099, daily 0900-1700*; all helpful and speak some English. Manta has public safety problems; enquire locally about the current situation.

MANTA TO PUERTO LOPEZ

South of Manta, the coast road heads to **San Lorenzo**, with its cape and lighthouse, and then through forested hills to **Puerto Cayo**, with a nice beach and surfing. Whale-watching tours may be organized in July and August. An alternative route heads inland from Manta 16 km to **Montecristi**, below an imposing hill. The town is renowned as the centre of the Panama hat industry. Also produced are varied straw- and basketware, and wooden barrels which are strapped to donkeys for carrying water. Ask for José Chávez Franco (Rocafuerte 203), where you can see Panama hats being made. From Montecristi the road continues south to the trading centre of Jipijapa where you turn right (west) to rejoin the coast road at Puerto Cayo.

ON THE ROAD
A whale of a time

Whale watching is a major tourist attraction along Ecuador's coast. A prime site to see these massive mammals is around Isla de La Plata but whales travel the entire length of Ecuador's shores and well beyond.

Between June and September each year, groups of up to 10 individuals of this gregarious species make the 7200-km trip from their Antarctic feeding grounds to the equator. They head for these warmer waters to mate and calve. Inspired by love, we presume, the humpbacks become real acrobats. Watching them breach (jump almost completely out of the water) is the most exciting moment of any tour. Not far behind, though, is listening to them 'sing'. Chirrups, snores, purrs and haunting moans are all emitted by solitary males eager to use their chat-up techniques on a prospective mating partner. These vocal performances can last half an hour or more.

Adult humpbacks reach a length of over 15 m and can exceed 30 tonnes in weight. The gestation period is about one year and newborn calves are 5-6 m long. The ventral side of the tail has a distinctive series of stripes which allows scientists to identify and track individual whales.

Humpbacks got their English name from their humped dorsal fins and the way they arch when diving. Their scientific name, *Megaptera novaeangliae* (which translates roughly as 'large-winged New Englanders') comes from the fact that they were first identified off the coast of New England, and from their very large wing-like pectoral fins. In Spanish they are called *ballena jorobada* or *yubarta*.

These whales have blubber up to 20 cm thick. Combined with their slow swimming, this made them all too attractive for whalers in the 19th and 20th centuries. During that period their numbers are estimated to have fallen from 100,000 to 2500 worldwide. Protected by international whaling treaties since 1966, the humpbacks are making a gradual recovery. Ironically, the same behaviour that once allowed them to be harpooned so easily makes the humpbacks particularly appealing to whale watchers today.

There is ongoing research about marine mammals. If you have good photos showing a whale's tail, a dolphin, orca or other creature, share them with scientists through www.museodeballenas.org; click on 'catálogos'.

→PUERTO LOPEZ AND PARQUE NACIONAL MACHALILLA

PUERTO LOPEZ

This pleasant fishing town is beautifully set in a horseshoe bay. The beach is best for swimming at the far north and south ends, away from the fleet of small fishing boats moored offshore. The town is popular with tourists for watching humpback whales from approximately mid-June to September, and for visiting Parque Nacional Machalilla and Isla de la Plata year-round. Whales can also be seen elsewhere on the coast of Ecuador but most reliably in Puerto López.

There is a good fleet of small boats (16-20 passengers) running whale-watching excursions, all have life jackets and a toilet; those with two engines are safer. All agencies offer the same tours for the same price. In high season: US$40 per person for whale watching, Isla de la Plata and snorkelling, with a snack and drinks, US$25 for whale watching only (available June and September). Outside whale season, tours to Isla de la Plata and snorkelling cost US$25. Trips depart around 0800 and return about 1700. Agencies also offer tours to the mainland sites of the national park. A day tour combining Agua Blanca and Los Frailes costs US$25 per person. There are also hiking, birdwatching, kayaking, diving (be sure to use a reputable agency, there have been accidents) and other trips. A visit to Salango (see below) is recommended.

PARQUE NACIONAL MACHALILLA

① *Park office in Puerto López, C Eloy Alfaro y García Moreno, daily 0800-1200, 1400-1600.*
The park extends over 55,000 ha, including Isla de la Plata, Isla Salango, and the magnificent beach of **Los Frailes** and preserves marine ecosystems as well as the dry tropical forest and archaeological sites on shore. At the north end of Los Frailes beach is a trail through the forest leading to a lookout with great views and on to the town of Machalilla (don't take valuables). The land-based part of the park is divided into three sections which are separated by private land, including the town of Machalilla. The park is recommended for birdwatching, especially in the cloud forest of Cerro San Sebastián (see below); there are also several species of mammal and reptile.

About 5 km north of Puerto López, at Buena Vista, a dirt road to the east leads to **Agua Blanca** (park kiosk at entry). Here, 5 km from the main road, in the national park, amid hot, arid scrub, is a small village and a fine, small **archaeological museum** ① *0800-1800, US$5 for a 2- to 3-hr guided tour of the museum, ruins (a 45-min walk), funerary urns and sulphur lake; horses can be hired for the visit, camping is possible and there's a cabin and 1 very basic room for rent above the museum for US$5 pp; pick-up from Puerto López US$8.* Exhibits include some fascinating ceramics from the Manteño civilization.

San Sebastián, 9 km from Agua Blanca, is in tropical moist forest at 800 m; orchids and birds can be seen and possibly howler monkeys. Although part of the national park, this area is administered by the Comuna of Agua Blanca, which charges its own fees; you cannot go independently. It's five hours on foot or by horse. A tour to the forest costs US$40 per day including guide, horses and camping (minimum two people), otherwise lodging is with a family at extra cost.

About 24 km offshore is **Isla de la Plata**. Trips are popular because of the similarities with Galápagos. Wildlife includes nesting colonies of waved albatross (April to November), frigates and three different booby species. Whales can be seen from June to September, as well as sea lions. It is also a pre-Columbian archaeological site with substantial pottery finds, and there is good diving and snorkelling, as well as walks. Take a change of clothes, water, precautions against sun and seasickness (most agencies provide snorkelling equipment). Staying overnight at the island is not permitted.

→ PUERTO LOPEZ TO GUAYAQUIL

SALANGO TO AYAMPE

South of Puerto López is **Salango**, with an ill-smelling fish processing plant, but worth visiting for the excellent **Salango archaeological museum** ① *at the north end of town, daily 0900-1200, 1300-1700, US$1*, housing artefacts from excavations right in town. It also has a craft shop and, at the back, nice rooms with bath in the **$** range. There is a place for snorkelling offshore, by Isla Salango. South of Salango are the villages of **Las Tunas**, **Puerto Rico** and **Río Chico**. There are places to stay all along this stretch of coast. Next comes the small, poor village of **Ayampe** with many popular places to stay at south end of the beach. A further 20 km south is **Olón**, with a spectacular long beach.

MONTAÑITA
Past an impressive headland and a few minutes south of Olón is Montañita, which has mushroomed into a major surf resort, packed with hotels, restaurants, surf-board rentals, tattoo parlours and craft/jewellery vendors. There are periodic police drug raids in Montañita and several foreigners are serving long sentences in jail. At the north end of the bay, 1 km away, is another hotel area with more elbow room, Baja Montañita (or Montañita Punta, Surf Point). Between the two is a lovely beach where you'll find some of the best surfing in Ecuador. Various competitions are held during the year. At weekends in season, the town is full of Guayaquileños.

MANGLARALTO
About 3 km south of Montañita, 180 km northwest of Guayaquil, this is the main centre of the region north of Santa Elena. There is a tagua nursery; ask to see examples of worked 'vegetable ivory' nuts. It is a nice place, with a quiet beach, good surf but little shade. **Pro-pueblo** ① *T04-268 3569, www.propueblo.com*, is an organization working with local communities to foster family-run orchards and cottage craft industry, using tagua nuts, *paja toquilla* (the fibre Panama hats are made from) and other local products. They have a craft shop in town (opposite the park), an office in San Antonio south of Manglaralto (T04-278 0230), and headquarters in Guayaquil. **Proyecto de Desarrollo Ecoturístico Comunitario** ① *contact Paquita Jara T09-9174 0143*, has a network of simple lodgings with local families (US$9 per person), many interesting routes into the Cordillera Chongón Colonche and whale-watching and island tours.

VALDIVIA
Continuing south, Valdivia and San Pedro are two unattractive villages which merge together. There are many fish stalls. This is the site of the 5000-year-old Valdivia culture. Many houses offer 'genuine' artefacts (it is illegal to export pre-Columbian artefacts from Ecuador). Juan Orrala, who makes excellent copies, lives up the hill from the **Ecomuseo Valdivia** ① *T09-8011 9856, daily, US$1.50*, which has displays of original artefacts from Valdivia and other coastal cultures. There is also a handicraft section, where artisans may be seen at work, and lots of local information. At the museum is a restaurant and five rooms with bath to let. Most of the genuine artefacts discovered at the site are in museums in Quito and Guayaquil.

PLAYAS AND SALINAS
The coast road continues south to Santa Elena, an important junction which provides access to the eponymous peninsula where Guayaquil goes to the beach. The resorts of Salinas and Playas are very popular with vacationing Guayaquileños and get crowded, especially at weekends during the *temporada de playa* (beach season), December to April.

Salinas, surrounded by miles of salt flats, is Ecuador's answer to Miami Beach. High-rise blocks of holiday flats and hotels line the seafront. There is safe swimming in the bay, but more appealing is the (still urban) beach of Chipipe, west of the exclusive Salinas Yacht Club. From December to April town is overcrowded, its services stretched to the limit. Even in the off season it is not that quiet.

Whalewatching (June to September) and birdwatching trips can be arranged. The **Museo de Ballenas** ⓘ *Av Enríquez Gallo, entre C 47 y C 50, T04-277 8329, www.museo deballenas.org, by appointment only, voluntary contributions welcome*, is a small whale museum at the home of naturalist Ben Haase, who also offers tours. This is the place to report beached whales or dolphins. On the museum's website is a catalogue with photos of individual whales and dolphins; contribute to marine mammal research with your photos. For more information on whales, see page 82. For general information, contact **Turismo Municipal** ⓘ *Eloy Alfaro y Mercedes de Jesús Molina, Chipipe, T04-277 3931, Tue-Fri 0800-1700, Sat 0800-1400*.

On the south shore of the Santa Elena peninsula, 8 km south of La Libertad and built on high cliffs, is **Punta Carnero**, with hotels in the **$$$-$$** range. To the south is a magnificent 15-km beach with wild surf and heavy undertow. Here too there is whale watching in season; some might even be spotted from the shore.

At El Progreso (Gómez Rendón), a secondary road goes south off the toll highway between Salinas and Guayaquil. It leads to **Playas** (General Villamil), the nearest seaside resort to Guayaquil; bottle-shaped *ceibo* (kapok) trees characterize the landscape as it turns into dry, tropical thorn scrub. In Playas a few single-sailed balsa rafts, very simple but highly ingenious, can still be seen among the motor launches returning laden with fish.

In high season (*temporada* – December to April), and at weekends, Playas is prone to severe crowding, although the authorities are trying to keep the packed beaches clean and safe (thieving is rampant during busy times). Out of season or midweek, the beaches are almost empty especially north towards Punta Pelado (5 km). Playas has six good surf breaks. There are showers, toilets and changing rooms along the beach, with fresh water, for a fee and many hotels in our **$$-$** ranges. Excellent seafood and typical dishes are served from over 50 beach cafés (all numbered and named). Many close out of season. The **tourist office** ⓘ *Tue-Fri 0800-1200, 1400-1800, Sat-Sun 0900-1600*, is in the Malecón.

PACIFIC COAST LISTINGS

WHERE TO STAY

Canoa

There are over 60 hotels in Canoa.

$$$ Canoa Beach Hotel, 10 mins' walk from town along the beach, T05-258 8062, www.canoabeachhotel.com. Upmarket 4-storey beachfront hotel, rooms with a/c, nice pool and deck.

$$ La Vista, on the beach towards the south end of town, T09-9228 8995. All rooms have balconies to the sea, palm garden with hammocks, good value.

$ Bambú, on the beach just north of C Principal, T09-8926 5225, www.hotel bambuecuador.com. Pleasant location and atmosphere. A variety of rooms and prices, good restaurant including vegetarian, private or shared bath, also dorm, camping possible, hot water, fan, surfing classes and board rentals. Dutch/ Ecuadorean-owned, very popular.

Bahía de Caráquez

$$$$ Casa Ceibo, Km 5 on the road to Chone, T05-239 9399, www.casaceibo.com. An opulent luxury hotel, includes breakfast, restaurant, pool, ample manicured grounds, large comfortable rooms, tours.

$$$ La Piedra, Circunvalación near Bolívar, T05-269 0154, www.hotellapiedra.com. Modern hotel with access to the beach and lovely views, good expensive restaurant, a/c, pool (US$2 for non-guests, only in low season), good service, bicycle rentals.

$$ La Herradura, Bolívar e Hidalgo, T05-269 0446, www.laherradurahotel.com. Older well-maintained hotel, restaurant, a/c, cheaper rooms with fan and cold water are good value, nice common areas.

$ Coco Bongo, Cecilio Intriago y Arenas, T09-8544 0978, www.cocobongohostal.com. Popular hostel with a pleasant atmosphere, private bath, cheaper in dorm, breakfast available, electric shower, ceiling fan, mosquito nets, cooking facilities, Australian-owned.

Puerto López

$$$-$$ Pacífico, Malecón y González Suárez, T05-230 0147, www.hotelpacifico ecuador.com. Restaurant, a/c, comfortable, cheaper in old wing with fan, pleasant grounds, pool, boat tours.

$$ La Terraza, on hill overlooking town (moto-taxi US$0.50), T09-8855 4887, www.laterraza.de. Spacious cabins, great views over the bay, gardens, restaurant for guests, crystal-clear pool and jacuzzi, parking. Organizes horse tours to see howler monkeys at **Bola de Oro**. German-run.

$$ Mandála, Malecón at north end of the beach, T05-230 0181, www.hosteria mandala.info. Attractive cabins decorated with art, lovely garden, excellent restaurant, fan, mosquito nets, games, music room, Swiss/Italian-run, English spoken, knowledgeable owners.

$ Sol Inn, Montalvo entre Eloy Alfaro y Lascano, T05-230 0248, hostal_solinn@ hotmail.com. Bamboo and wood construction, private or shared bath, fan, laundry and cooking facilities, parking, garden, pool table. Popular, nice atmosphere, English and French spoken, good value.

Montañita

$$ Balsa Surf Camp, 50 m from the beach in Montañita Punta, T04-206 0075, www.balsasurfcamp.com. Includes breakfast, very nice clean and spacious cabins with terrace, hammocks in garden, fan, parking, surf classes and rentals, French/Ecuadorian-run.

$$ La Casa del Sol, in Montañita Punta, T09-9210 8931, www.casadelsolsurfcamp. com. Includes breakfast, nice oceanfront rooms, some in older section are dark, fan, beach-side restaurant/bar, surf classes and rentals, yoga drop-in (US$5).

RESTAURANTS

Canoa

$$-$ Surf Shak, at the beach. Daily 0800-2400. Good for pizza, burgers and breakfast, best coffee in town, Wi-Fi US$1 per hr, popular hangout for surfers, English spoken.

Bahía de Caráquez

$$ Puerto Amistad, on the pier at Malecón y Vinueza. Mon-Sat 1200-2400. Nice setting over the water, international food and atmosphere, popular with yachties.

$$-$ Arena-Bar Pizzería, Riofrío entre Bolívar y Montúfar. Daily 1700-2400. Restaurant/bar serving good pizza, salads and other dishes, nice atmosphere, also take-away and delivery service.

$$-$ Muelle Uno, by the pier where canoes leave for San Vicente. Daily 1000-2400. Good grill and seafood, lovely setting over the water.

$ Doña Luca, Cecilio Intriago y Sergio Plaza, towards the tip of the peninsula. Daily 0800-1800. Simple little place serving excellent local fare, *ceviches*, *desayuno manabita* (a wholesome breakfast) and set lunches. Friendly service, recommended.

Puerto López

$$$-$$ Bellitalia, Montalvo y Abdón Calderón, 1 block back from the Malecón. Open 1800-2100. Excellent Italian food, try their spinach soup, pleasant garden setting, Italian-run. Highly recommended.

Montañita

$$ Happy Donkey, near the beachfront. Good grill, Chinese food, seafood, frequently recommended.

WHAT TO DO

Canoa

Canoa Thrills, at the beach next to **Surf Shak**, www.canoathrills.com. Surfing tours and lessons, sea kayaking. Also rent boards and bikes. English spoken.

Río Muchacho Organic Farm, J Santos y Av 3 de Noviembre, T05-258 8184, www.riomuchacho.com. Bookings for the organic farm and eco-city tours. Hikes from Canoa to Río Muchacho and around Río Muchacho. Knowledgeable and helpful with local information. Recommended.

Wings and Waves, T09-8519 8507 or ask around for Greg. Paragliding flights and lessons.

Bahía de Caráquez

Bahía Dolphin Tours, at Hotel Casa Grande, T05-269 0257, www.bahiadolphintours.com. Tours to Chirije and other local attractions.

Puerto López

Bosque Marino-Expediciones Oceánicas, Malecón y Sucre, T05-260 4106 or T09-9707 1067. Experienced dive guides, some speak English.

Cercapez, at the Centro Comercial on the highway, T05-230 0173. All-inclusive trips to San Sebastián, with camping, local guide and food, US$40 pp per day.

Exploramar Diving, Malecón y Gral Córdova, T05-230 0123, www.exploradiving.com. Quito-based, T02-256 3905. Have 2 boats for 8-16 people. PADI divemaster accompanies qualified divers to various sites, but advance notice is required, US$95 pp for all-inclusive diving day tour (2 tanks). Also offer diving lessons. Recommended.

Mares Dive Center, Malecón y Gral Córdova, T05-230 0137, www.mares ecuador.com. 1 day (2 tanks) US$95. They also offer a 4-day course.

Montañita

Surfboard rentals from US$4 per hr, US$15 per day.

Montañita Adventures, around the corner from **Hotel Casa Blanca**. Kayaks, bicycles, surfing lessons, snorkelling tours.

GUAYAQUIL AND AROUND

Guayaquil traditionally receives fewer tourists than Quito but, as a point of arrival or departure, it can be a good alternative to the capital for those who wish to avoid the altitude of the highlands or are heading directly to the beach or Galápagos. Good hotels and restaurants abound but are not cheap. There are several agencies with whom you can make bookings for Galápagos as well as other tours.

Guayaquil is hotter, faster and louder than Quito. It is Ecuador's largest city, the country's chief seaport and main commercial centre, some 56 km from the Río Guayas' outflow into the Gulf of Guayaquil. Industrial expansion continually fuels the city's growth. Founded in 1535 by Sebastián de Benalcázar, then again in 1537 by Francisco Orellana, the city has always been an intense political rival to Quito. Guayaquileños are certainly more lively, colourful and open than their Quito counterparts. Since 2000, Guayaquil has cleaned-up and 'renewed' some of its most frequented downtown areas, it boasts a modern airport and bus terminal, and the Metrovía transit system.

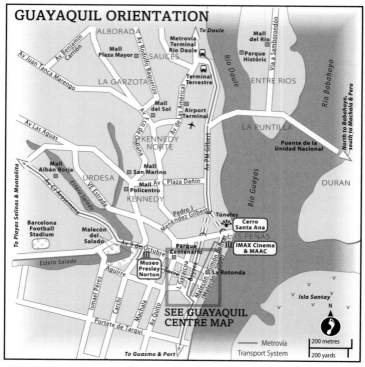

ON THE ROAD

Choosing a hotel in Guayaquil

If your budget is up to it, Guayaquil has some of the best top-class accommodation in Ecuador. Hotels include various international chains as well as excellent local establishments. There are also many mid-priced hotels, offering comfortable rooms and attentive service in varied surroundings.

Many establishments are clustered in the busy downtown core, where you can find everything from a quaint boutique B&B and the practical international hotel catering to business people, to basic cheap lodging. The best location in the centre is along the Malecón Simón Bolívar, opposite the Malecón 2000 riverside promenade. Another good option is around the east end of Boulevard 9 de Octubre, close to the Malecón. A number of good hotels are clustered near Parque Bolívar, around Calle Chile and Clemente Ballén. Since the city is noisy, select a room away from the street. Cheap hotels are concentrated around Parque Centenario. This area is not recommended, however, since it is unsafe and many hotels here are used by short-stay couples. The downtown core also has a few good economy hotels.

To the north of downtown, a number of luxury hotels are located in the neighbourhood of Kennedy Norte, to the west of the airport. This area also has good restaurant options, as does Urdesa, further west. There are a few mid-priced hostels near the airport but, being on the flight path, they are very noisy.

Those seeking real peace and quiet, plus gardens and swimming pools, can do very well in a number of suburban hotels. They would be ideal were they not so hard to find. Best call to book in advance and try to get precise instructions for the taxi driver or arrange to be picked up on arrival.

→ ARRIVING IN GUAYAQUIL

GETTING THERE

Air Guayaquil's **José Joaquín de Olmedo** airport receives many international flights and has domestic air service throughout Ecuador, including to the Galápagos Islands.

Bus There is ample bus service throughout the country. From Puerto López, **Cooperativa Jipijapa** runs inland via Jipijapa, 10 daily (US$4, four hours). To do this trip along the coast, transfer in Olón or Santa Elena.

MOVING ON

From Guayaquil you can fly to Galápagos (see page 155), back to Quito (see page 35) or to Cuenca (see page 118) or Coca (see page 140) to connect with any of the other routes in this book. You can also take an international flight home or to another South American country.

ORIENTATION

The international airport is 15 minutes north of the city centre by car. Not far from the airport is the **Terminal Terrestre** long-distance bus station. Opposite this terminal is the northern terminus of the **Metrovía** rapid transit system.

A number of hotels are centrally located in the downtown core, along the west bank of the Río Guayas, where you can get around on foot. The city's suburbs sprawl to the north and south of the centre, with middle-class neighbourhoods and some very upscale areas in the north, where some elegant hotels and restaurants are located, and poorer working-class neighbourhoods and slums to the south. Road tunnels under Cerro Santa Ana link the northern suburbs to downtown. Outside downtown, addresses are hard to find; ask for a nearby landmark to help orient your driver.

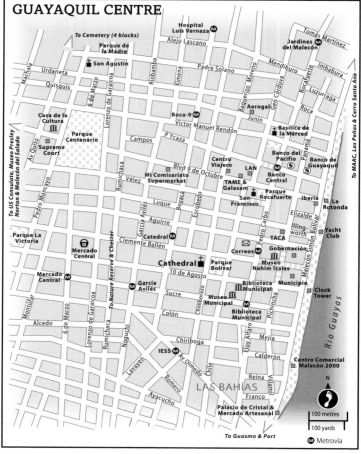

BEST TIME TO VISIT

From May to December the climate is dry with often overcast days but pleasantly cool nights, whereas the hot rainy season from January to April can be oppressively humid.

TOURIST INFORMATION

Centro de Información Turística del Municipio ① *Clemente Ballén y Pichincha, at Museo Nahim Isaías, T04-232 4182, Tue-Sat 0900-1630*, has pamphlets and city maps. There are also information booths at the Malecón 2000 by the clock tower, and at the Terminal Terrestre. The Ministerio de Turismo, Subsecretaría del Litoral ① *Av Francisco de Orellana, Edif Gobierno del Litoral, p 8 and counter on the ground floor, Ciudadela Kennedy, T04-268 4274, www.ecuador.travel, Mon-Fri 0900-1700*, has information about the coastal provinces of Ecuador and whale-watching regulations. See also www.visitaguayaquil.com.

SAFETY

The Malecón 2000, parts of Avenida 9 de Octubre, Las Peñas and Malecón del Estero Salado are heavily patrolled and reported safe. The rest of the city requires precautions. Do not go anywhere with valuables, for details see page 201. The area around Parque Centenario is unsafe, day or night. 'Express kidnappings' are of particular concern in Guayaquil. Enquire locally as to which taxis are currently considered safest.

→ PLACES IN GUAYAQUIL

A wide, tree-lined waterfront avenue, the Malecón Simón Bolívar runs alongside the Río Guayas from the Palacio de Cristal, past Plaza Olmedo, the Moorish clock tower, by the imposing Palacio Municipal and Gobernación and the old Yacht Club to Las Peñas. The riverfront along this avenue is an attractive promenade, known as Malecón 2000 ① *open daily 0700-2400*, where visitors and locals can enjoy the fresh river breeze and take in the views. There are gardens, fountains, childrens' playgrounds, monuments, walkways and an electric vehicle for the less able (daily 1000-2000, US$2). You can dine at upmarket restaurants, cafés and food courts. Towards the south end are souvenir shops, a shopping mall and the Palacio de Cristal (prefabricated by Eiffel 1905-1907), which is used as a gallery housing temporary exhibits.

At the north end of the Malecón is an IMAX large-screen cinema, and downstairs the Museo Miniatura ① *Tue-Sun 0900-2000, US$1.50*, with miniature historical exhibits. Beyond is the Museo Antropológico y de Arte Contemporaneo (MAAC) ① *T04-230 9400, Tue-Fri 0900-1630, Sat-Sun and holidays 1000-1630, free,* with excellent collections of ceramics and gold objects from coastal cultures and an extensive modern art collection.

North of the Malecón 2000 is the old district of Las Peñas, the last picturesque vestige of colonial Guayaquil with its brightly painted wooden houses and narrow, cobbled main street (Numa Pompilio Llona). It is an attractive place for a walk to Cerro Santa Ana, which offers great views of the city and the mighty Guayas. It has a bohemian feel, with bars and restaurants. A large open-air exhibition of paintings and sculpture is held here during the Fiestas Julianas (24-25 July). North of La Peñas is Puerto Santa Ana, with upmarket apartments, a promenade and three museums: to the romantic singer Julio Jaramillo, to beer in the old brewery, and to football.

By the pleasant, shady Parque Bolívar, also known as Parque Seminario, stands the cathedral, in Gothic style, inaugurated in the 1950s. In the park are many iguanas and it is also popularly referred to as Parque de las Iguanas. The nearby **Museo Municipal** ① *in the Biblioteca Municipal, Sucre y Chile, Tue-Sat 0900-1700, free, city tours on Sat, also free*, has paintings, gold and archaeological collections, shrunken heads, a section on the history of Guayaquil and a good newspaper library.

Between the Parque Bolívar and the Malecón is the **Museo Nahim Isaías** ① *Pichincha y Clemente Ballén, T04-232 4283, Tue-Sat 0900-1630, US$1.50, free on Sat*, a colonial art museum with a permanent religious art collection and temporary exhibits.

Halfway up 9 de Octubre is **Parque Centenario** with a towering monument to the liberation of the city erected in 1920. Overlooking the park is the museum of the **Casa de la Cultura** ① *9 de Octubre 1200 y P Moncayo, T04-230 0500, Tue-Fri 1000-1800, Sat 0900-1500, US$1, English-speaking guides available*, which houses an impressive collection of prehistoric gold items in its archaeological museum, and a photo collection of old Guayaquil.

West of Parque Centenario, the **Museo Presley Norton** ① *Av 9 de Octubre y Carchi, T04-229 3423, Tue-Sat 0900-1700, free*, has a good collection of coastal archaeology in a beautifully restored house. At the west end of 9 de Octubre are **Plaza Baquerizo Moreno** and the **Malecón del Estero Salado**, another pleasant waterfront promenade along a brackish estuary. It has various monuments, eateries specializing in seafood, and rowing boats and pedal-boats for hire.

→ AROUND GUAYAQUIL

Parque Histórico Guayaquil ① *Vía Samborondón, near Entrerríos, T04-283 2958, Wed-Sun 0900-1630, free*, recreates Guayaquil and its rural surroundings as they were at the end of the 19th century. There is a natural area with native flora and fauna, a traditions section where you can learn about rural life, an urban section with old wooden architecture, and eateries. It's a pleasant place for a family outing. CISA buses to Samborondón leave from the Terminal Terrestre every 20 minutes (US$0.25).

The **Botanical Gardens** ① *Av Francisco de Orellana, in Ciudadela Las Orquídeas (bus line 63), T04-289 9689, daily 0800-1600, US$3, guiding service US$5*, are to the northwest of Guayaquil. There are over 3000 plants, including 150 species of Ecuadorean and foreign orchids (most flower August to December).

A **Tourist Train** ① *station, T04-215 4254, reservations T1-800-873637, www.trenecuador. com, Thu-Sun 0900 and 1315, US$10, 2 hrs return, tickets sold at Malecón 2000, Malecón y Aguirre*, runs through rice paddies from Durán, across the river from Guayaquil, to Yaguachi and back.

Bosque Protector Cerro Blanco ① *Vía a la Costa, Km 16, T04-287 4947, US$4, additional guiding fee US$7-12 depending on trails visited, camping US$7 pp, lodge available*, run by **Fundación Pro-Bosque**, is set in tropical dry forest with an impressive variety of birds (over 200 species), many reptiles and with sightings of monkeys and other mammals. Unfortunately it is getting harder to see the animals due to human encroachment in the area. Reservations are required on weekdays and for groups larger than eight at weekends, and for birders wishing to arrive before or stay after normal opening hours (0800-1530). Take a **CLP** bus from the Terminal Terrestre or a taxi (from US$5 up). On the other side of the road, at Km 18 is **Puerto Hondo** ① *T04-287 1900*. Canoe trips through the mangroves can be arranged on the spot at weekends from the **Fundación Pro-Bosque** kiosk (US$12 for a group of eight), or during the week with the Cerro Blanco office (see above).

Heading east then south from Guayaquil, 22 km beyond the main crossroads at Km 50 on the road to Machala lies the **Reserva Ecológica Manglares Churute** ① *arrange trips several days ahead through the Dirección Regional, Ministerio del Ambiente in Guayaquil, 9 de Octubre y Pichincha, Edif Banco Central, p 6, T04-230 6645, ext 106,* a rich natural area with five different ecosystems created to preserve mangroves in the Gulf of Guayaquil and forests of the Cordillera Churute. Many waterbirds, monkeys, dolphins and other wildlife can be seen. There is a trail through the dry tropical forest (1½ hours' walk) and you can also walk (one hour) to Laguna Canclón or Churute, a large lake where ducks nest. Boat tours cost US$15 per hour for up to 15 passengers (two to four hours recommended to appreciate the area. Basic cabins (US$5) and camping (US$3) are available. Near the park, **Monoloco Lodge ($)**, www.monoloco.ec, can also organize tours. Buses (CIFA, Ecuatoriano Pullman, 16 de Junio) leave the Terminal Terrestre every 30 minutes, going to Naranjal or Machala; ask to be let off at the Churute information centre. The reserve can also be reached by river.

GUAYAQUIL AND AROUND LISTINGS

WHERE TO STAY

For tips on choosing a hotel, see page 89.

$$$$-$$$ Mansión del Río, Numa Pompilio Llona 120, Las Peñas, T04-256 6044, www.mansiondelrio-ec.com. Elegant boutique hotel in a 1926 European-style mansion, river view, buffet breakfast, airport transfers, 10 mins from city centre.

$$$ Ramada, Malecón 606 e Imbabura, T04-256 5555, www.hotelramada.com. Excellent location on the Malecón, rooms facing river are more expensive, includes buffet breakfast, restaurant, a/c, pool, spa.

$$ Las Peñas, Escobedo 1215 y Vélez, T04-232 3355. Nice hotel in a refurbished part of downtown, ample modern rooms, includes breakfast, cafeteria, a/c, quiet despite being in the centre of town, good value. Recommended.

$$ Manso, Malecón 1406 y Aguirre, upstairs, T04-252 6644, www.manso.ec. Attractively refurbished hostel in a great location opposite the Malecón. Rooms vary from fancy with a/c, private bath and river view, to simpler with shared bath and fan, and a 4-bed dorm (**$** pp), includes breakfast, English spoken.

$$ Tangara Guest House, Manuela Sáenz y O'Leary, Manzana F, Villa 1, Ciudadela Bolivariana, T04-228 4445, www.tangara-ecuador.com. Comfortable hotel in a pleasant area by the university and near the Estero Salado, includes breakfast, a/c, fridge, one airport transfer, convenient for airport and bus terminal but also along the flight path, so it can be noisy.

$$-$ Elite Internacional, Baquerizo Moreno 902 y Junín, T04-256 5385. Completely refurbished old downtown hotel, better rooms have a/c, private bath, hot water; **$** with fan, shared bath and cold water.

RESTAURANTS

$$$ Lo Nuestro, VE Estrada 903 e Higueras, Urdesa, T04-238 6398. Daily 1100-1530, 1900-2330. Luxury restaurant with typical coastal cooking, good seafood platters and stuffed crabs, colonial decor.

$$$-$$ Cangrejo Criollo, Av Rolando Pareja, Villa 9, La Garzota, T04-262 6708. Daily 0900-0100. Excellent, varied seafood menu.

$$$-$$ La Parrilla del Ñato, VE Estrada 1219 y Laureles in Urdesa; Av Francisco de Orellana opposite the Hilton Colón; Luque y Pichincha downtown; and several other locations, T04-268 2338. Daily 1200-2200. Large variety of dishes, salad bar, also pizza by the metre, good quality, generous portions. Try the *parrillada de mariscos*, available only at the Urdesa and Kennedy locations.

$$ La Canoa, at Hotel Continental, Chile 512 y 10 de Agosto, T04-232 9270. Open 24 hrs. Regional dishes rarely found these days, with different specials during the week, a Guayaquil tradition.

$ Ollantay, Tungurahua 508 y 9 de Octubre, west of downtown. Good vegetarian food.

WHAT TO DO

Centro Viajero, Baquerizo Moreno 1119 y 9 de Octubre, No 805, T04-230 1283, T09-9235 7745. 24-hr service, www.centroviajero.com. Custom-designed tours all over Ecuador, information and bookings, car and driver service, well informed about Galápagos, helpful, English spoken.

La Moneda, Av de las Américas 406, Centro de Convenciones Simón Bolívar, oficina 2, T04-269 0900, ecuador@lamoneda.com.ec. City and coastal tours, whale watching, also tours to other parts of the country.

Xavier Ávalos, T04-603 0824 or T09-9709 8400, is an English-speaking biologist who offers tours to the islands and all natural sites in the region.

DREAM TRIP 2
Quito→Riobamba→Cuenca→Vilcabamba 14 days

Quito 3 nights, page 35

Latacunga 1 night, page 101
Bus/van/train from Quito (2 hrs) or full-day
tour via Parque Nacional Cotopaxi and
Saquisilí market (Thu only)

Quilotoa or Chugchilán 1 night,
pages 102 and 103
Bus/taxi from Latacunga to Quilotoa (2 hrs).
Bus from Quilotoa to Chugchilán (1 hr) or
tour from Latacunga

Baños 2 nights, page 107
Bus/tour/private transport from Latacunga
(2 hrs), Quilotoa or Chugchilán (4-5 hrs;
change bus in Latacunga).

Riobamba 2 nights, page 110
Bus/taxi from Baños (1½ hrs)

Cuenca 3 nights, page 118
Direct bus from Riobamba (5½ hrs) or
indirect via Alausí, El Tambo and Ingaparica
(2 days). Or tour from Riobamba via Alausí
and Ingapirca (full day)

Saraguro en route, page 125
Bus from Cuenca (2½ hrs)

Vilcabamba 2 nights, page 127
Bus/van/taxi from Cuenca (5 hrs;
change in Loja)

From Vilcabamba there are several options:
bus/taxi to Catamayo airport (2 hrs;
change in Loja) for flight to Quito (1 hr)
or Guayaquil (30 mins); or bus to Quito
(12 hrs, direct) or Guayaquil (10 hrs, change
in Loja) for connection to Galápagos or
international flight home.

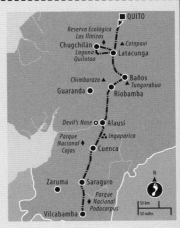

QUITO
Reserva Ecológica
Los Ilinizas
Chugchilán ▲ Cotopaxi
Laguna Latacunga
Quilotoa
Chimborazo ▲ Baños
Guaranda ▲ Tungurahua
Riobamba
Devil's Nose ○ Alausí
∴ Ingaparica
Parque
Nacional ♦
Cajas Cuenca
Zaruma Saraguro
Parque
Nacional ♦
Podocarpus
Vilcabamba
N
50 km
50 miles

GOING FURTHER

Guaranda page 115
Bus from Ambato (2 hrs) or
Riobamba (2 hrs)

Zaruma page 129
Bus from Cuenca (6 hrs) or Loja (5 hrs)

DREAM TRIP 2
Quito→Riobamba→Cuenca→Vilcabamba 14 days

In the early 19th century, German explorer Alexander Von Humboldt dubbed the Ecuadorean Andes the 'Avenue of the Volcanoes'. It's easy to see why when you follow his footsteps along the impressive roll call of towering peaks which extend south of Quito. Two hours from the capital by road is Cotopaxi, one of the world's highest active volcanoes and Ecuador's most popular summit. The area obviously attracts its fair share of climbers and trekkers, while the less active tourist can browse through many teeming indigenous markets and colonial towns.

After exploring the mountains and villages, rest up and pamper yourself in one of the historic haciendas which have opened their doors to visitors, or in the resort town of Baños. Located 3½ hours south of Quito, Baños is named and famed for its thermal baths and proximity to the Tungurahua volcano, which occasionally puts on spectacular displays of fireworks. An hour from Baños is the city of Riobamba, with access to the country's highest mountain, Chimborazo (6310 m), and the famous Devil's Nose train ride.

South of Riobamba the majestic solitary volcanoes give way to a more convoluted mountain landscape as you make your way to Incapirca, Ecuador's most important Inca site, and Cuenca, its most congenial big city. Cuenca is an important craft centre with a thriving cultural and expat scene, as well as providing access to the high moorlands of Parque Nacional Cajas.

Five hours south of Cuenca, the rainbow at the south end of Ecuador's Andean trail is unquestionably the small town of Vilcabamba, where an eclectic population of resident foreigners thrives amid the foothills of Parque Nacional Podocarpus. It's a great place to relax at the end of your own epic journey before returning to Quito by air, via the nearby city of Loja.

COTOPAXI, LATACUNGA AND QUILOTOA

The second Dream Trip starts with three nights in Ecuador's capital city, Quito (see pages 35-56). As you travel the Panamerican Highway south from Quito, the perfect cone of Cotopaxi volcano is ever present and is one of the country's main tourist attractions. Machachi and Latacunga are good bases from which to explore Reserva Ecológica Los Ilinizas and Parque Nacional Cotopaxi as well as the beautiful Quilotoa Circuit of small villages and vast expanses of open countryside.

→ ARRIVING FROM QUITO

GETTING THERE
Air Latacunga has a regional airport north of the centre.

Road The best way to visit Cotopaxi and to enjoy the Quilotoa Circuit is with a tour from Quito or Latacunga, or by private vehicle. **Servicio Express**, T03-242 6828 (Ambato) or T09-9924 2795, offers door-to-door van service from Quito to Latacunga, US$10, 1½ hours, nine daily, fewer on Sunday. There are frequent bus services from Quito's Terminal Quitumbe to Latacunga, US$2, 2½ hours. Buses for villages along the Quilotoa Circuit run from Latacunga; several daily except Thursday, when most leave from the Saquisilí market instead.

Train A tourist train runs from Quito to Latacunga Thursday-Sunday, see page 52.

MOVING ON
Buses from Latacunga to Baños (see page 107) leave from Puente San Felipe, every 20 minutes, US$2, two hours.

→ COTOPAXI AND LATACUNGA

MACHACHI
In a valley between the summits of Pasochoa, Rumiñahui and Corazón, lies the town of **Machachi**, famous for its horsemen (*chagras*), horse-riding trips, mineral water springs and crystal-clear swimming pools. The water, 'Agua Güitig' or 'Tesalia', is bottled in a plant 4 km from the town, where there is also a sports/recreation complex with one warm and two cold pools (entry US$5). The annual highland 'rodeo', El Chagra, takes place the third week in July. There's a tourist information office on the plaza. Just north of Machachi is Alóag, an important crossroads where a major highway runs west to Santo Domingo and the coast.

RESERVA ECOLOGICA LOS ILINIZAS
Machachi is a good starting point for a visit to the northern section of the Reserva Ecológica Los Ilinizas, a 150,000-ha nature reserve created to preserve remnants of western slope forest and *páramo*. It includes El Corazón, Los Ilinizas and Quilotoa volcanoes. The area is suitable for trekking and the twin peaks of Ilinizas are popular among climbers. The southern section is reached from Latacunga.

There is a **refugio** ⓘ *T09-8663 0971, US$15 per night, meals available,* (shelter) below the saddle between the two peaks, at 4740 m, with capacity for 20 people and cooking facilities; take a mat and sleeping bag. Iliniza Norte (5105 m) although not a technical climb, should not be underestimated, a few exposed, rocky sections require utmost caution. Some climbers suggest using a rope and a helmet is recommended if other parties are there because of falling rock; allow two to four hours for the ascent from the refuge. Take a compass, it's easy to mistake the descent. Iliniza Sur (5245 m) involves ice climbing despite the deglaciation: full climbing gear and experience are absolutely necessary. Access to the reserve is through a turn-off west of the Panamericana 6 km south of Machachi, then it's 7 km to the village of El Chaupi, which is a good base for day-walks and climbing **Corazón** (4782 m, not trivial). A dirt road continues from El Chaupi 9 km to 'La Virgen' (statue), pickup US$10. Nearby are woods where you can camp. El Chaupi hotels arrange for horses with muleteer (US$20 per animal).

PARQUE NACIONAL COTOPAXI
ⓘ *Visitors to the park must register at the entrance. Park gates are open 0700-1500, although you can stay until 1800. Visitors arriving with guides not authorized by the park are turned back at the gate.*
The beautiful snow-capped cone of Volcán Cotopaxi (5897 m) is at the heart of this lovely national park and is one of the prime tourist destinations in the country. If you only climb one of Ecuador's many volcanoes, then this should be the one. Many agencies run tours here, both the route and shelter can get crowded.

Historical records describe various spectacular and destructive eruptions of Cotopaxi, most recently in 1904, and volcanic material can be seen strewn about the *páramo* surrounding the volcano. It remains active and is monitored by the National Geophysics Institute (see www.igepn.edu.ec).

The park administration, a small **museum** ⓘ *0800-1200, 1300-1700,* and the Paja Blanca restaurant and shelter, are 10 km from the park gates, just before Limpio Pungo. The museum has a 3D model of the park, information about the volcano and stuffed animals.

The northwest flank of Cotopaxi is most often visited. Here is a high plateau with a small lake (Laguna Limpio Pungo), a lovely area for walking and admiring the delicate flora, and fauna including wild horses and native bird species such as the Andean lapwing and the Chimborazo hillstar hummingbird. The lower slopes are clad in planted pine forests, where llamas may be seen. The southwest flank, or Cara Sur, has not received as much impact as

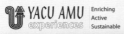

the west side. Here too, there is good walking, and you can climb Morurco (4881 m) as an acclimatization hike; condors may sometimes be seen. Just north of Cotopaxi are the peaks of Rumiñahui (4722 m), Sincholagua (4873 m) and Pasochoa (4225 m). To the southeast, beyond the park boundary, are Quilindaña (4890 m) and an area of rugged *páramos* and mountains dropping down to the jungle. The area has several large haciendas which form the **Fundación Páramo** (www.fundacionparamo.org), a private reserve with restricted access.

The **main entrance** to Parque Nacional Cotopaxi is approached from Chasqui, 25 km south of Machachi, 6 km north of Lasso. Once through the national park gates, go past Laguna Limpio Pungo to a fork, where the right branch is mostly paved and climbs steeply to a parking lot (4600 m). From here it's a 30-minute to one-hour walk to the José Ribas refuge, at 4800 m; beware of altitude sickness. Walking from the highway to the refuge takes an entire day or more.

The **El Pedregal entrance**, from the northwest, is accessed from Machachi via Santa Ana del Pedregal (21 km from the Panamericana), or from Sangolquí via Rumipamba and the

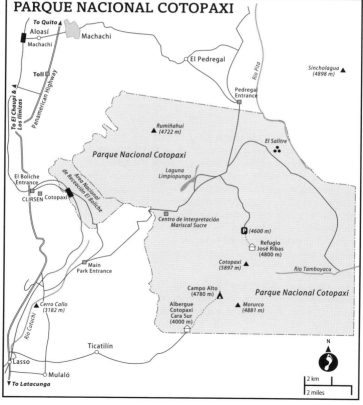

Río Pita Valley. From Pedregal to the refuge car park is 14 km. There are infrequent buses to Pedregal (two a day) then the hike in is shorter but still a couple of hours.

The **Ticatilín access** leads to the southwest flank. Just north of Lasso, a road goes east to the village of San Ramón and on to Ticatilín (a contribution of US$2 per vehicle may be requested at the barrier here; be sure to close all gates) and Rancho María. From the south, San Ramón is accessed from Mulaló. Beyond Rancho María is the private Albergue **Cotopaxi Cara Sur** (4000 m), run by Eduardo Agama (T09-9800 2681, www.cotopaxicarasur.com). Walking four hours from here you reach **Campo Alto** (4760 m), a climbers' tent camp.

Climbing Cotopaxi There is no specific best season to climb Cotopaxi, weather conditions are largely a matter of luck year-round. The ascent from the Ribas refuge takes between five and eight hours; start climbing at 0100 as the snow deteriorates in the sun. A full moon is both practical and a magical experience. Check out snow conditions with the guardian of the refuge before climbing. The route changes from year to year due to deglaciation. Because of the altitude and weather conditions, Cotopaxi is a serious climb and both equipment and experience are required. To maximize your chances of reaching the summit, make sure you are well acclimatized beforehand. Take a guide if you are inexperienced on ice and snow. Agencies in Quito and throughout the Central Highlands offer Cotopaxi climbing trips. Note that some guides encourage tourists to turn back at the first sign of tiredness, don't be pressured; insist on going at your own pace. You can also climb on the southwest flank, where the route is reported easier and safer than on the northwest face, but a little longer. To reach the summit in one day, you have to stay at Campo Alto (see above). The last hour goes around the rim of the crater with impressive views.

Climbing Rumiñahui Rumiñahui can be climbed from the park road, starting at Laguna Limpio Pungo from where it takes about one to 1½ hours to the base of the mountain. The climb itself is straightforward and not technical, though it is quite a scramble on the rockier parts and it can be very slippery and muddy in places after rain. There are three summits: Cima Máxima (the highest, at 4722 m), Cima Sur and Cima Central. The quickest route to Cima Máxima is via the central summit, as the climb is easier and not as steep. Note that the rock at the summits is unstable. There are excellent views of Cotopaxi and the Ilinizas. From the base to the summits takes about three to four hours. Allow around three to 3½ hours for the descent to Limpio Pungo. This is a good acclimatization climb. Take cold- and wet-weather gear. Even outside the rainy season there can be hail and sleet.

LASSO
Some 30 km south of Machachi is the small town of Lasso, on the railway line and off the Panamericana. In the surrounding countryside are several *hosterías* (converted country estates) offering accommodation and meals. Intercity buses bypass Lasso.

LATACUNGA

The capital of Cotopaxi Province is a place where the abundance of light grey pumice has been artfully employed. Volcán Cotopaxi is much in evidence, though it is 29 km away. Provided they are not hidden by clouds, which unfortunately is all too often, as many as nine volcanic cones can be seen from Latacunga; try early in the morning. The colonial character of the town has been well preserved. The central plaza, **Parque Vicente León**, is a beautifully maintained garden (locked at night). There are several other gardens in the town including **Parque San Francisco** and **Lago Flores** (better known as 'La Laguna'). **Casa de los Marqueses de Miraflores** ① *Sánchez de Orellana y Abel Echeverría, T03-280 1382, Mon-Fri 0800-1200, 1400-1800, Sat 0900-1300, free,* in a restored colonial mansion, has a modest museum, with exhibits on Mama Negra, colonial art, archaeology, numismatics and a library.

Casa de la Cultura ① *Antonia Vela 3-49 y Padre Salcedo T03-281 3247, Tue-Fri 0800-1200, 1400-1800, Sat 0800-1500, US$1,* built around the remains of a Jesuit Monastery and the old Monserrat watermill, houses a decent museum with pre-Columbian ceramics, weavings, costumes and models of festival masks; also an art gallery, library and theatre. It has week-long festivals with exhibits and concerts for all the local festivities. There is a Saturday **market** on the Plaza de San Sebastián (at Juan Abel Echeverría). Goods for sale include *shigras* (fine stitched, colourful straw bags) and homespun wool and cotton yarn. The produce market, Plaza El Salto, has daily trading and larger fairs on Tuesday, Friday and Saturday. A tourist **train** runs from Quito to Latacunga.

The **Cámara de Turismo de Cotopaxi** ① *Sánchez de Orellana y Guayaquil, at Plaza de Santo Domingo, T03-281 4968, Mon-Fri 0800-1200, 1400-1700,* provides local and regional information, Spanish only. The **Oficina de Turismo** ① *2nd floor, Terminal Terrestre, Mon-Fri 0900-1200, 1330-1800, Sat 0900-1600, Sun 0900-1400,* is staffed by high school students and has local and some regional information.

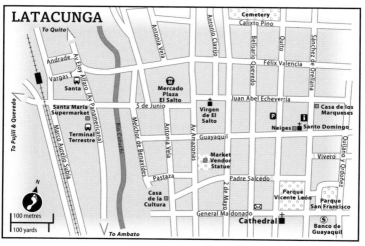

LATACUNGA

The popular and recommended 200-km round trip from Latacunga to Pujilí, Zumbahua, Quilotoa crater, Chugchilán, Sigchos, Isinliví, Toacazo, Saquisilí and back to Latacunga, can be done in two to three days by bus; less by private vehicle. It is also a great route for biking and only a few sections of the loop are cobbled or rough. Access is from either Pastocalle, north of Lasso or Latacunga. Hiking from one town to another can be challenging, especially when the fog rolls in. For these longer walks hiring a guide is advisable if you don't have a proper map or enough experience.

LATACUNGA TO ZUMBAHUA

A fine paved road leads west from Latacunga to **Pujilí** (15 km, bus US$0.25), which has a beautiful church. There's a good market on Sunday and a smaller one on Wednesday. Corpus Christi celebrations are colourful here. Beyond Pujilí, many interesting crafts are practised by the *indígenas* in the **Tigua** valley: paintings on leather, hand-carved wooden masks and baskets. **Chimbacucho**, also known as Tigua, is home to the Toaquiza family, most famous of the Tigua artists. The road goes on to Zumbahua, then over the Western Cordillera to La Maná and Quevedo. This is a great downhill bike route. It carries very little traffic and is extremely twisty in parts but is one of the most beautiful routes connecting the highlands with the coast. Beyond Zumbahua are the pretty towns of **Pilaló** (two restaurants and petrol pumps), **Esperanza de El Tingo** (two restaurants and lodging at **Carmita's**, T03-281 4657) and **La Maná** (two hotels).

ZUMBAHUA

Zumbahua lies 800 m from the main road, 62 km from Pujilí. It has an interesting Saturday market (starts at 0600) for local produce and some tourist items. Just below the plaza is

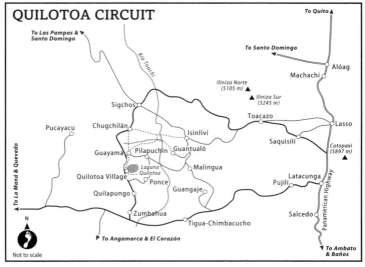

ON THE ROAD

After Otavalo, Saquisilí is perhaps the best known and most frequently visited market in the country. There are also a great many others and everyone should visit at least one market in the highlands of Ecuador. Fortunately, there is a market for every day of the week.

Monday: Ambato and Guantualó (on the Quilotoa Circuit).

Tuesday: Latacunga.

Wednesday: Pujilí.

Thursday: Guamote, Salcedo and Saquisilí.

Friday: Salarón (near Riobamba).

Saturday: Azogues, Guaranda, Latacunga, Otavalo, Pelileo, Riobamba and Zumbahaua.

Sunday: Alausí, Cajabamba, Cañar, Cayambe, Gualaceo, Machachi, Sangolquí and Saraguro, as well as Guangaje and Sigchos (both on the Quilotoa Circuit).

a shop selling dairy products and cold drinks. Friday nights involve dancing and drinking. Take a warm fleece, as it can be windy, cold and dusty. There is a good hospital in town, Italian-funded and run. The Saturday trip to Zumbahua market and the Quilotoa crater makes an excellent excursion.

QUILOTOA

ⓘ *Entry fee US$2.*

Zumbahua is the point to turn off for a visit to Quilotoa, a volcanic crater filled by a beautiful emerald lake. From the rim of the crater, 3850 m, several snow-capped volcanoes can be seen in the distance. The crater is reached by a paved road which runs north from Zumbahua (about 12 km, three to five hours' walk). There's a 300-m drop down from the crater rim to the water. The hike down takes about 30 minutes (an hour or more to climb back up). The trail starts to the left of the parking area down a steep, canyon-like cut. You can hire a mule to ride up from the bottom of the crater (US$8); best arranged before heading down. There is a basic hostel by the lake and kayaks for rent. Everyone at the crater tries to sell the famous naïve Tigua pictures and carved wooden masks, so expect to be besieged (also by begging children). To hike around the crater rim takes 4½ to six hours in clear weather. Be prepared for sudden changes in climate; it gets very cold at night and thick fog can roll in at any time. Always stay on the trail as trekkers have got lost and hurt themselves.

CHUGCHILAN, SIGCHOS AND ISINLIVI

Chugchilán, a village in one of the most scenic areas of Ecuador, is 16 km by road from Quilotoa. An alternative to the road is a five- to six-hour walk around part of the Quilotoa crater rim, then down to Guayama and across the canyon (Río Sigüí) to Chugchilán (11 km). Outside town is a cheese factory and nearby, at Chinaló, a woodcarving shop. The area has good walking.

Continuing from Chugchilán the road runs through **Sigchos**, the starting point for the Toachi Valley walk, via Asache to San Francisco de las Pampas (0900 bus daily to Latacunga). There is also a highland road to Las Pampas, with two buses from Sigchos. Southeast of Sigchos is **Isinliví**, on the old route to Toacazo and Latacunga. It has a fine woodcarving shop and a pre-Inca *pucará* (fortress). Trek to the village of Guantualó, which has a fascinating market on Monday. You can hike to or from Chugchilán (five hours), or from Quilotoa to Isinliví in seven to nine hours.

From Sigchos, a paved road leads to **Toacazo** (**$$ La Quinta Colorada**, T03-271 6122, www.quintacolorada.com, price includes breakfast and dinner) and on to Saquisilí.

SAQUISILI

Some 16 km southwest of Lasso, and 6 km west of the Panamericana is the small but very important market town of Saquisilí. Its Thursday market (0500-1400) is famous throughout Ecuador for the way in which its seven plazas and some of its streets become jam-packed with people, the great majority of them local *indígenas* with red ponchos and narrow-brimmed felt hats. The best time to visit the market is 0900-1200 (before 0800 for the animal market). Be sure to bargain as there is a lot of competition. This area has colourful Corpus Christi processions.

COTOPAXI, LATACUNGA AND QUILOTOA LISTINGS

WHERE TO STAY

Machachi

$$$ PapaGayo, in Hacienda Bolivia, west of the Panamericana, take a taxi from Machachi, T02-231 0002, www.hosteria-papagayo.com. Nicely refurbished hacienda, pleasant communal areas with fireplace and library, restaurant, includes breakfast, jacuzzi, parking, central heating, homely atmosphere, horse riding, biking, tours, popular.

Parque Nacional Cotopaxi and around

The **José Ribas refuge** (entry US$1) has a kitchen, water, and 60 bunks with mattresses; US$24.40 pp per night, bring sleeping bag and mat, also bring padlock or use the luggage deposit, US$2.50.

$$$$ Hacienda San Agustín de Callo, 2 access roads from the Panamericana, 1 just north of the main park access (6.2 km); the other, just north of Lasso (4.3 km), T03-271 9160, Quito T02-290 6157, www.incahacienda.com. Exclusive hacienda, the only place in Ecuador where you can sleep and dine in an Inca building. Rooms and suites have fireplace and bathtub, includes breakfast and dinner, horse rides, treks, bicycles and fishing. Restaurant (**$$$**) and buildings open to non-guests (US$5-10).

$$$$ Hacienda Santa Ana, Santa Ana del Pedregal on the road to the park, T02-222 4950, www.santaanacotopaxi.com. 17th-century former Jesuit hacienda in beautiful surroundings, 7 mins from the park. 7 comfortable rooms with fireplaces, great views, horse riding, biking, trekking and climbing.

$$$-$$ Tambopaxi, 3 km south of the El Pedregal access (1-hr drive from Machachi) or 4 km north of the turn-off for the climbing shelter, T02-222 0242 (Quito), www.tambopaxi.com. Comfortable straw-bale mountain shelter at 3750 m.

3 double rooms and several dorms (US$20 pp), duvets, includes breakfast, other meals available, camping US$7.50 pp, horse riding with advance notice.

$$$-$$ Tierra del Volcán, T09-9498 0121, Quito T02-600 9533, www.tierradelvolcan.com. 3 haciendas: **Hacienda El Porvenir**, a working ranch by Rumiñahui, between El Pedregal and the northern access to the park, 3 types of rooms, includes breakfast, set meals available, horses and mountain bikes for hire, camping, zipline; **Hacienda Santa Rita**, by the Río Pita, on the Sangolquí–El Pedregal road, with ziplines, entry US$6, camping US$5 pp; and the more remote, rustic **Hacienda El Tambo** by Quilindaña, southeast of the park. Also offers many adventure activities in the park.

$$$-$$ Cuello de Luna, 2 km northwest of the park's main access on a dirt road, T09-9970 0330, www.cuellodeluna.com. Comfortable rooms with fireplace, includes breakfast, meals available. US$22 pp in dorm (a very low loft). Can arrange tours to Cotopaxi, horse riding and biking.

$$ Huagra Corral, 200 m east of Panamericana along the park's main access road, T03-271 9729, Quito T02-380 8427, www.huagracorral.com. Nicely decorated, includes breakfast, restaurant, private or shared bath, heaters, convenient location, helpful, reserve ahead.

Latacunga

$$ Rodelú, Quito 16-31, T03-280 0956, www.rodelu.com.ec. Comfortable popular hotel, restaurant, good suites and rooms except for a few which are very small, breakfast included starting the second day.

$$-$ Tiana, Luis F Vivero N1-31 y Sánchez de Orellana, T03-281 0147, www.hostaltiana.com. Includes breakfast, drinks and snacks available, private or shared bath, US$10 pp in dorm.

Zumbahua

$ Cóndor Matzi, overlooking the market area, T09-8906 1572 or 03-281 2953 to leave message. Basic but best in town, shared bath, hot water, dining room with wood stove, kitchen facilities, try to reserve ahead, if closed when you arrive ask at **Restaurante Zumbahua** on the corner of the plaza.

Quilotoa

Humberto Latacunga, a good painter who also organizes treks, runs 3 good hostels, T09-9212 5962, all include breakfast and dinner: **Hostería Alpaca (\$\$)**, www.alpacaquilotoa.com, the most upmarket, rooms with wood stoves; **Cabañas Quilotoa (\$\$-\$)**, on the access road to the crater, www.cabanasquilotoa.com, private or shared bath, wood stoves; **Hostal Pachamama (\$)**, at the top of the hill by the rim of the crater, private bath.

Chugchilán

\$\$\$\$-\$\$\$ Black Sheep Inn, below the village on the way to Sigchos, T03-270-8077, www.blacksheepinn.com. A lovely eco-friendly resort which has received several awards. Includes 3 excellent vegetarian meals, private and shared bath, **\$\$** pp in dorms, spa, water slide, zipline, arrange excursions.

\$\$ Hostal Mama Hilda, on the road in to town, T03-270 8015. Pleasant family-run hostel, warm atmosphere, large rooms some with wood stoves, includes good dinner and breakfast, private or shared bath, camping, parking, arrange trips.

\$\$-\$ Hostal Cloud Forest, at the entrance to town, T03-270 8016, www.cloudforest hostal.com. Simple, popular family-run hostel, sitting room with wood stove, includes dinner and breakfast, restaurant open to public for lunch, private or shared bath, also dorm, parking, very helpful.

Isinliví

\$\$ Llullu Llama, T09-9258 0562, www.llullullama.com. Nicely refurbished farmhouse, cosy sitting room with wood stove, tastefully decorated rooms, private, semiprivate and dorm (**\$** pp), cabins with private bath under construction in 2013, includes good hearty dinner and breakfast, warm and relaxing atmosphere, a lovely spot.

RESTAURANTS

Machachi

\$\$\$-\$\$ Café de la Vaca, 4 km south of town on the Panamericana. Daily 0800-1730. Very good meals using produce from their own farm, popular.

Latacunga

\$\$-\$ Pizzería Buon Giorno, Sánchez de Orellana y Maldonado. Mon-Sat 1300-2200. Great pizzas and lasagne, large selection, popular.

Coffee Andes Alpes, Guayaquil 6-07 y Quito, by Santo Domingo church. Mon-Sat 1400-2100, Sun 1600-2100. Pleasant café/bar, strong drinks, sweets and sandwiches.

WHAT TO DO

Latacunga

The following operators offer day trips to **Cotopaxi** and **Quilotoa** (US\$40 pp, includes lunch and a visit to a market town if on Thu or Sat, minimum 2 people). Climbing trips to Cotopaxi are around US\$170 pp for 2 days (plus *refugio*), minimum 2 people. Trekking trips US\$70-80 pp per day.

Greivag, Guayaquil y Sánchez de Orellana, Plaza Santo Domingo, L5, T03-281 0510, www.greivagturismo.com.

Neiges, Guayaquil 6-25, Plaza Santo Domingo, T03-281 1199, neigestours@hotmail.com.

Tovar Expediciones, at Hostal Tiana, T281 1333. Specializes in climbing and trekking.

BAÑOS AND RIOBAMBA

After the chill of Cotopaxi or Quilotoa, Baños is the ideal spot to warm up, or to cool off if you are coming from the jungle on Dream Trip 3. Both this resort town and the nearby city of Riobamba are good bases for exploring the Central Sierra, and their close proximity to high peaks gives more great opportunities for climbing, cycling and trekking (but check for volcanic activity before you set out). The thermal springs at Baños are an added lure and the road east is one of the best ways to get to and from the jungle lowlands (see Dream Trip 3). On the other hand, anyone with the faintest interest in railways stops in Riobamba to ride the train on the famous section of the line from the Andes to Guayaquil, around the Devil's Nose.

→ BAÑOS AND AROUND

Baños is nestled between the Río Pastaza and the Tungurahua volcano, only 8 km from its crater. Baños bursts at the seams with hotels, *residenciales*, restaurants and tour agencies. Ecuadoreans flock here at weekends and on holidays for the hot springs, to visit the Basílica and enjoy the local *melcochas* (toffees), while escaping the Andean chill in a subtropical climate (wettest in July and August). Foreign visitors are also frequent, using Baños as a base for trekking, organizing a visit to the nearby jungle, making local day trips on horseback or by mountain bike, or just plain hanging out. The nearest big city is **Ambato**, 40 km west of Baños, a busy commercial and transportation centre with all services but few special attractions.

ARRIVING IN BAÑOS
Getting there There are frequent buses from Latacunga, US$2, two hours. If coming from Qutio, there is frequent service from Terminal Quitumbe (US$3, three hours) but unfortunately this route is regularly worked by thieves – be wary and keep your carry-on luggage on your lap at all times. A better option is to take **Servicio Express** (T03-242 6828 or T09-9924 2795) to Ambato (US$12 including hotel pickup) and ask them to let you off at the bus stop for Baños; local buses depart from there every few minutes. When travelling by bus from Baños to Quito, theft has not been an issue to date.

Getting around Baños is small enough to enjoy on foot. City buses run from Alfaro y Martínez east to Agoyán and from Rocafuerte by the market, west to El Salado and the zoo. The long-distance bus station is on the Ambato–Puyo road (Avenida Amazonas). To Río Verde take any Puyo-bound bus; through buses don't go in the station, 20 minutes, US$0.50.

Moving on To Riobamba, the direct Baños–Riobamba road is sometimes closed due to Tungurahua's volcanic activity (also dangerous after rain), so most buses go via Mocha, two hours, US$2.

Tourist information iTur ① *Oficina Municipal de Turismo, at the Municipio, Halflants y Rocafuerte, opposite Parque Central, Mon-Fri 0800-1230, 1400-1730, Sat-Sun 0800-1600,* is helpful, they have colourful maps of the area and some English is spoken. There are several private 'tourist information offices' run by travel agencies near the bus station; high-pressure tour sales, maps and pamphlets available. Local artist, J Urquizo, produces an accurate pictorial map of Baños (12 de Noviembre y Ambato), which is also sold in many shops. Enquire with **iTur** (see above) or at your hotel about the current safety situation. Robberies have taken place along the trail to the Bellavista cross and on the cycling route to Puyo.

Safety In 1999, after over 80 years of dormancy, Tungurahua became active again and has remained so until the close of this edition. The level of activity is variable, the volcano can be quiet for days or weeks and then suddenly bursts into life with a spectacular and at times frightening display of fireworks. Baños however continues to be a safe and popular destination and will likely remain so unless the overall level of volcanic activity greatly increases. **Tungurahua is closed to climbers** and the direct road to Riobamba is often closed, but all else is normal. Since the level of volcanic activity can change quickly, you should enquire locally before visiting Baños. The National Geophysical Institute posts daily reports at www.igepn.edu.ec.

PLACES IN BAÑOS

The **Manto de la Virgen** waterfall at the southeast end of town is a symbol of Baños. The **Basílica** attracts many pilgrims. The paintings of miracles performed by Nuestra Señora del Agua Santa are worth seeing. The restaurants and cafés of Baños, clustered around the Parque Central, Parque de la Basílica and Calle Ambato are an attraction in themselves, while many other worthwhile sights are located just outside town.

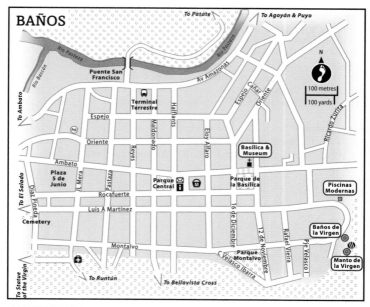

HOT SPRINGS AND SPAS

There are various thermal baths in town, all charge US$2 unless otherwise noted. The **Baños de la Virgen** ① *0430-1700*, are by the waterfall. They get busy so best visit very early in the morning. Two small hot pools are open evenings only (1800-2200, US$3). The **Piscinas Modernas** ① *Fri-Sun and holidays 0900-1700*, with a water slide, are next door. **El Salado baths** ① *0500-1700, US$3*, has several hot pools, plus icy cold river water, repeatedly destroyed by volcanic debris (not safe when activity is high), 1.5 km out of town off the Ambato road. The **Santa Ana baths** ① *Fri-Sun and holidays 0900-1700*, have hot and cold pools in a pleasant setting, just east of town on the road to Puyo. All the baths can be very crowded at weekends and holidays; the brown colour of the water is due to its high mineral content.

As well as the medicinal baths, there is a growing number of independent spas in hotels and many massage therapists. These offer a combination of sauna, steam bath (Turkish or box), jacuzzi, clay and other types of baths, a variety of massage techniques (Shiatsu, Reiki, Scandinavian) and more.

AROUND BAÑOS

There are many interesting **walks** in the Baños area. The **San Martín shrine** is an easy 45-minute walk from town that overlooks a deep rocky canyon with the Río Pastaza thundering below. Beyond the shrine, crossing to the north side of the Pastaza, is the **Ecozoológico San Martín** ① *T03-274 0552, 0800-1700, US$2.50*, with the **Serpentario San Martín** ① *daily 0900-1800, US$2*, opposite. Fifty metres beyond is a path to the **Inés María waterfall**, cascading down, but sadly polluted. Further, a *tarabita* (cable car) and ziplines span the entrance to the canyon. You can also cross the Pastaza by the **Puente San Francisco** road bridge, behind the kiosks across the main road from the bus station. From here a series of trails fans out into the hills, offering excellent views of Tungurahua from the ridge-tops in clear weather. A total of six bridges span the Pastaza near Baños, so you can make a nice round trip.

On the hillside behind Baños, it is a 45-minute hike to the **statue of the Virgin** (good views). Go to the south end of Calle JL Mera, before the street ends, take the last street to the right, at the end of which are stairs leading to the trail. A steep path continues along the ridge, past the statue. Another trail begins at the south end of JL Mera and leads to the **Hotel Luna Runtún**, continuing on to the village of Runtún (five- to six-hour round-trip). Yet another steep trail starts at the south end of Calle Maldonado and leads in 45 minutes to the **Bellavista cross**, where there is a café (open 0900-2400). You can continue from the cross to Runtún.

The scenic road to Puyo (58 km) has many waterfalls tumbling down into the Pastaza. Several *tarabitas* (cable cars) span the canyon offering good views. The paved road goes through seven tunnels between Baños and Río Negro. The older gravel road runs parallel to the new road, just above the Río Pastaza, and is the preferred route for cyclists who, coming from Baños, should only go through one tunnel at Agoyán and then stay to the right avoiding the other tunnels. Between tunnels there is only the paved road, cyclists must be very careful as there are many buses and lorries. The area has excellent opportunities for walking and nature observation.

At the junction of the Río Verde and Río Pastaza, 17 km from Baños, is the town of **Río Verde** with snack bars, restaurants and a few places to stay. The Río Verde has crystalline green water and is nice for bathing. The paved highway runs to the north of town, between it and the old road, the river has been dammed forming a small lake where rubber rafts are rented for paddling. Before joining the Pastaza the Río Verde tumbles down several falls, the most spectacular of which is **El Pailón del Diablo** (the Devil's Cauldron). Cross the Río Verde on the old road and take the path to the right after the church, then follow the trail down towards the suspension bridge over the Pastaza for about 20 minutes. Just before the bridge take a side trail to the right (signposted) which leads you to **Paradero del Pailón**, a nice restaurant, and viewing platforms above the falls (US$1.50). The **San Miguel Falls**, smaller but also nice, are some five minutes' walk from the town along a different trail. Cross the old bridge and take the first path to the right where you'll come to **Falls Garden** (US$1.50), with lookout platforms over both sets of falls. Cyclists can leave their bikes at one of the snack bars while visiting the falls and then return to Baños by bus.

→RIOBAMBA AND AROUND

Riobamba and Guaranda are good bases for exploring the Sierra. Riobamba is the bigger of the two and is on the famous railway line from Quito to Guayaquil. Many indigenous people from the surrounding countryside can be seen in both cities on market days. Because of their central location Riobamba and the surrounding province are known as 'Corazón de la Patria' – the heartland of Ecuador – and the city boasts the nickname 'La Sultana de Los Andes' in honour of lofty Mount Chimborazo.

ARRIVING IN RIOBAMBA
Getting there There are buses from Baños throughout the day, US$2, 1½ hours. Note that these and buses to and from Oriente arrive and depart from the **Terminal Oriental** at Espejo y Cordovez, while most other long-distance buses use the main **Terminal Terrestre** on Epiclachima y Avenida Daniel L Borja. From Quito, buses run throughout the day from Terminal Quitumbe, US$3.75, four hours.

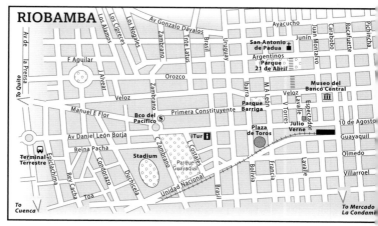

Moving on Buses run throughout the day from the **Terminal Terrestre** to Alausí (for the Devil's Nose train ride), US$1.50, two hours. There are also several daily departures to Cuenca, US$6, 5½ hours, via El Tambo and Cañar if you would like to visit Ingapirca on your own. To ride the train, visit Ingarpirca and make it to Cuenca all in the same day it is best to book a tour or private vehicle.

Getting around Riobamba is a bit spread out but many of its attractions are not far from the train station. Taxis are cheap and plentiful for getting in from the bus stations and moving around.

Tourist information: iTur ① *Av Daniel León Borja y Brasil, T03-296 3159, Mon-Fri 0830-1230, 1430-1800,* is the municipal information office. The **Ministerio de Turismo** ① *3 doors from iTur, in the Centro de Arte y Cultura, T03-294 1213, Mon-Fri 0830-1700, is* very helpful and knowledgeable.

RIOBAMBA
The capital of Chimborazo Province has broad streets and many ageing but impressive buildings. The main square is **Parque Maldonado** around which are the **cathedral**, the **municipality** and several colonial buildings with arcades. The cathedral has a beautiful colonial stone façade and an incongruously modern interior. Four blocks northeast of the railway station is the **Parque 21 de Abril**, named after the Batalla de Tapi, 21 April 1822, the city's independence from Spain. The park, better known as **La Loma de Quito**, affords an unobstructed view of Riobamba as well as Chimborazo, Carihuairazo, Tungurahua, El Altar and occasionally Sangay. It also has a colourful tile tableau of the history of Ecuador. The **Convento de la Concepción** ① *Orozco y España, entrance at Argentinos y J Larrea, T03-296 5212, Tue-Sat 0900-1230, 1500-1730, US$3,* has a religious art museum. **Museo del Ministerio de Cultura** ① *Veloz y Montalvo, T03-296 5501, Mon-Fri 0900-1700, free,* has well displayed exhibits of archaeology and colonial art. **Museo de la Ciudad** ① *Primera Constituyente y Espejo, at Parque Maldonado, T03-294 4420, Mon-Fri 0800-1230, 1430-1800, free,* in a beautifully restored colonial building, has an interesting historical photograph exhibit and temporary displays.

Riobamba is an important **market centre** where people from many communities congregate. Saturday is the main day when the city fills with colourfully dressed *indígenas* from all over Chimborazo, each wearing their distinctive costume; trading overflows the markets and buying and selling go on all over town. Wednesday is a smaller market day. The 'tourist' market in the small **Plaza de la Concepción or Plaza Roja** ① *Orozco y Colón, Sat and Wed only 0800-1500,* is a good place to buy local handicrafts and authentic indigenous clothing. The main produce market is **San Alfonso** ⓘ *Argentinos y 5 de Junio, Sat*, spills over into the nearby streets and also sells clothing, ceramics, baskets and hats. Other markets in the colonial centre are **La Condamine** ⓘ *Carabobo y Colombia, daily, largest market on Fri*, **San Francisco** and **La Merced**, near the churches of the same name.

   Guano is a carpet-weaving, sisal and leather-working town 8 km north of Riobamba. Many shops sell rugs and you can arrange to have these woven to your own design. Buses leave from the Mercado Dávalos, García Moreno y New York, every 15 minutes (US$0.25, taxi US$4).

ALAUSÍ AND THE DEVIL'S NOSE TRAIN RIDE

Alausí is a picturesque town perched on a hillside. It offers good walking, a Sunday market and a **Fiesta de San Pedro** on 29 June. In mid-2013 the Devil's Nose Train was departing from and returning to Alausí (Tuesday-Sunday at 0800, 1100 and 1500, 2½ hours return, US$25-35); the price includes a snack and folklore dance performance. An *autoferro* (motorized rail car) was also running from Riobamba to Urbina (Thursday-Sunday at 0800, US$11) and from Riobamba to Colta (Thursday-Sunday at 1200, US$15). Dress warmly. Services between Riobamba and Alausí are scheduled to resume in late 2013. The train rides are popular with Ecuadorean and foreign tourists alike. Purchase tickets well in advance for weekends and holidays at any train station (Riobamba, T03-296 1038, Monday-Wednesday 0800-1630, Thursday-Sunday 0700-1600; Alausí, T03-293 0126, Tuesday-Sunday 0700-1600) or by email (reservasriobamba@ferrocarrilesdelecuador. gob.ec, then you have to make a bank deposit). Procedures change frequently, so enquire locally and check www.trenecuador.com. See also box, opposite.

RESERVA FAUNÍSTICA CHIMBORAZO

ⓘ *Information from Ministerio del Ambiente, Av 9 de Octubre y Quinta Macají, Riobamba, T03-261 0029, Mon-Fri 0800-1300, 1400-1700. Visitors arriving with guides not authorized by the ministry are turned back at the gate.*

   The most outstanding features of this reserve, created to protect the camelids (vicuñas, alpacas and llamas) which were re-introduced here, are the beautiful snow-capped volcano of **Chimborazo** and its neighbour **Carihuayrazo**. Chimborazo, inactive, is the highest peak in Ecuador (6310 m), while Carihuayrazo, at 5020 m, is dwarfed by its neighbour. Day visitors can enjoy lovely views, a glimpse of the handsome vicuñas and the rarefied air above 4800 m. There are great opportunities for trekking on the eastern slopes, accessed from **Urbina**, west of the Ambato–Riobamba road, and of course climbing Ecuador's highest peak. Horse-riding and trekking tours are offered along the Mocha Valley between the two peaks and downhill cycling from Chimborazo is fun and popular.

   To the west of the reserve runs the Vía del Arenal which joins San Juan, along the Riobamba–Guaranda road, with Cruce del Arenal on the Ambato–Guaranda road. A turn-off from this road leads to the main park entrance and beyond to the **Refugio Hermanos Carrel**, a shelter at 4800 m, from where it is a 45-minute walk to **Refugio Whymper** at 5000 m. There are plans to renovate both shelters in late 2013. The access from Riobamba (51 km, paved to the park entrance) is very beautiful. Along the Vía del Arenal past San Juan are a couple of small indigenous communities which grow a few crops and raise llamas and alpacas. They offer lodging and *guías nativos*; the area is good for acclimatization. The Arenal is a large sandy plateau at about 4400 m, to the west of Chimborazo, just below the main park entrance. It can be a harsh, windy place, but it is also very beautiful; take the time to admire the tiny flowers which grow here. This is the best place to see vicuñas,

ON THE ROAD
The railway that refused to die

As you climb aboard for the Devil's Nose, consider the rich history of this train. What is today an exhilarating tourist ride was once the country's pride and joy. Its construction was internationally acclaimed, the 11-year US$26 million project of Ecuadorean president Eloy Alfaro and US entrepreneur Archer Harman.

A spectacular 464-km railway line (1.067-m gauge), which ran from Durán (outside Guayaquil) up to Riobamba, was opened in 1908. It passed through 87 km of delta lands and then, in another 80 km, climbed to 3238 m. The highest point (3619 m) was reached at Urbina, between Riobamba and Ambato. It then fell and rose before reaching Quito at 2850 m.

This was one of the great railway journeys of the world and a fantastic piece of engineering, with a maximum gradient of 5.5%. Rail lines also ran from Riobamba south to Cuenca, and from Quito north to Ibarra, then down to the coast at San Lorenzo. There were even more ambitious plans, never achieved, to push the railhead deep into the Oriente Jungle, from Ambato as far as Leticia (then Ecuador, today Colombia). Time and neglect subsequently took their toll and by the turn of the millennium only a few short rail segments remained in service, basically as cheap tourist rides. There was often talk of reviving the Ecuadorean railway as a whole but most Ecuadoreans, including the authors, found it hard to take such promises seriously.

Since 2007 however, the Ecuadorean government has undertaken a complete rehabilitation of the line from Quito to Durán, which is scheduled to re-open in 2013. From new concrete ties to modern rolling stock, this is unquestionably a formidable achievement, but what remains in doubt is the purpose of the refurbished railway. At the close of this edition it still consisted of a series of short, but no longer cheap, tourist rides and an all-inclusive four-day/three-night package for train buffs costing US$1270.

In the meantime, what happened to the dream of Eloy Alfaro and Archer Harman? Surely a working railway to transport local passengers and freight could serve Ecuador today as much as, if not more than, it did in the past.

which congregate either in family groups, one male and its harem, or lone males which have been expelled from a group.

Climbing Chimborazo This is a difficult climb owing to the altitude and variable snow conditions. No one without mountaineering experience should attempt it before doing other summits; rope, ice-axe, crampon and helmet must be used, ice screws may be useful, and acclimatization is essential. To make the most of it, climb some lower mountains before meeting your guide for the Chimborazo climb. The best season is November to January and June to September.

From the Whymper refuge (see above) to the summit the climb is six to eight hours and the descent about four hours. The path from the hut to the glacier is marked but difficult to follow at midnight, so it's best to check it out the day before. Parts of the route on the glacier are marked with flags, but it can be tricky in cloud or mist. There are several crevasses on the way, so you need to rope up. There are three routes depending on your experience and snow conditions. It is highly recommended to go with a guide and start at

2400 or 0100. There are avalanche problems on the entire mountain and danger of falling rocks and black ice in the dry season. *Penitentes*, which are conical ice formations, may obstruct the final portion between the Veintimilla and Whymper summits.

PARQUE NACIONAL SANGAY

ⓘ *Information from Ministerio del Ambiente, see Reserva Chimborazo, above.*

Riobamba provides access to the central highland region of Sangay National Park, a beautiful wilderness area with excellent opportunities for trekking and climbing. A spectacular but controversial road runs from Riobamba to Macas in the Oriente, cutting through the park. Near Cebadas (with a good cheese factory) a branch road joins from **Guamote**, a quiet, mainly indigenous town on the Pan-American Highway, which comes to life during its colourful Thursday market. At **Atillo**, south of Cebadas, an area of lovely *páramo* dotted with lakes, there is basic lodging (US$6 per person) and restaurant at **Cabaña Saskines**, T03-230 3290, atillosaskines@hotmail.com.

Sangay (5230 m) is an active volcano. Access to the mountain takes at least three days and is only for those who can endure long, hard days of walking and severe weather. Climbing Sangay can be dangerous even on a quiet day and a helmet to protect against falling stones is vital, November to January is a good time to climb it. Agencies in Quito and Riobamba offer tours or you can try to organize an expedition independently. A guide is essential, porters can be hired in the access towns of **Alao** and **Guarguallá**. The latter has a community tourism project with accommodation (US$12 per person, T03-302 6688, kitchen facilities) and *guías nativos*. Also in Sangay National Park is the beautiful **El Altar** volcano (5315 m), whose crater is surrounded by nine summits. The most popular climbing and trekking routes begin beyond Candelaria at **Hacienda Releche**.

GOING FURTHER
Guaranda

This quaint town, capital of Bolívar Province, proudly calls itself 'the Rome of Ecuador' because it is built on seven hills. There are fine views of the mountains all around and a colourful market. Locals traditionally take an evening stroll in the palm-fringed main plaza, **Parque Libertador Simón Bolívar**, around which are the Municipal buildings and a large stone **cathedral**. Towering over the city, on one of the hills, is an impressive statue of **El Indio Guaranga** with a museum (free) and art gallery. Although not on the tourist trail, there are many sights worth visiting in the province, for which Guaranda is the ideal base. Of particular interest is the highland town of **Salinas**, with its many successful community development projects, as well as the *subtrópico* region, the lowlands stretching west towards the coast. Salinas is only 45 minutes from Guaranda by bus and has a simple **Hotel Refugio** (**$**, T03-221 0044, www.salinerito.com), advance booking advised.

Market days in Guaranda are Friday (till 1200) and Saturday (larger), when many indigenous people in typical dress trade at the market complex at the east end of Calle Azuay, by Plaza 15 de Mayo (9 de Abril y Maldonado), and at Plaza Roja (Avenida General Enríquez). Carnival in Guaranda is among the best known in the country. The **Oficina Municipal de Turismo** ⓘ *García Moreno entre 7 de Mayo y Convención de 1884, T03-298 5877, www.guaranda.gob.ec (multilingual), Mon-Fri 0800-1200, 1400-1800*, provides information in Spanish and maps. For more information (also in Spanish) about regional attractions, go to www.gobiernodebolivar.gob.ec.

There are several places to stay in Guaranda, including **Mansión del Parque ($$**, 10 de Agosto y Sucre, T03-298 4468), in a nicely restored colonial house; **La Bohemia** (Convención de 1884 y 10 de Agosto), which serves good meals. Several daily buses go to **Guaranda**, from both Riobamba (sit on the right for best views) and Ambato, US$2, two hours.

BAÑOS AND RIOBAMBA LISTINGS

WHERE TO STAY

Baños

$$$$ Luna Runtún, Caserío Runtún Km 6, T03-274 0882, www.lunaruntun.com. A classy hotel in a beautiful setting overlooking Baños. Includes dinner, breakfast and spa, very comfortable rooms with balconies and superb views, lovely gardens. Good service, English, French and German spoken, tours, nanny service.

$$$-$$ Sangay, Plazoleta Isidro Ayora 100, next to waterfall and thermal baths, T03-274 0490, www.sangayspahotel.com. A traditional Baños hotel and spa with 3 types of rooms, includes buffet breakfast, good restaurant specializes in Ecuadorean food, pool and spa open to non-residents 1600-2000 (US$10), parking, tennis and squash courts, games room, car hire, disco, attentive service, mid-week discounts, British/Ecuadorean-run.

$$ La Floresta, Halflants y Montalvo, T03-274 1824, www.laflorestahotel.com. Pleasant hotel with large comfortable rooms set around a lovely garden, includes excellent buffet breakfast, wheelchair accessible, parking, attentive service. Warmly recommended.

$ La Chimenea, Martínez y Rafael Vieira, T03-274 2725, www.hostalchimenea.com. Nice hostel with terrace café, breakfast available, private or shared bath, US$6 pp in dorm, small pool, jacuzzi extra, parking for small cars, quiet, helpful and good value.

Riobamba

$$$ Mansión Santa Isabella, Veloz 28-48 y Carabobo, T03-296 2947, www.mansionsantaisabella.com. Lovely restored house with pleasant patio, comfortable rooms most with bathtub, duvets, includes breakfast, restaurant serves set lunches and à la carte, bar in stone basement, parking, attentive service, British/Ecuadorean-run.

$$$ San Pedro de Riobamba, Daniel L Borja 29-50 y Montalvo, opposite the train station, T03-294 0586, www.hotelsanpedro deriobamba.com. Elegant hotel in a beautifully restored house in the centre of town, ample comfortable rooms, includes breakfast, cafeteria, bathtubs, parking, covered patio, reservations required.

$$-$ Tren Dorado, Carabobo 22-35 y 10 de Agosto, near the train station, T03-296 4890, www.hoteltrendorado.com. Modern hotel with large rooms, buffet breakfast available (starting 0730, open to non-guests), restaurant, reliable hot water, good value.

$ Oasis, Veloz 15-32 y Almagro, T03-296 1210, www.oasishostelriobamba.com. Small, pleasant, family-run hostel in a quiet location, laundry facilities, some rooms with kitchen and fridge, shared kitchen for the others, parking, garden, popular with backpackers.

Alausí

$$$ La Quinta, Eloy Alfaro 121 y M Muñoz, T03-293 0247, www.hosteria-la-quinta.com. Nicely restored old house along the railway line to Riobamba. Ample rooms, includes breakfast, restaurant, gardens, excellent views.

$$-$ San Pedro, 5 de Junio y 9 de Octubre, T03-293 0089, hostalsanpedro@hotmail.com. Modern hotel with comfortable rooms, a few cheaper rooms in older section, restaurant downstairs, parking, nice owner.

Reserva Faunística Chimborazo

$ Posada de la Estación, opposite the Urbina railway station at 3619 m, 2 km west of the highway, T09-9969 4867, aventurag@yahoo.com. Comfortable rooms, shared bath, meals available, wood stoves, magnificent views, trips and equipment arranged, helpful. Also run **Urcu Huasi ($)**, cabins at 4150 m, 10 km from Urbina, in an area where reforestation is taking place.

RESTAURANTS

Baños

$$ Mariane, on a small lane by Montalvo y Halflants. Mon-Sat 1200-2200, Sun 1800-2200. Excellent authentic Provençal cuisine, large portions, lovely setting, pleasant atmosphere, good value and attentive service. Highly recommended. **Hotel Mariane ($)**, at the same location, is very clean and pleasant.

$$-$ Casa Hood, Martínez between Halflants and Alfaro. Open 1200-2200. Largely vegetarian, but also serve some meat dishes, juices, milkshakes, varied menu including Indonesian and Thai dishes, good set lunch and desserts. Travel books and maps sold, book exchange, cinema, occasional cultural events, good atmosphere, popular.

$ La Chimenea, Oriente y 16 de Diciembre. 1830-2300, closed Tue. Simple place serving good filling grilled chicken.

Riobamba

Most places close after 2100 and on Sun.

$$$ Le Piaf Bistro, Veloz 10-41 y Puruha. Daily except Tue and Sun night, 1300-1500 and 1700-2300. Excellent French and Mediterranean cuisine in a nice ambiance.

$$ Mónaco Pizzería, Av de la Prensa y Francisco Aguilar. Mon-Fri 1500-2200, Sat-Sun 1200-2200. Delicious pizza and pasta, tasty salads, very good food, service and value.

$ Naranjo's, Daniel L Borja 36-20 y Uruguay. Tue-Sun 1200-1500. Excellent economical set lunch, friendly service, popular with locals.

Helados de Paila, Espejo y 10 de Agosto. Daily 0900-1900. Very good home-made ice cream, coffee, sweets, popular.

La Abuela Rosa, Brasil y Esmeraldas. Mon-Sat 1600-2100. *Cafetería* in grandmother's house serving typical Ecuadorean snacks. Great atmosphere and good service.

WHAT TO DO

Baños

Adrenalin sports are popular in Baños, including mountaineering, whitewater rafting, canyoning, canopying and bridge jumps. Safety standards vary greatly between tour operators; check their equipment before signing up and avoid guides and agencies who seek out customers on the street.

Geotours, Ambato y Halflants, next to Banco Pichincha, T03-274 1344, www.geotoursbanios.com. Also offer paragliding.

Sachayacu Explorer, Bolívar 229 y Urbina, in Píllaro, T03-287 3292, www.parquellanganates.com. Trekking in the Llanganates, jungle tours as far as Peru, English spoken.

Riobamba

Most companies offer mountain biking (US$45-55 pp per day), climbing trips (US$180 pp for 2 days to Chimborazo or Carihuayrazo) and trekking (US$85-100 pp per day).

Incañán, Brasil 20-28 y Luis A Falconí, T03-294 0508, www.incanian.com.ec. Trekking, cycling and cultural tours.

Julio Verne Travel, El Espectador 22-25 y Daniel L Borja, 2 blocks from the train station, T03-296 3436, www.julioverne-travel.com. Climbing, trekking, excellent cycling, jungle and Galápagos trips, transport, equipment rental, English spoken, Ecuadorean/Dutch-run, very conscientious and reliable. Uses official guides. Highly recommended.

Pro Bici, Primera Constituyente 23-51 y Larrea, T03-295 1759, www.probici.com. Bike tours and rentals.

CUENCA AND VILCABAMBA

Founded in 1557 on the site of the Inca settlement of Tomebamba, much of Cuenca's colonial air has been preserved and many of its old buildings have been renovated. Its cobblestone streets, flowering plazas and whitewashed buildings with old wooden doors and ironwork balconies make it a pleasure to explore. The climate is spring-like, but the nights are chilly. In 1999 Cuenca was designated a UNESCO World Heritage Site. Cuenca is the favourite city of many visitors to Ecuador and, in recent years, it has become home to a growing expatriate retiree community.

The city is surrounded by scenic countryside, where you are likely to see the 'chola cuencana' – women dressed in traditional costume, with colourful pleated skirt, lace blouse and Panama hat. To the north live the Cañari people, who wear bright attire and small white felt hats. They are the custodians of Ingapirca, Ecuador's most important archaeological site. There is much to explore in the area. Beautiful Parque Nacional Cajas, with over 200 lakes, is a short ride from Cuenca. Here, and in several other locations, are very good opportunities for trekking. There are also craft towns producing weavings, jewellery, basketry and Panama hats, all of which can be purchased in Cuenca.

→CUENCA

ARRIVING IN CUENCA

Air The **airport** is five minutes beyond the Terminal Terrestre (see below), T07-280 6709; taxis charge US$1.50-2.50 to the centre. There are several daily flights to Quito and Guayaquil with **TAME, Aerogal** and LAN.

Bus The main **Terminal Terrestre** is on Avenida España, 15 minutes' ride northeast of the centre, T07-284 2811. There are several daily buses from Riobamba (US$6, 5½ hours) and Alausí (US$5, four hours). If you are coming from further north, buses for Cuenca depart from Quito's Terminal Quitumbe (US$10-12, nine hours); **Flota Imbabura** also has several overnight buses which depart from their own terminal in central Quito. As Ecuador's third city, Cuenca has bus links with most of the country.

Moving on There are several daily buses from Cuenca to Loja (for Vilcabamba, see page 127) (US$7.50, four hours, see www.viajerosinternacional.com); also van service to Loja with **Elite Tours** (Remigio Crespo 14-08 y Santa Cruz, T07-245 5851, US$12, three hours); a taxi from Cuenca to Loja costs about US$60. From the Terminal Terrestre in Loja, **Vilcabambaturis** vans run every 15 minutes throughout the day to Vilcabamba (US$1.30, 1½ hours); taxi from Loja to Vilcabamba US$15.

Loja airport (located in Catamayo) has two to three daily flights to Quito and one daily flight to Guayaquil with TAME; tickets can be purchased in Vilcabamba as well as Loja. Taxi from Vilcabamba to Catamayo US$35, or make van and bus connection through Loja.

There is one overnight bus from Vilcabamba to Quito's Terminal Quitumbe with **Transportes Loja** (US$20, 12 hours). Alternatively, take the van to Loja, from where there are more buses to Quito, Guayaquil and throughout the country.

Orientation The city is bounded by the Río Machángara to the north and the Ríos Yanuncay and Tarqui to the south. The Río Tomebamba separates the colonial heart from the newer districts to the south. Avenida Las Américas is a ring road around the north and west of the city and the *autopista*, a multi-lane highway bypasses the city to the south. The **Terminal Sur**, for regional buses, is by the Feria Libre El Arenal, on Avenida Las Américas. Many city buses also pass here but it is not a safe area. Taxis are a good option for getting around town.

Tourist information Ministerio de Turismo ① *Sucre y Benigno Malo, on Parque Calderón next to the Municipio, T07-282 2058/1035, Mon-Fri, 0830-1700*, is helpful. **Cámara de Turismo** ①*Terminal Terrestre, T07-286 8482, Mon-Sat 0830-1200, 1230-1800*, is also at the airport. For general information see www.cuenca.com.ec; to locate an establishment see www.ubicacuenca.com.

Safety Though safer than Quito or Guayaquil, routine precautions are advised. Outside the busy nightlife area around Calle Larga, the city centre is deserted and unsafe after 2300. The river banks, the Cruz del Vado area (south end of Juan Montalvo), the Terminal Terrestre and all market areas, are not safe after dark.

BACKGROUND

From AD 500 to around 1480, Cuenca was a Cañari settlement, called Guapondeleg, which roughly translates as 'an area as large as heaven'. The suffix 'deleg' is still found in several local place names, a vestige of the now extinct Cañari language.

Owing to its geographical location, this was among the first parts of what is now Ecuador to come under the domination of the Inca empire, which had expanded north. The Incas settled the area around Cuenca and called it Tomebamba, which translates as 'Valley of Knives'. The name survives as one of the region's rivers. Some 70 km north of Cuenca, in an area known as Jatun Cañar, the Incas built the ceremonial centre of Ingapirca, which remains the most important Inca site in the country (see page 123). Ingapirca and Tomebamba were, for a time, the hub of the northern part of the Inca empire.

The city as it is today was founded by the Spanish in 1557 on the site of Tomebamba and named Santa Ana de los Cuatro Ríos de Cuenca. It then became an important and populous regional centre in the crown colony governed from Quito. The conquistadors and the settlers who followed them were interested in the working of precious metals, for which the region's indigenous peoples had earned a well deserved reputation. Following independence from Spain, Cuenca became capital of one of three provinces that made up the new republic, the others being Quito and Guayaquil.

PLACES IN CUENCA

On the main plaza, **Parque Abdón Calderón**, are the Old Cathedral, **El Sagrario** ① *Mon-Fri 0900-1600, Sat-Sun 1000-1500, US$1*, begun in 1557, and the immense 'New' **Catedral de la Inmaculada**, started in 1885. The latter contains a famous crowned image of the Virgin,

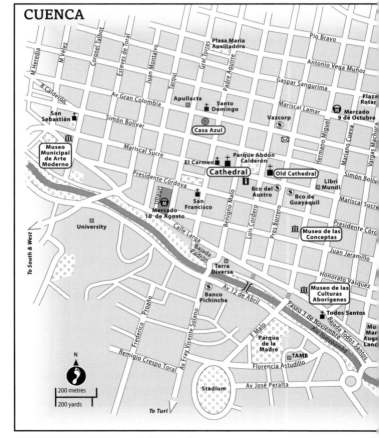

a beautiful altar and an exceptional play of light and shade through modern stained glass. Other churches which deserve a visit are **San Blas**, **San Francisco** and **Santo Domingo**. Many churches are open at irregular hours only and for services. The church of **El Carmen de la Asunción**, close to the southwest corner of La Inmaculada, has a flower market in the tiny **Plazoleta El Carmen** in front. There is a colourful daily market in **Plaza Rotary** where pottery, clothes, guinea pigs and local produce, especially baskets, are sold. Thursday is the busiest day.

Museo del Monasterio de las Conceptas ① *Hermano Miguel 6-33 entre Pdte Córdova y Juan Jaramillo, T07-283 0625, www.museodelasconceptas.org.ec, Mon-Fri 0900-1830, Sat and holidays 1000-1300, US$2.50*, in a cloistered convent founded in 1599, houses a well displayed collection of religious and folk art, in addition to an extensive collection of lithographs by Guayasamín.

Pumapungo ① *C Larga y Huayna Capac, T07-283 1255, Mon-Fri 0900-1700, Sat 0900-1300*, is a mueum complex on the edge of the colonial city, at the actual site of Tomebamba excavations. Part of the area explored is seen at the **Parque Arqueológico Pumapungo**. The **Sala Arqueológica** section contains all the Cañari and Inca remains and artefacts found at this site. Other halls in the premises house the **Sala Etnográfica**, with information on different Ecuadorean cultures, including a special collection of *tsantsas* (shrunken heads from Oriente), the **Sala de Arte Religioso**, the **Sala Numismática** and temporary exhibits. There are also book and music libraries, free cultural videos and music events. Three blocks west of Pumapungo, **Museo Manuel Agustín Landívar** ① *C Larga 2-23 Y Manuel Vega, T07-282 1177, Mon-Fri 0800-1700, Sat 0900-1300, US$1*, is at the site of the small Todos los Santos ruins, with Cañari, Inca and colonial remains; ceramics and artefacts found at the site are also displayed.

Museo de las Culturas Aborígenes ① *C Larga 5-24 y Hermano Miguel, T07-283 9181, Mon-Fri 0830-1800, Sat 0900-1400, US$2; guided tours in English, Spanish and French, has a craft shop and restaurant*, the private collection of Dr J Cordero López, has an impressive selection of pre-Columbian archaeology. **Museo del Sombrero** ① *C Larga 10-41 y Gral Torres, T07-283 6972, Mon-Fri 0900-1800, Sat 0900-1700*, is a shop with all the old factory machines for hat finishing.

On Plaza San Sebastián the **Museo Municipal de Arte Moderno** ① *Sucre 1527 y Talbot, T07-282 0638, Mon-Fri 0830-1300, Sat-Sun 0900-1300, free*, has a permanent contemporary art collection and art library. It holds a biennial international painting competition and other cultural activities. Across the river from the Museo Pumapungo, the **Museo de Artes de Fuego** ① *Las Herrerías y 10 de Agosto, T07-409 6510, Mon-Fri 0800-1330, 1500-1730, free except for special events*, has a display of wrought-iron work and pottery. It is housed in the beautifully restored Casa de Chaguarchimbana. Also south of city, accessed via Avenida Fray Vicente Solano, beyond the football stadium, is Turi church, orphanage and mirador; a tiled panorama explains the magnificent views.

BAÑOS

There are sulphur baths, 5 km southwest of Cuenca at Baños, with its domed, blue church in a delightful landscape. Water temperatures at the source are measured at 76°C making these the hottest commercial baths in the country, but bathing pools are at various temperatures. There are three complexes: **Rodas, Merchán and Durán** ① *dawn till 2100, US$3.50-5*. Durán is by far the largest and best maintained and, although associated with the **Hostería Durán** (**$$$**), the numerous hot pools and tubs and steam baths are open to the public. They are very crowded at weekends. The country lanes above the village offer some pleasant walks. City buses marked 'Baños' go to and from Cuenca; it takes 1½ hours to walk.

INGAPIRCA

ⓘ *Daily 0800-1800, closed public holidays, US$6, including museum and tour in Spanish; bags can be stored. Small café.*

Ecuador's most important Inca archaeological site, at 3160 m, lies 8.5 km east of the colonial town of Cañar, less than two hours from Cuenca.

Although it is famed as a classic Inca site, Ingapirca, which translates as 'Wall of the Inca', had probably already been sacred to the native Cañari people for many centuries. It is also known as 'Jatun Cañar' (great Cañar). The Inca Huayna Capac took over the site from the conquered Cañaris when his empire expanded north into Ecuador in the third quarter of the 15th century. Ingapirca was strategically placed on the Royal Highway that ran from Cuzco to Quito and soldiers may have been stationed there to keep the troublesome Cañaris under control.

The site, first described by the French scientist Charles-Marie de la Condamine in 1748, shows typical imperial Cuzco-style architecture, such as tightly fitting stonework and trapezoidal doorways, which can be seen on the *castillo* and governor's house. The central structure may have been a solar observatory. There is considerable debate as to Ingapirca's precise function. From what remains of the site, it probably consisted of storehouses, baths and dwellings for soldiers and other staff, suggesting it could have been a royal *tambo*, or inn. It could also have been used as a sun temple, judging by the beautiful ellipse, modelled on the Qoricancha in Cuzco. Furthermore, the length of the site is exactly three times the diameter of the semi-circular ends, which may have been connected with worship of the sun in its morning, midday and afternoon positions.

Nearby is a throne cut into the rock, the **Sillón del Inca** (Inca's Chair) and the **Ingachugana**, a large rock with carved channels. This may have been used for offerings and divination with water, *chicha* or the blood of sacrificial animals. A 10-minute walk away from the site is the **Cara del Inca**, or 'Face of the Inca', an immense natural formation in the rock looking over the landscape. On Friday there is an interesting indigenous market at Ingapirca village.

A tourist train runs from El Tambo 7 km to the small Cañari-Inca archaeological site of **Baños del Inca** or **Coyoctor** ⓘ *site open daily 0800-1700, US$1; 2 departures Wed-Fri, 5 departures Sat, Sun and holidays, US$7, includes entry to El Tambo museum and Coyoctor site*, a massive rock outcrop carved to form baths, showers, water channels and seats overlooking a small amphitheatre. There is an interpretation centre with information about the site, a hall with displays about regional fiestas and an audiovisual room with tourist information about all of Ecuador.

Many Cuenca operators offer tours to Ingapirca or you can visit independently. Access is from **Cañar** or **El Tambo,** both have simple *hostales* and there are others plus and an upmarket *posada* near the archeological site. Direct buses run from Cuenca to Ingapirca with **Transportes Cañar** Monday-Friday at 0900 and 1220, Saturday-Sunday at 0900, returning 1300 and 1545, US$2.50, two hours. Frequent buses also run from Cuenca to El Tambo and Cañar; from there take a local bus or taxi (pick-up) to Ingapuirca. If you are coming from the north (Qutio, Riobamba or Alausí) then you can get off the bus in El Tambo or Cañar, visit Ingapirca, and then carry on to Cuenca.

INCA TRAIL TO INGAPIRCA

The three-day hike to Ingapirca starts at **Achupallas** (lively Saturday market, one hostel), 25 km from Alausí. Local buses and pick-ups from Alausí to Achupallas leave as they fill 1100-1600 daily, US$1, one hour. The walk is covered by three 1:50,000 *IGM* topographic maps, Alausí, Juncal and Cañar. The Juncal sheet is most important, the name Ingapirca does not appear on the latter, you may have to ask directions near the end. Also take a compass and GPS. Good camping equipment is essential. Take all food and drink with you as there is nothing along the way. A shop in Achupallas sells basic foodstuffs. There are persistent beggars the length of the hike, especially children. Tour operators in Riobamba and Cuenca offer this trek for about US$250-310 per person, three days, everything included.

EAST OF CUENCA

Northeast of Cuenca, on the road to Méndez in the Oriente, is **Paute**, with a pleasant park and modern church. South of Paute, **Gualaceo** is a rapidly expanding, modern town set in beautiful landscape, with a charming plaza and Sunday market. The iTur ① *at the Municipio, Gran Colombia y 3 de Noviembre, Parque Central, T07-225 5131, Mon-Fri 0800-1300, 1400-1700* is very helpful, Spanish only. CIDAP ① *Loja y Sucre, Wed-Sun 0900-1300, free*, is a small crafts museum. A scenic road goes from Gualaceo to Limón in Oriente (closed for paving in 2013). Many of Ecuador's 4000 species of orchids can be seen at **Ecuagénera** ① *Km 2 on the road to Cuenca, T07-225 5237, www.ecuagenera.com, Mon-Sat 0730-1630, Sun 0930-1630, US$5 (US$3 pp for groups of 3 or more).*

South of Gualaceo is **Chordeleg**, a touristy village famous for its crafts in wood, silver and gold filigree, pottery and Panama hats. At the Municipio is the **Centro de Interpretación** ① *C 23 de Enero, Mon-Fri 0800-1300, 1400-1700*, an exhibition hall with fascinating local textiles, ceramics and straw work, some of which are on sale at reasonable prices. It's a good uphill walk from Gualaceo to Chordeleg, and a pleasant hour downhill in the other direction. South of Gualaceo, 83 km from Cuenca, **Sígsig**, an authentic highland town where women can be seen weaving hats 'on the move'. It has a Sunday market, two *residenciales* and an archaeology museum. A poor but scenic road goes from Sígsig to Gualaquiza in Oriente.

Buses from the Terminal Terrestre in Cuenca go to all of the above towns throughout the day. All are one to 1½ hours from the city and make a convenient day-trip or overnight excursion; there are various places to stay.

PARQUE NACIONAL CAJAS

① *The park office in Cuenca is at Presidente Córdova 7-56 y Luis Cordero, Edif Morejón, p 2, T07-282 9853, www.etapa.net.ec/PNC, Mon-Fri 0800-1300 and 1500-1800. Entry free, overnight stay US$4 per night.*
Northwest of Cuenca, Cajas is a 29,000-ha national park with over 230 lakes. The *páramo* vegetation, such as *chuquiragua* and lupin, is beautiful and the wildlife interesting. Cajas is very rich in birdlife; 125 species have been identified, including the condor and many varieties of hummingbird (the violet-tailed metaltail is endemic to this area). On the lakes are Andean gulls, speckled teal and yellow-billed pintails. On a clear morning the views are superb, even to Chimborazo, some 300 km away.

There are two access roads. The paved road from Cuenca to Guayaquil via Molleturo goes through the northern section and is the main route for **Laguna Toreadora**, the visitor centre and Laguna Llaviuco. Skirting the southern edge of the park is a poor secondary road, which goes from Cuenca via San Joaquín to the **Soldados** entrance and the community of Angas beyond. There is nowhere to stay after the *refugio* at Laguna Toreadora until you reach the lowlands between Naranjal and La Troncal.

The park offers ideal but strenuous walking, at 3150-4450 m altitude, and the climate is wet and cold. There have been deaths from exposure. The best time to visit is August-January, when you may expect clear days, strong winds, night-time temperatures to -8°C and occasional mist. From February to July temperatures are higher but there is much more fog, rain and snow. It is best to arrive in the early morning since it can get very cloudy, wet and cool after about 1300. Cuenca tourist office has a good, one-page map of Cajas, but other local maps are not always exact. It is best to get the IGM maps in Quito (Chaucha, Cuenca, San Felipe de Molleturo, and Chiquintad 1:50,000) and take a compass and GPS. It is easy to get lost.

Many Cuenca operators offer tours to Cajas. To get there on your own, take any Guayaquil-bound bus from the Terminal Terrestre that goes via Molleturo, not Zhud (US$2); it's 30 minutes to the turn-off for Llaviuco, 45 minutes to Toreadora. **Coop Occidental** runs to Molleturo, eight a day from the Terminal Sur/Feria Libre; this is a slower bus and may wait to fill. For the Soldados entrance, catch a bus from Puente del Vado in Cuenca (daily at 0600, US$1.25, 1½ hours); the return bus passes the Soldados gate at about 1600.

→CUENCA TO VILCABAMBA

From Cuenca various routes go to the Peruvian border, fanning out from the pleasant city of Loja, due south of which is Vilcabamba, famous for its invigorating climate and lovely countryside.

SOUTH TO LOJA VIA SARAGURO

The Pan-American Highway divides about 20 km south of Cuenca. One branch runs south to Loja, the other heads southwest to Machala on the coast. The scenic road between Cuenca and Loja climbs to high cold *páramo* before dropping to the deep desert-like canyon of the Río León.

Further along the road to Loja is the old town of **Sarguro** (all buses between Cuenca and Loja pass through Saraguro), where the local people, the most southerly indigenous Andean group in Ecuador, dress all in black. The men are notable for their black shorts and the women for their pleated black skirts, necklaces of coloured beads and silver *topos*, ornate pins fastening their shawls. The town has a picturesque Sunday market and interesting Mass and Easter celebrations. Traditional festivities are held during solstices and equinoxes in surrounding communities. Above the altar of the church, with its imposing stone façade, are inscribed the three Inca commandments in Quichua: *"Ama Killa, Ama Llulla, Ama Shua"*. (Do not be lazy, do not lie, do not steal.)

Necklaces and other crafts are sold around the plaza. Saraguro has a community tourism programme with tours and homestay opportunities with indigenous families. Contact **Fundación Kawsay** ① *18 de Noviembre y Av Loja, T07-220 0331*, or the **Oficina Municipal de Turismo** ① *C José María Vivar on the main plaza, T07-220 0100 ext 18, Mon-Fri 0800-1200, 1400-1800; see also www.saraguro.org*. **Bosque Washapampa**, 6 km south, has good birdwatching.

LOJA

For most tourists, Loja serves as a transport link between Vilcabamba and Cuenca, as well as Quito, Guayaquil and other destinations (see Moving on, page 118). It is also a friendly pleasant city, encircled by hills, which has won international awards for its parks and its recycling programme. If you need to stay overnight here, there are many hotel and restaurant options as well as all services. **iTur** ① *José Antonio Eguiguren y Bolívar, Parque Central, T07-258 1251, Mon-Fri 0800-1300, 1500-1800, Sat 0900-1300*, has local and regional information and a map; helpful, some English spoken.

PARQUE NACIONAL PODOCARPUS

① *Headquarters at Cajanuma entrance, T07-302 4862. Limited information from Ministerio del Ambiente in Loja, Sucre 04-55 y Quito, T07-257 9595, parquepodocarpus@gmail.com, Mon-Fri 0800-1700. In Zamora at Sevilla de Oro y Orellana, T07-260 6606. Their general map of the park is not adequate for navigation; buy topographic maps in Quito.*

Podocarpus (950 to 3700 m) is one of the most diverse protected areas in the world. It is particularly rich in birdlife, including many rarities, and includes one of the last major habitats for the spectacled bear. The park protects stands of *romerillo* or podocarpus, a native, slow-growing conifer. UNESCO has declared Podocarpus-El Cóndor (Cordillera del Cóndor) as a biosphere reserve. It includes a large area (1.14 million ha) in the provinces of Loja and Zamora Chinchipe. The park itself is divided into two areas, an upper premontane section with spectacular walking country, lush cloud forest and excellent birdwatching; and a lower subtropical section, with remote areas of virgin rainforest and unmatched quantities of flora and fauna. Both zones are wet (rubber boots recommended) but there may be periods of dry weather between October and January. The upper section is also cold, so warm clothing and waterproofs are indispensable year-round.

There are entrances to the upper section at **Cajanuma**, 8 km south of Loja on the Vilcabamba road, from the turn-off it is a further 8 km uphill to the vistor centre and trailheads; and at **San Francisco**, 24 km from Loja along the road to Zamora. Entrances to the lower section are at **Bombuscaro**, 6 km from Zamora (see Going further, page 150), the visitor centre is a 30-minute walk from the car park. Cajanuma is the starting point for the demanding eight-hour hike to **Lagunas del Compadre**, a series of beautiful lakes set amid rock cliffs, camping is possible there (no services). Another trail from Cajanuma leads in one hour to a lookout with views over Loja.

A popular Podocarpus day trip is from Vilcabamba to Cajanuma for hiking and birdwatching. Taxis charge US$15 one way, more with wait, or you can walk 8 km down to the main road and flag a van going from Loja to Vilcabamba.

At **San Francisco**, the *guardianía* (ranger station) operated by **Fundación Arcoiris**, offers good accommodation. This section of the park is a transition cloud forest at around 2200 m and is very rich in birdlife. This is the best place to see podocarpus trees: a trail (four hours return) goes from the shelter to the trees. The **Bombuscaro** lowland section, also very rich in birdlife, has several trails leading to lovely swimming holes on the Río Bombuscaro and waterfalls; Cascada La Poderosa is particularly nice.

VILCABAMBA

Once an isolated village, Vilcabamba is today home to a thriving and colourful expatriate community. It is also popular with travellers and the ideal place to pamper yourself and rest up at the end of your long overland journey from Quito. The whole area is beautifully tranquil, with a very agreeable climate. There are many great places to stay and a selection of good restaurants. The surroundings offer excellent day-walks and longer treks, as well as ample opportunities for horse riding. A number of lovely private nature reserves are situated east of Vilcabamba, towards Parque Nacional Podocarpus. Trekkers can continue on foot through orchid-clad cloud forests to high *páramos*.

Artisans sell their crafts in front of the school on weekends. For tourist information iTur ① *Diego Vaca de Vega y Bolívar, on the corner of the main plaza, T07-264 0090, daily 0800-1300, 1500-1800*, has various pamphlets and is helpful.

Rumi Wilco ① *10-min walk northeast of town, take C Agua de Hierro towards C La Paz and turn left, follow signs, US$2 valid for the duration of your stay in Vilcabamba*, is a 40-ha private nature reserve with several signed trails. Many of the trees and shrubs are labelled with their scientific and common names. There are great views of town from the higher trails, and it is a very good place to go for a walk. Over 100 species of bird have been identified here. Volunteers are welcome.

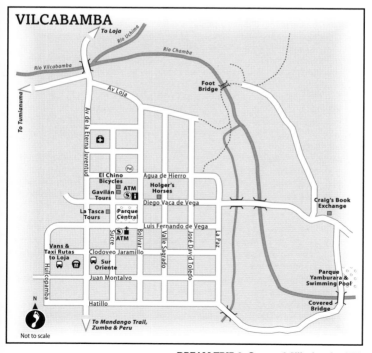

ON THE ROAD
The Vilcabamba syndrome

At the time a tiny isolated village, Vilcabamba attracted international attention in the 1960s when researchers announced that it was home to one of the oldest living populations in the world. It was said that people here often lived well over 100 years, some as old as 135.

Although doubt was subsequently cast on some of this data, there is still a high incidence of healthy, active elders in Vilcabamba. It is not unusual to find people in their 70s and 80s working in the fields and covering several miles a day on foot to get there. Such longevity and vitality has been ascribed to the area's famously healthy climate and excellent drinking water, but other factors must also be involved: perhaps physical activity, diet and lack of stress.

Attracted in part by Vilcabamba's reputation for nurturing a long and tranquil life, a number of outsiders – both Ecuadoreans and foreigners – settled in the area. Some of the earliest arrivals followed the footsteps of Doctor Johnny Lovewisdom, a California-born ascetic who arrived in 1969 to establish his Pristine Order of Paradisiacal Perfection. Others just came for a few days and never left.

For a time drugs were in vogue in Vilcabamba, especially a hallucinogenic cactus extract called San Pedro, and the flashbacks associated with its use became known as the 'Vilcabamba syndrome'. Later, the fashion turned to UFO sightings, with plans to build a large observation platform. Then people arrived to escape the impending end of the world when the Mayan calendar expired in 2012.

Through it all, more and more foreign residents, ranging from retirees to young families, continue to settle in Vilcabamba. Real-estate speculation is rife and brokers' offices line the plaza alongside the cafés where the expats congregate. Catering to their needs has become the town's growth industry while, in a delightfully ironic reversal of roles, urban middle-class Ecuadoreans from Cuenca, Guayaquil and Quito come to spend their holidays and watch the colourful gringos. Today's Vilcabamba syndrome has more to do with postmodern colonialism than hallucinogenic cactus juice. Similar scenarios are being played out in expatriate enclaves from Cuenca to Cotacachi in Ecuador, as well as many other parts of the world.

Come check it out for yourself and, if you are really interested, read the anonymously authored history: *Valley of the Rare Fruits*, available at **Caballos Gavilán** tour agency. Do you think the outsiders will still be able to benefit from the once famous tranquility and longevity of Vilcabamba? Or have we brought with us the seeds of our own destruction?

Climbing **Mandango**, 'the sleeping woman' mountain, just outside town, is a scenic half-day walk. The signed access is along the highway, 250 m south of the bus terminal. Be careful on the higher sections when it is windy and always enquire beforehand about public safety; armed robberies have taken place and tourists have been hurt.

In several out-of-the-way locations around Vilcabamba are permaculture, environmental conservation and **alternative lifestyle projects** that welcome visitors and volunteers. If you are interested and have a few weeks to spare, contact **Yves Zender** ① *T09-143 1689, www.sacredsuenos.com.*

GOING FURTHER
Zaruma

This delightful old gold-mining town is far off the tourist trail and reached from Loja or Cuenca along scenic back roads, or by paved road from Machala on the coast. All these routes have bus services.

Founded in 1549, Zaruma is scenically perched on a hilltop, with steep, twisting streets and painted wooden buildings. The **tourist office** ① *in the Municipio, at the plaza, T07-297 3533, Mon-Fri 0800-1200, 1400-1800, Sat 0900-1600, Sun 0900-1300,* is very friendly and helpful. They can arrange for guides and accommodation with local families. Next door is the small **Museo Municipal** ① *free, ask for the key at the tourist office if closed.* It has a collection of local historical artefacts. Family-run **Hostería El Jardín ($$)**, in Barrio Limoncito, a 10-minute walk from the centre, T07-297 2706, has a lovely palm garden and terrace with views and is a great place to stay.

The Zaruma area has a number of pre-Hispanic archaeological sites and petroglyphs are also found in the region. Tours can be arranged with **Oroadventure** ① *at the Parque Central, T07-297 2761,* or with English-speaking guide **Ramiro Rodríguez** ① *T07-297 2523.* Zaruma is also known for its excellent Arabica coffee freshly roasted in the agricultural store basement; the proud owner will show you around if the shop is not busy.

On top of the small hill beyond the market is a public swimming pool (US$1), from where there are amazing views over the hot, dry valleys. For even grander views, walk up **Cerro del Calvario** (follow Calle San Francisco); go early in the morning as it gets very hot. At **Portovelo**, south of Zaruma, is the largest mine in the area. Its history is told inside a mine shaft at the **Museo Magner Turner** ① *T07-294 9345, daily 0900-1100, 1400-1700, US$1.* The area has virtually no tourists and is well worth a visit.

Piñas, 19 km west of Zaruma, along the road to Machala is a pleasant town which conserves just a few of its older wooden buildings. Northwest of Piñas, 20 minutes along the road to Saracay and Machala, is **Buenaventura**, to the north of which lies an important area for bird conservation, with over 310 bird species recorded, including many rare ones. **The Jocotoco Foundation** (www.fjocotoco.org) protects a 1500-ha forest in this region, with 13 km of trails, entry US$15, lodge (**$$$$**), advance booking required.

CUENCA AND VILCABAMBA LISTINGS

WHERE TO STAY

Cuenca

$$$$ Mansión Alcázar, Bolívar 12-55 y Tarqui, T07-282 3918, www.mansionalcazar. com. Beautifully restored house, a mansion indeed, central, very nice rooms, includes breakfast, restaurant serves gourmet international food, lovely gardens, quiet relaxed atmosphere.

$$$ Carvallo, Gran Colombia 9-52, entre Padre Aguirre y Benigno Malo, T07-283 2063, www.hotelcarvallo.com. ec. Combination of an elegant colonial-style hotel and art/antique gallery. Very comfortable rooms all have bath tubs, includes breakfast, restaurant, boutique with exclusive crafts and clothing.

$$$ La Posada Cuencana, Tarqui 9-46 y Bolívar, T07-282 6831, www.laposada cuencana.com. Small family run hotel, beautiful colonial style rooms, includes breakfast, personalized service by owners.

$$$ Victoria, C Larga 6-93 y Borrero, T07-283 1120, www.grupo-santaana.net. Elegant refurbished hotel overlooking the river, comfortable modern rooms, includes breakfast, excellent restaurant, nice views.

$$ Posada del Angel, Bolívar 14-11 y Estévez de Toral, T07-284 0695, www. hostalposadadelangel.com. A nicely restored colonial house, comfortable rooms, includes breakfast, good Italian restaurant, parking, patio with plants, some noise from restaurant, English spoken, helpful staff.

$$ Macondo, Tarqui 11-64 y Lamar, T07-284 0697, www.hostalmacondo.com. Restored colonial house, large rooms, includes buffet breakfast, private or shared bath, laundry and cooking facilities, pleasant patio with plants, garden, very popular, US-run. Highly recommended.

$$-$ Casa Naranja, Lamar 10-38 y Padre Aguirre, T07-285 3234. Artistically decorated colonial house with 2 inner patios, breakfast available, private or shared bath, cooking facilities, terrace, safety deposit boxes, storage room, long-stay discounts.

Vilcabamba

$$-$ Izhcayluma, 2 km south on road to Zumba, T07-302 5162, www.izhcayluma. com. Popular inn with comfortable rooms and cabins with terrace and hammocks. Includes very good buffet breakfast, excellent restaurant with wonderful views, private or shared bath, also dorm, lovely grounds, pool, massage centre, lively bar, billiards, ping-pong, parking, walking map and route descriptions, English and German spoken, helpful. Highly recommended.

$$-$ Las Margaritas, Sucre y Clodoveo Jaramillo, T07-264 0051. Small family-run hotel with comfortable well-furnished rooms, includes good breakfast, intermittent solar-heated water, parking, garden.

$$-$ Le Rendez-Vous, Diego Vaca de Vega 06-43 y La Paz, T09-9219 1180, www. rendezvousecuador.com. Very comfortable rooms with terrace and hammocks around a lovely garden. Includes breakfast, private or shared bath, pleasant atmosphere, attentive service, French and English spoken.

$ Rumi Wilco, 10-min walk northeast of town, take C Agua de Hierro towards C La Paz and turn left, follow the signs from there, www.rumiwilco.com. Cabins in the Rumi Wilco reserve. Lovely setting on the shores of the river, very tranquil, private or shared bath, laundry facilities, fully furnished kitchens, discounts for long stays and volunteers, camping US$3.50 pp, friendly Argentine owners, English spoken.

RESTAURANTS

Cuenca

Cuenca has many good dining options.

$$$-$$ Tiestos, J Jaramillo 7-34 y Borrero, T07-283 5310. Tue-Sat 1230-1500, 1830-

2200, Sun 1230-1500. Superb international cuisine prepared on *tiestos* (shallow clay pans), comfortable feel-at-home atmosphere, very popular, reserve ahead.

$$ Café Austria, Benigno Malo 5-99 y J Jaramillo. Daily 0900-2400. A traditional Cuenca café serving international food and great Austrian pastries, pleasant atmosphere.

$$ Café Eucalyptus, Gran Colombia 9-41 y Benigno Malo. Mon-Fri 1700-2300 or later, Sat 1900-0200. A pleasant restaurant, café and bar in an elegantly decorated house. Large menu with dishes from all over the world. British-run, popular.

$$ Raymipampa, Benigno Malo 8-59, at Parque Calderón. Mon-Fri 0830-2300, Sat-Sun 0930-2230. Good typical and international food in a central location, economical set lunch on weekdays, fast service, very popular, at times it is hard to get a table.

$$-$ Viejo Rincón, Pres Córdova 7-46 y Borrero. Mon-Fri 0900-2100, Sat 0900-1500. Tasty Ecuadorean food, very good set lunch and à la carte, popular.

Vilcabamba

Around the Parque Central are many café/bar/restaurants with pleasant sidewalk seating. The restaurant at hotel **Izhcayluma** is highly recommended.

$$ Shanta's, 800 m from the centre on the road to Yamburara. Tue-Sun 1300-2100. Specialities are pizza (excellent), trout, frogs legs, filet mignon and *cuy* (with advance notice). Also vegetarian options, good fruit juices and drinks. Attractively decorated rustic setting, pleasant atmosphere and attentive service.

WHAT TO DO

Cuenca
Language schools
Centro de Estudios Interamericanos (CEDEI), Gran Colombia 11-02 y General Torres, Casilla 597, T07-283 9003, www.cedei.org. Spanish and Quichua lessons, immersion/volunteering programmes. Also run the attached **Hostal Macondo**.
Sí Centro de Español e Inglés, Borrero 7-67 y Sucre, T07-282 0429, www.sicentrospanishschool.com. Good teachers, competitive prices, homestays, volunteer opportunities, helpful and enthusiastic, tourist information available.

Tour operators
Apullacta, Gran Colombia 11-02 y Gral Torres, p2, T07-283 7815, www.apullacta.com. Run city and regional tours (Cajas, Ingapirca, Saraguro), also adventure tours (cycling, horse riding, canopy, canyoning), sell jungle, highland and Galápagos trips; also hire camping equipment.
Pazhuca Tours, T07-282 3231, info@pazhucatours.com.ec. Run regional tours

and offer transport through **Van Service**, T07-281 6409, www.van service.com.ec, which also run city tours on a double-decker bus.

Terra Diversa, C Larga 8-41 y Luis Cordero, T07-282 3782, www.terradiversa.com. Lots of useful information, helpful staff, a pleasant sitting area, small library and bulletin boards. Ingapirca, Cajas, community tourism in Saraguro, jungle trips, horse riding, mountain biking and other options. The more common destinations have fixed departures. Also sell Galápagos tours and flights.

Vilcabamba
Horse riding
Horse riding is very popular. All of the following are experienced and have good horses.
Gavilán Tours, Sucre y Diego Vaca de Vega, T07-264 0209, gavilanhorse@yahoo.com.
Holger's Horses, Diego Vaca de Vega y Valle Sagrado, T09-8296 1238. German spoken.
La Tasca Tours, Sucre at the plaza, T09-8556 1188. Horse and bike tours.

DREAM TRIP 3
Quito→Oriente→Baños 14 days

Quito 3 nights, page 35

Papallacta or Baeza 1 night, page 136
Bus/tour/private transport from Quito
(2 hrs to Papallacta, 2½ hrs to Baeza)

Lago Agrio or Coca 1 night, page 137
Bus from Papallacta or Baeza to Lago Agrio
(6 hrs); bus to Coca (7-8 hrs); or tour from
Quito. Flight from Quito (45 mins)

Tena and around 2 nights, page 141
Bus from Lago Agrio (7 hrs) or Coca (5 hrs)

Puyo en route, page 143

Jungle lodges, tours and river cruises
4 nights, page 144
Accessed from Lago Agrio, Coca or Quito

Baños 2 nights, page 107 and 149
Bus from Tena (3½ hrs)

From Baños you can head directly back
to Quito for a flight to Galápagos or an
international flight home. Alternatively
you can join Dream Trip 2 northbound
to Latacunga, the Quilotoa Circuit and/or
Cotopaxi, or southbound to Riobamba
and beyond.

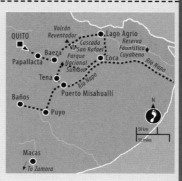

DREAM TRIP 3
Quito → Oriente → Baños

East of the Andes the hills fall away to the vast green carpet of Amazonia. Some of this beautiful wilderness remains unspoiled and sparsely populated, with indigenous settlements along the tributaries of the Amazon. Yet the Ecuadorean jungle has the advantage of being easily accessible and tourist infrastructure here is well developed.

From Quito you can fly in less than an hour to Lago Agrio or Coca, gateways to the Cuyabeno Wildlife Reserve and the Lower Río Napo, respectively, which have most of the jungle lodges in the country. Or you can enjoy the spectacular transition from the Andes to the Amazon by travelling overland and taking in attractions such as Papallacta, the country's finest thermal baths, and San Rafael, Ecuador's highest waterfall, along the way. A good choice is to go one way by road and the other by air.

The eastern foothills of the Andes, where the jungle begins, offer the easiest access and a good introduction to the rainforest for those with limited time or money. Here is the pleasant city of Tena, five hours from Quito by paved road, and surrounded by opportunities for whitewater sports and ethno-tourism. Downriver lie the remaining tracts of primary rainforest, teeming with life, where many world-class lodges offer an unforgettable immersion into life in the rivers, canopy and understorey. Although not cheap, this is Ecuadorean jungle tourism at its best.

Most tourists love the exotic feeling of El Oriente, as the Ecuadorean Amazon is known, and El Oriente needs tourists. Large tracts of jungle are under threat; colonists have cleared many areas for agriculture, while others are laid waste by petroleum exploration or mining. The region's irreplaceable biodiversity and traditional ways of life can only be protected if sustainable ecotourism provides a viable economic alternative.

QUITO TO ORIENTE

After three nights in Quito (see pages 35-56) you'll be ready to head east to El Oriente. If you are in a hurry, you can fly from Quito to Coca or Lago Agrio, visit a jungle lodge and fly back to the capital in just four days. For those with plenty of time, we recommend doing the complete circuit from Quito to the Oriente and back by road. In about two weeks you can take in the fascinating transition from Andes to Amazon and vice versa, as well as various worthwhile attractions along the way. For most visitors the best option will probably be an intermediate one: travelling one way by road and the other by air.

→ ARRIVING FROM QUITO

GETTING TO THE ORIENTE

There are commercial flights from Quito to Lago Agrio, Coca and Macas; and from Guayaquil to Coca via Latucunga. From Quito, Macas and Shell, light aircraft can be chartered to any jungle village with a landing strip. Western Oriente is also accessible by scenic roads which wind their way down from the highlands. Quito, via Baeza, to Lago Agrio and Coca, Baños to Puyo and Tena, and Loja to Zamora are all fully paved, as is almost all of the lowland road from Lago Agrio south to Zamora.

Some roads from the highlands to Oriente are narrow and tortuous and subject to landslides in the rainy season, but all have regular bus services and all can be attempted in a jeep or in an ordinary car with good ground clearance. Deeper into the rainforest, motorized canoes provide the only alternative to air travel.

If you are in a hurry, you can fly from Quito to Coca or Lago Agrio, visit a jungle lodge and fly back to the capital in just four days. For those with plenty of time, we recommend doing the complete circuit from Quito to the Oriente and back by road. In about two weeks you can take in the fascinating transition from Andes to Amazon and vice versa, as well as various worthwhile attractions along the way. For most visitors the best option will probably be an intermediate one: travelling one way by road and the other by air.

If you are travelling by bus from Quito to the Oriente and wish to stop en route at Papallacta, Baeza or San Rafael Falls then you will have to get on and off the long-distance buses that run between Quito and Tena, Coca or Lago Agrio. This is not difficult as services are frequent, but you cannot buy tickets in advance and you are not guaranteed a seat. This is not an issue between larger centres such as Quito, Coca, Lago Agrio, Tena and Baños.

HEALTH AND SAFETY

A yellow fever vaccination is required. Anti-malarial tablets are recommended, as is an effective insect repellent. There may be police and military checkpoints in the Oriente, so always have your passport handy. Caution is advised in the province of Sucumbíos, enquire about public safety before visiting sites near the Colombian border.

From Quito to Baeza, a paved road goes via the Guamaní pass (4064 m). It crosses the Eastern Cordillera just north of Volcán Antisana (5705 m), and then descends via the small village of Papallacta to the old mission settlement of Baeza. The trip between the pass and Baeza has beautiful views of Antisana (clouds permitting), high waterfalls, *páramo*, cloud forest and a lake contained by an old lava flow.

ARRIVING IN PAPALLACTA AND BAEZA

Papallacta is two hours east of Quito, most easily reached with a tour or driving. The **Termas de Papallacta Resort** (see below) offers private van service, which is convenient for groups. From Quito, buses bound for Tena, Lago Agrio or Coca, which depart from Terminal Quitumbe, and buses to Baeza (30 minutes past Papallacta), which depart from La Marín near the colonial city, pass close to the village of Papallacta. From where the bus lets you off, you can take a taxi or walk 1 km to the village or 3 km uphill to the Termas resort.

MOVING ON

From Papallacta to Baeza, get on any bus coming from Quito. One kilometre before Baeza is an important crossroads, where one branch of the paved highway heads north to Lago Agrio via the San Rafael Falls, and the other branch runs to Tena, with a turn-off at Narupa for Coca via Loreto. Buses coming from Quito serve all of these routes.

PAPALLACTA HOT SPRINGS

At the **Termas de Papallacta** ① *64 km east from Quito, 2 km from the town of Papallacta, 0600-2100, T02-256 8989 (Quito), www.papallacta.com.ec*, the best developed hot springs in the country, are 10 thermal pools, three large enough for swimming, and four cold plunge pools. There are two public complexes of springs: the **regular pools** ① *US$7.50*, and the **spa centre** ① *US$18 (massage and other special treatments extra)*. There are additional pools at the Termas hotel and cabins for the exclusive use of their guests. The complex is tastefully done and recommended.

In addition to the Termas there are pleasant, municipal pools in the village of Papallacta (US$3) and several more economical places to stay (some with pools) on the road to the Termas and in the village. On a clear day, the view of Antisana while enjoying the thermal waters is superb. There are several pleasant walking paths in the **Rancho del Cañón** ① *US$2 for use of a short trail, to go on longer walks you are required to take a guide for US$6-15 pp*, a private reserve behind the Termas.

To the north of this private reserve is **Reserva Cayambe-Coca** ① *T02-211 0370*. A scenic road starts by the Termas information centre, crosses both reserves and leads in 45 km to Oyacachi. A permit from Cayambe Coca headquartes (write to lbenitez@ambiente.gob.ec) is required to travel this road even on foot. It is a lovely two-day walk; there is a ranger station and camping area 1½ hours from Papallacta. Reserva Cayambe-Coca is also accessed from La Virgen, the pass on the road to Quito. **Fundación Ecológica Rumicocha** ① *T02-321 4833, www.rumicocha.org.ec*, and **Ríos Ecuador** ① *T06-288 6727, www.riosecuador.com*, offer guiding service here.

BAEZA

The mountainous landscape and high rainfall in this area have created spectacular waterfalls and dense vegetation. Orchids and bromeliads abound. Baeza, in the beautiful

Quijos valley, is about 1 km from the main junction of roads from Lago Agrio and Tena. The town itself is divided in two parts: a faded but pleasant **Baeza Colonial** (Old Baeza) and **Baeza Nueva** (New Baeza), where most shops and services are located. There are various hiking trails and rafting possibilities in the area.

From Baeza a road heads south to Tena, with a branch going east at Narupa to Coca via Loreto, all paved. Another paved road goes northeast from Baeza to Lago Agrio, following the Río Quijos past the villages of **Borja** (8 km from Baeza, very good *comedor* Doña Cleo along the highway, closed Sunday) and **El Chaco** (12 km further, simple accommodation and kayaking at **$ La Guarida del Coyote**) to the slopes of the active volcano **Reventador** (3560 m). There is good trekking here but check www.igepn.edu.ec and enquire locally about volcanic activity beforehand. There is a simple **Hostería El Reventador** (**$**) near the bridge over the Río Reventador; **Ecuador Journeys** (www.ecuadorianjourney.com) offers tours.

Half a kilometre south of the bridge is signed access to the impressive 145-m **San Rafael Falls**, part of Reserva Ecológica Cayambe-Coca and believed to be the highest in Ecuador. It is a pleasant 45-minute hike through cloud forest to a mirador with stunning views of the thundering cascade. Many birds can be spotted along the trail, including cock-of-the-rock, also monkeys and coatimundis. In 2013 the falls could still be visited but the former ranger station had been converted to headquarters of a hydroelectric project (www.ccs.gob.ec), which will use up to 70% of the water in the Río Quijos, leaving only 30% to go over the falls – the death knell for Ecuador's most beautiful cascade.

➜ LAGO AGRIO, COCA AND AROUND

Much of the Northern Oriente is taken up by the Parque Nacional Yasuní, the Cuyabeno Wildlife Reserve and the Cayambe-Coca Ecological Reserve. The main towns for access are Lago Agrio and Coca.

ARRIVING IN LAGO AGRIO AND COCA
There are several daily flights from Quito to both of these jungle cities with **TAME** (www.tame.com.ec) and **Aerogal** (www.aerogal.com.ec). Buses from Quito run via Papallacta and Baeza: eight hours to Lago Agrio, nine to 10 hours to Coca. From Quito to Coca you can take either the northern route via San Rafael Falls (see above) or the southern route via Parque Nacional Sumaco (see page 140). Frequent local buses run between Coca and Lago Agrio, two hours.

MOVING ON
For flights back to Quito, see above. There is also one daily flight with **TAME** from Coca via Latacunga to Guayaquil, for connections to Galápagos (see page 155). See page 97 to connect with Dream Trip 2 and the highlands south of Quito. Several daily buses run from Lago Agrio (seven hours) and Coca (five hours) to Tena via Parque Nacional Sumaco (see page 140).

LAGO AGRIO
The capital of Sucumbíos province is an old oil town with close ties to neighbouring Colombia; it is among the places in Ecuador which has been most affected by conflict there. The name comes from Sour Lake, the US headquarters of Texaco, the first oil company to exploit the Ecuadorean Amazon in the 1970s. It is also called Nueva Loja or just 'Lago'.

ON THE ROAD

The legends of the Incas fuelled the greed and ambition of the Spanish invaders, dreaming of untold riches buried deep in the Amazon jungle. The most famous and enduring of these was the legend of El Dorado, which inspired a spate of ill-fated expeditions deep into this mysterious and inhospitable world.

Francisco Pizarro, conqueror of the Incas, had appointed his younger brother, Gonzalo, as governor of Quito. Lured by tales of fresh lands to be conquered to the east and riches in cinnamon and gold, an expedition under the command of Gonzalo Pizarro left Quito at the end of February 1541. It was made up of 220 Spanish soldiers, 4000 indigenous slaves, 150 horses and 900 dogs, as well as a great many llamas and other livestock. They headed across the Andes not far from Papallacta and down through the cloud forest until they reached a place they called Zumaco. Here Pizarro was joined by Francisco de Orellana, founder of Guayaquil, accompanied by 23 more *conquistadores* who had left Quito a few weeks after the main expedition.

After proceeding to the shores of the Río Coca, the Spaniards began to run out of food and built a small ship, the *San Pedro*. Rumours that they would find food once they reached the Río Napo led Pizarro to dispatch Orellana and his men to look for this river and bring back provisions. Orellana and his party sailed downriver in the *San Pedro* but found nothing for many days, and claimed they could not return against the current. Pizarro, for his part, was convinced that he had been betrayed and abandoned by Orellana.

On February 12, 1542, Orellana reached the confluence of the Napo and the Amazon – so called by him because he said he had been attacked by the legendary women warriors of the same name. Perhaps a more appropriate name for the mighty new river, but one which never caught on, was El Río de Orellana.

On August 26, 1542, 559 days after he had left Guayaquil, Orellana and his men arrived at the mouth of the Amazon, having become the first Europeans to cross the breadth of South America and follow the world's greatest river from the Andes to the Atlantic. Totally lost, they then followed the coastline north and managed to reach the port of Cubagua in Venezuela. In the meantime, Gonzalo Pizarro had suffered enormous losses and limped back to Quito at about the same time, with only 80 starving survivors.

Orellana returned to Spain and, with great difficulty, organized a second expedition which sailed up the Amazon in 1544 only to meet with disaster. Three of his four vessels were shipwrecked and many of the survivors, including Orellana himself, died of fever.

Dominican friar Gaspar de Carvajal, who accompanied Orellana on his first voyage, penned a 31-page chronicle of this odyssey. Carvajal's manuscript survives to this day and the story has been re-told countless times. Orellana is a national hero in Ecuador and his journey is a pillar of the country's assertion that it "is, was, and will be" an Amazonian nation. Some 200 years later, a less famous but no less valiant Ecuadorean named Isabela Godin travelled from Riobamba to the mouth of the Amazon under even harsher conditions than Orellana.

These and other Amazon-size tales are beautifully told in *Explorers of the Amazon* and *The Lost Lady of the Amazon*, both by Anthony Smith, and *The Mapmaker's Wife*, by Robert Whitaker.

GOING FURTHER
Sailing to Peru and beyond

Ever since the days of Francisco de Orellana (see box, opposite), sailing down the Amazon has been the romantic dream of many a visitor to South America. Following in Orellana's own footsteps, such an epic journey can begin in Coca. Beyond the romance, it is a rough adventurous trip requiring plenty of time, patience and stamina. It is also very beautiful and an entirely unforgettable experience.

There are two options: one using public river transport, the other taking a private tour. For public transport, take a motorized canoe from Coca to Nuevo Rocafuerte on the Peruvian border. These 50-passenger canoes leave from the Coca dock (Sunday-Friday 0730, 10-12 hours; returning at 0500, 12-14 hours; US$15). Details change often so enquire locally; buy tickets at the dock a day in advance and arrive early for boarding.

Pañacocha is about halfway between Coca and the border, near a magnificent lagoon and reserve. Here is the **Amazon Dolphin Lodge** (see Lodges on the lower Río Napo, page 146) and Coca agencies and guides also run tours to the area. There are basic places to stay and eat in Pañacocha village. **Nuevo Rocafuerte** is a tranquil riverside town with simple accommodation (**$ Casa Blanca**, Malecón y Nicolás Torres, T06-238 2184), eateries and basic shops. This can be a base for exploring the endangered southeastern section of **Parque Nacional Yasuní**, while you wait for a Peruvian riverboat (see below). **Juan Carlos Cuenca**, T06-238 2257, offers tours here for about US$60 per day.

Ecuadorean immigration for exit stamps is located next to the navy dock in Nuevo Rocafuerte. Peruvian entry stamps are given in the Peruvian border town of **Pantoja**, where there is a decent municipal *hospedaje* (**$ Napuruna**). Shopkeepers in Nuevo Rocafuerte and Pantoja change money at poor rates; Peruvian soles cannot be purchased in Coca. In addition to immigration, you may have to register with the navy on either side of the border so have your passport to hand.

There is no public river transport from Nuevo Rocafuerte to Pantoja but boats can be hired for the 30-km trip downriver, US$60 per boat, you can try to share the ride. Sailings of Peruvian riverboats from Pantoja to **Iquitos** are irregular, once or twice a month, so you must be prepared for a long wait. The trip takes four or five days downriver but may be a bit easier to organize in reverse, upriver from Iquitos to Pantoja, because information about departure dates is more readily available in Iquitos. Crowding and poor sanitation are problems on some of the boats. Take a hammock, cup, bowl, cutlery, extra food and snacks, drinking water or purification, insect repellent, toilet paper, soap, towel, cash dollars and soles in small notes.

The second option for river travel to Iquitos is to arrange a private tour with a Coca agency, taking in various attractions en route and continuing to Iquitos or closer Peruvian ports from where you can catch onward public river transport. Enquire carefully about these tours as they are neither cheap nor luxurious, and may involve many hours of sitting in a small cramped boat.

Experienced jungle guide Juan Medina from **Sachayacu Explorer** in Píllaro near Baños (T03-287 3292, www.rio-amazonas.banios.com) offers recommended jungle tours and trips to Iquitos. Make arrangements well in advance. Luis Duarte, at **Casa del Maito** in Coca (T06-288 2285, cocaselva@hotmail.com) also organizes regional tours and trips to Iquitos, as does Robert Vaca from **Wildlife Amazon** at Hotel San Fermín in Coca (see page 152).

From Iquitos it is possible to continue to the Brazilian Amazon.

Lago is not a safe place, return to your hotel by 2000. Alternatively you can overnight at more tranquil **Cascales** (**$ Paraíso Dorado**, small, simple but pleasant), 35 minutes before Lago Agrio, and still meet your tour party in Lago the following morning. Local advice is available from the **Ministerio de Turismo** ⓘ *Narváez y Añazco, upstairs, T06-283 2488, Mon-Fri 0830-1300, 1400-1800*. For lodges and cruises, see page 144; for other listings, see page 152.

CUYABENO WILDLIFE RESERVE
This large tract of rainforest, covering 602,000 ha, is located about 100 km east of Lago Agrio along the Río Cuyabeno, which eventually drains into the Aguarico. In the reserve are many lagoons and a great variety of wildlife, including river dolphins, tapirs, capybaras, five species of caiman, ocelots, 15 species of monkey and over 500 species of bird. This is among the best places in Ecuador to see jungle animals. The reserve is very popular with visitors but there have been occasional armed hold-ups of tour groups here; best enquire before booking a tour. Access is either by road from Lago Agrio or by river along the Río Aguarico. Within the reserve, transport is mainly by canoe. In order to see as many animals as possible and minimally impact their habitat, seek out a small tour group which scrupulously adheres to responsible tourism practices. Most Cuyabeno tours are booked through agencies in Quito. For tour operators and jungle lodges, see page 144.

COCA
Officially named **Puerto Francisco de Orellana**, Coca is a hot, noisy, bustling oil town at the junction of the Ríos Payamino and Napo. It is the capital of the province of Orellana and is a launch pad from where to visit many jungle lodges on the lower Río Napo (see page 146). The view over the water is nice, and the riverfront **Malecón** can be a pleasant place to spend time around sunset; various indigenous groups have craft shops here. Hotel and restaurant provision is adequate, but electricity, water and, ironically for an oil-producing centre, petrol supplies are erratic. Information is available from **iTur** ⓘ *Chimborazo y Amazonas, by the Malecón, T06-288 0532, Mon-Sat 0800-1200, 1400-1800, www.orellanaturistica.gob.ec* and the **Ministerio de Turismo** ⓘ *Cuenca y Quito, upstairs, T06-288 1583, Mon-Fri 0830-1700*.

In addition to the lower Río Napo lodges, Coca also provides access to **Parque Nacional Yasuní** and the **Huaorani Reserve**. The majority of tours out of Coca are booked through agencies in Quito but there are a few local operators. Quality varies considerably so try to get a personal recommendation. For lodges and cruises, see page 146; for other listings, see page 152.

PARQUE NACIONAL SUMACO
The paved road west from Coca via Loreto (to Tena and Baños, or Baeza and Quito) passes through **Wawa Sumaco**, where a rough road heads north to Parque Nacional Sumaco; 7 km along it is **$$$$-$$$ Wildsumacom** (T06-301 8343, www.wildsumaco.com), a comfortable birdwatching lodge with full board, excellent trails and many rare species. Just beyond is the village of Pacto Sumaco from where a trail runs through the park to the *páramo*-clad summit of **Volcán Sumaco** (3732 m), a six- to seven-day round-trip. Local guides may be hired, there are three nice shelters along the route and a basic community-run hostel in the village (www.sumacobirdwatching.com, T06-301 8324 – not always staffed).

Tena and its surroundings make a very good stop en route to or from the deeper jungle. Closer to Quito than either Coca or Lago Agrio, the area around Tena is an alternative for getting just a glimpse of the jungle for those with limited time or money. For lodges and tours on the Upper Río Napo, see page 149; for other listings, see page 152.

ARRIVING IN TENA

There is an airport at Ahuano and frequent talk of starting flights from Quito, but none were operating in 2013. From Quito's Terminal Quitumbe, several buses a day run to Tena in five hours. Buses from Lago Agrio to Tena take seven hours, from Coca five hours.

MOVING ON

There are frequent local bus services from Tena (Amazonas y Bolívar by the market) to Archidona, 15 minutes; and to Misahuallí (from the Terminal), 45 minutes. Buses from Tena to Baños take 3½ hours but if you are coming from Misahuallí then you can take the local bus towards Tena as far as the highway at Puerto Napo, and catch a Tena-to-Baños bus from there.

ON THE ROAD
Monkey business in Misahuallí

Misahuallí's experience with white-fronted capuchin monkeys (*Cebus albifrons*) apparently dates back to the 1980s. At the time, the story goes, a pet male monkey named Octavio escaped from his owner, who then tried to lure him back with a female. Instead, she also escaped and the young couple took up residence in a tree by the river.

Among their progeny was Peco, another male who became famous for his mischievous antics with tourists. Peco and his family eventually moved from the outskirts to an abandoned house right on the plaza, where he came to an untimely end in the jaws of a local Great Dane. Peco's troop, however, not only multiplied but also thoroughly integrated themselves into Misahuallí society.

The monkeys' interaction with humans is a subtle and unusual one, in which both sides appear to benefit. The monkeys have gained a steady source of food and shelter from the town's shops and tourists, and the townspeople have gained an important tourist attraction.

The capuchins have proven amazingly adaptable due to their ability to consume a wide variety of foods, as well as their behavioural complexity which has enabled them to learn how to unscrew the tops off of bottles, unzip tourist luggage, turn doorknobs to get into houses and open refrigerators for a snack.

The commensal relationship of Misahuallí's two species of urban primates (those with and those without a camera) also attracted serious scientific attention when an anthropology student did her PhD research here, comparing the town monkeys with their country cousins.

TENA

Relaxed and friendly, Tena is the capital of Napo Province. It occupies a hill above the confluence of the Ríos Tena and Pano, there are good views of the Andean foothills often shrouded in mist. Tena is Ecuador's most important centre for whitewater rafting and also offers ethno-tourism. The road from the north passes the old airstrip and market and heads through the town centre as Avenida 15 de Noviembre on its way to the bus station, nearly 1 km south of the river. Tena is quite spread out. A pedestrian bridge and a vehicle bridge link the two halves of town. **iTur** and **Ministerio de Turismo** ① *Malecón, sector El Balneario, Mon-Fri 0730-1230, 1400-1700*, has several information offices under one roof.

ARCHIDONA

Archidona, 65 km south of Baeza and 10 km north of Tena, has a striking, small painted church and not much else, but there are some interesting reserves in the surrounding area. The road leaving Archidona's plaza to the east goes to the village of **San Pablo**, and beyond to the Río Hollín. Along this road, 15 km from Archidona, is **Reserva El Para** ① *owned by Orchid Paradise (see page 153); guided tours US$5 per person plus US$20 for transport.* This 500-ha forest reserve has many rare birds and a nice waterfall. Tours can also be arranged to the **Izu Mangallpa Urcu (IMU) Foundation** ① *contact Elias Mamallacta in Archidona, T06-288 9383 or T08-9045 6942, www.izu-mangallpa-urcu.freehomepage.com, US$50 per day for accommodation (private rooms, mosquito nets) and guiding, minimum 2 people.* This reserve was set up by the Mamallacta family to protect territory on Galeras mountain. There is easy walking as well as a tougher trek, and the forest is wonderful.

MISAHUALLI

This small port, at the junction of the Napo and Misahuallí rivers, is perhaps the best place in Ecuador from which to visit the 'near Oriente', but your expectations should be realistic. The area has been colonized for many years and there is no extensive virgin forest nearby (except at **Jatun Sacha** and **Liana Lodge**. Access is very easy however, prices are reasonable and, while you will not encounter large animals in the wild, you can still see birds, butterflies and exuberant vegetation – enough to get a taste for the jungle. There is a fine, sandy beach on the Río Misahuallí, but don't camp on it as the river can rise unexpectedly. A narrow suspension bridge crosses the Río Napo at Misahuallí and joins the road along the south shore. There is an interesting **Mariposario** (butterfly farm) ① *arrangements through Ecoselva tour agency, US$2.50,* where several colourful species can be observed and photographed close up, and also an orchid garden and entomologica display. At Chichicorumi, outside Misahuallí, is **Kamak Maki** ① *T09-8118 4977, www.museokamakmaki.com*, an ethno-cultural museum run by the local Kichwa community.

→ PUYO

Eighty kilometers south of Tena on the way to Baños, the capital of the province of Pastaza feels more like a lowland city anywhere in Ecuador rather than a typical jungle town. Visits can nonetheless be made to nearby forest reserves and tours deeper into the jungle can also be arranged from Puyo. It is the junction for road travel into the northern and Southern Oriente, and for traffic heading to or from Quito via Baños (all on paved roads). The Sangay and Altar volcanoes can occasionally be seen from town. Tourist information available at **iTur** ① *Francisco de Orellana y 9 de Octubre, T03-288 5122, daily 0800-1600; also at Treminal Terrestre, Wed-Sun 0900-1600.*

Omaere ① *T03-288 3174, Tue-Sun 0900-1700, US$3, access by footbridge off the Paseo Turístico, Barrio Obrero,* is a 15.6-ha ethnobotanical reserve located in the north of Puyo. It has three trails with a variety of plants, an orchidarium and traditional indigenous homes. There are other private reserves of varying quality in the Puyo area and visits are arranged by local tour operators (see box, page 147). You cannot, however, expect to see large tracts of undisturbed primary jungle here.

ON THE ROAD
Ecotourism in Oriente

Jungle tours

These fall into four basic types: lodges, guided tours, indigenous ecotourism and river cruises. When staying at a jungle lodge, you will need to take a torch (flashlight), insect repellent, protection against the sun and a rain poncho that will keep you dry when walking and when sitting in a canoe. All jungle lodges must be booked in advance.

Guided tours of varying length are offered by tour operators and independent guides. These should, in principle, be licensed by the Ecuadorean Ministerio de Turismo. Tour operators and guides are mainly concentrated in Quito, Baños, Puyo, Tena, Misahuallí, Coca and to a lesser extent, Macas and Zamora.

A number of indigenous communities and families offer their own ecotourism programmes in their territories. These are either community controlled and operated, or organized as joint ventures between the indigenous community or family and a non-indigenous partner. The programmes usually involve guides who are licensed as *guías nativos* with the right to guide within their communities. You should be prepared to be more self-sufficient on such a trip than on a visit to a jungle lodge or a tour with a high-end operator. Take a light sleeping bag, rain jacket, trousers (not only shorts), long-sleeved shirt for mosquitoes, binoculars, torch, insect repellent, sunscreen and hat, water-purifying tablets, and a first-aid kit. Wrap everything in several plastic bags to keep it dry. Most lodges provide rubber boots, independenednt guides may not.

River cruises offer a better appreciation of the grandeur of Amazonia, but less intimate contact with life in the rainforest. Passengers sleep and take their meals onboard comfortable river boats, stopping en route to visit local communities and make excursions into the jungle.

Jungle travel without a guide is not recommended. Some indigenous groups prohibit the entry of outsiders to their territory, navigation in the jungle is difficult, and there are a variety of dangerous animals. For your own safety as well as the need to be a responsible tourist, the jungle is not a place to wander off on your own.

Choosing a rainforest

A tropical rainforest is one of the most exciting things to see in Ecuador, but it isn't easy to find a good one. The key is to have realistic expectations and choose accordingly. Think carefully about your interests. If you simply want to relax in nature and see some interesting plants, insects, small birds and mammals, you have many choices, including some that are quite economical and easily accessible. If you want to experience something of the cultures of rainforest people, you must go further. If you want the full experience,

---

→JUNGLE LODGES, TOURS AND RIVER CRUISES

LODGES AND TOURS IN CUYABENO WILDLIFE RESERVE
① *Visited from Lago Agrio.*
Dracaena ① *Pinto 446 y Amazonas, Quito, T02-290 6643, www.amazondracaena.com.* Has a long-standing reputation for good budget tours to Cuyabeno. US$260 for four days. Recommended.

with large mammals and birds, you will have to go further still and spend more money, because large creatures have been hunted or driven out of settled areas.

A visit to a rainforest is not like a visit to the Galápagos. The diversity of life in a good rainforest far exceeds that of the Galapagos, but creatures don't sit around and let themselves be seen. Even in the best forests, your experiences will be unpredictable – none of this 'today is Wednesday, time to see sea lions'. A rainforest trip is a real adventure; the only guarantee is that the surprises will be genuine, and hence all the more meaningful.

There are things that can increase the odds of really special surprises. One of the most important is the presence of a canopy tower or walkway. Even the most colourful rainforest birds are mere specks up in the branches against a glaring sky, unless you are above them looking down. Towers and walkways add an important dimension to bird- and mammal watching. A good guide is another necessity. Avoid guides (and lodges) that emphasize medicinal plants over everything else. This usually means that there isn't anything else around to show. If you are interested in exploring indigenous cultures, give preference to a guide from the same ethnic group as the village you will visit.

If you want to see real wilderness, with big birds and mammals, you should generally avoid any lodges you can drive to. Expect to travel at least a couple of hours in a motorized canoe. Don't stay near villages even if they are in the middle of nowhere. In remote villages people hunt a lot for food, and animals will be scarce. Indigenous villages are no different in this regard; most indigenous groups (except for a very few, such as certain Cofán villages that now specialize in eco-tourism) are ruthlessly efficient hunters.

Responsible jungle tourism

Some guides or their boatmen may try to hunt meat for your dinner – don't let them, and report such practices to other tourists and to guidebooks. Don't buy anything made with animal or bird parts. Avoid making a pest of yourself in indigenous villages; don't take photographs or videos without permission, and don't insist. Many native people believe that photographs can steal one's soul. In short, try to minimize your impact on the forest and its people. Also remember when choosing a tour agency or guide, that the cheapest is not the best. What happens is that agencies undercut each other and offer services that are unsafe or harm local communities and the environment. Do not encourage this practice.

A number of *centros de rescate* (wild animal rescue centres) have sprung up in Oriente, ostensibly to prepare captive animals to return to their natural habitats. They are convenient for observing fauna close-up but, while some may be genuine, others are really just zoos with small cages.

Ecuador Verde País ① *Calama E6-19 y Reina Victoria, Quito, T02-222 0614, www.cabanasjamu.com*. Operate **Jamu Lodge** in the Cuyabeno Reserve, good service, US$230-265 for four days.

Galasam ① *Cordero y Amazonas N24-214, Quito, T02-290 3909, www.galasam.com*. Well-established tour agency which operates **Siona Lodge** (www.sionalodge.com), US$360 for four days.

Magic River Tours ① *Lago Agrio, T09-9736 0670, www.magicrivertours.com.* Offers innovative good-quality and value five- to eight-day canoe tours, half-day paddling, half-day motorized, camping and accommodation in rustic cabins. US$330-800, book well in advance.

Neotropic Turis ① *Pinto E4-360, Quito, T02-252 1212, www.neotropicturis.com.* Operate the **Cuyabeno Lodge** by the Laguna Grande in Cuyabeno, English-speaking guides. US$220-350 for four nights.

LODGES AND CRUISES ON THE LOWER RIO NAPO
① *Visited from Coca.*
All of the following lodges count travel days as part of their package, which means that a 'three-day tour' would spend only one day actually in the forest. A minimum of four days is recommended. Most lodges have fixed departure days from Coca (eg Monday and Friday) and it is very expensive to get a special departure on another day.

Amazon Dolphin Lodge ① *Amazonas N24-236 y Colón, Quito, T02-250 4037, www.amazondolphinlodge.com*, is located on Laguna de Pañacocha, 4½ hours downriver

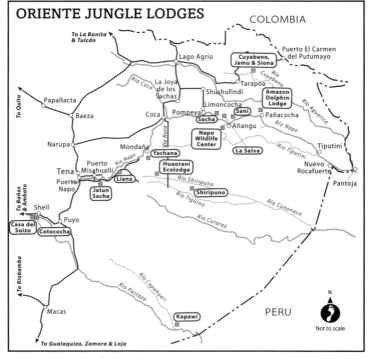

ON THE ROAD

Jungle tours cost from Puyo cost US$25-50 per person per day. Rafting tours around Tena are very popular and cost US$65-100 per day. Safety standards vary. Avoid touts selling tours on the street.

Coka Tours, 27 de Febrero y Ceslao Marín, Puyo, T03-288 6108, denisecoka@gmail.com. Jungle tours.

Ecoselva, Santander on the plaza, Misahuallí, T06-289 0019, ecoselva@yahoo.es. Recommended guide Pepe Tapia speaks English and has a biology background. Well organized and reliable.

Ecu-Astonishing, near Hotel La Missión, Coca, T06-288 0251, jjarrin1@msn.com. Julio Jarrín offers tours to his own cabins near Pañacocha, along the lower Río Napo.

Naveda Santos, Terminal Terrestre, upstairs, Puyo, T03-288 3974. Jungle tours organized by owner, Marco Naveda.

Papangu Tours, 27 de Febrero y Sucre, Puyo, T03-288 7684. Jungle tours operated by the Organización de Pueblos Indígenas de Pastaza (OPIP) and their guías nativos.

Ríos Ecuador, Tarqui 230 y Díaz de Pineda, Tena, T06-288 6727, www.riosecuador.com. Highly recommended whitewater rafting and kayak trips, and a four-day kayaking school (US$320).

River People, 15 de Noviembre y 9 de Octubre, Tena, T06-288 8384. Rafting and kayaking.

Runawa Tours, in La Posada hotel, on the plaza, Misahuallí, T09-9818 1961, www.misahualliamazon.com. Owner Carlos Santander organizes tubing, kayaking and jungle tours.

from Coca. Special wildlife here includes Amazon river dolphins and giant river otters as well as over 500 species of bird. Cabins with private bath, US$600-700 for four days.

Napo Wildlife Center ① *Pje Yaupi N31-90 y Mariana de Jesús, Quito, T02-600 5893, USA T1-866-750 0830, UK T0-800-032 5771, www.ecoecuador.org*, is operated by and for the local Añangu community, 2½ hours downstream from Coca. This area of hilly forest is rather different from the low flat forest of some other lodges, and the diversity is slightly higher. There are big caimans and good mammals, including giant otters, and the birdwatching is excellent with two parrot clay-licks and a 35-m canopy tower. US$820 for four days. Recommended.

Manatee ① *Advantage Travel, Gaspar de Villarroel 1100 y 6 de Diciembre, Quito, T02-336 0887, www.manateeamazonexplorer.com*. This 30-passenger vessel sails between Coca and Pañacocha. US$795 for four days.

La Selva ① *Mariana de Jesús E7-211 y La Pradera, Quito, T02-255 0995, www. laselvajunglelodge.com*, is an upmarket lodge, 2½ hours downstream from Coca on a picturesque lake. Surrounded by excellent forest, especially on the far side of Mandicocha. Bird and animal life is exceptionally diverse and many species of monkey are seen regularly. A total of 580 bird species have been found, one of the highest totals in the world for a single elevation. Comfortable cabins and excellent meals. High standards, most guides are biologists and there is a 45-m canopy tower. US$765-1100 for four days.

Sacha ① *Julio Zaldumbide y Valladolid, Quito, T02-256 6090, www.sachalodge.com*. An upmarket lodge 2½ hours downstream from Coca. Very comfortable cabins, excellent meals. The bird list is outstanding; the local bird expert, Oscar Tapuy (Coca T06-2881486), can be requested in advance. They have a canopy tower and 275-m canopy walkway. Several species of monkey are commonly seen. Nearby river islands provide access to a distinct habitat. US$790 for four days.

Sani ① *Washington E4-71 y Amazonas, Quito, T02-222 8802, www.sanilodge.com*. All proceeds go to the Sani Isla community, who run the lodge with the help of outside experts. It is located on a remote lagoon which has 4- to 5-m-long black caiman. This area is rich in wildlife and birds, including many species such as the scarlet macaw which has disappeared from most other Napo area lodges. There is good accommodation and a 35-m canopy tower. An effort has been made to make the lodge accessible to people who have difficulty walking; the lodge can be reached by canoe (total 3½ hours from Coca) without a walk. US$715 for four days. Good value, recommended.

LODGES IN THE HUAORANI RESERVE
① *Visited from Coca or Quito.*

Huaorani Ecolodge ① *Pasaje Sánchez Melo Oe1-37 y 10 de Agosto, Quito, T02-240 8741, www.tropiceco.com*. This is a joint venture with several Huaorani communities who staff the lodge, and it has won sustainable tourism awards. The small (10 guests) wooden cabins have solar lighting. Expect a spontaneous, rewarding and at times challenging experience, including much community involvement. Also rainforest hikes, kayaking (US$40 per day) and dug-out canoe trips. Tours arrive by small plane from Shell and leave on the Vía Auca to Coca. River journeys are non-motorized except the last stretch from Nenkepare to the road. US$940 for four days includes land and air transport from Quito; return from Coca to Quito is extra.

Otobo's Amazon Safari ① *www.rainforestcamping.com*. Offers eight-day/seven-night camping expeditions in Huaorani territory; access by flight from Shell to Bameno (US$1540 pp), or by road from Coca then two-day motorized canoe journey on the Ríos Shiripuno and Cononaco (US$1050 per person). All meals and guiding included.

Shiripuno ① *T02-227 1094 (Quito), www.shiripunolodge.com*. A lodge with capacity for 20 people, in a very good location on the Río Shiripuno, a four-hour canoe ride downriver from the Vía Auca. Cabins have private bath. The surrounding area has seen relatively little human impact to date. US$360 for four days, plus US$20 entry to Huaorani territory.

LODGES ON THE UPPER RIO NAPO

ⓘ *Visited from Tena and Misahualli.*

Jatun Sacha Biological Station ⓘ *east of Ahuano and easily accessible by bus, T02-331 7163 (Quito), www.jatunsacha.org.* This is a 2500-ha reserve for education, research and tourism. So far, 507 bird, 2500 plant and 765 butterfly species have been identified. There are basic cabins with shared bath, cold water, good self-guided trails and a canopy tower. US$30 per night, day visit US$6, guiding US$20 per group. Good value.

Liana Lodge ⓘ *on Río Arajuno near its confluence with the Napo, T06-301 7702 (Tena), www.amazoonico.org.* These are comfortable cabins with terraces and river views on a 1700-ha reserve. The *centro de rescate* has animals on site. US$250 for four days. They can also arrange stays at **Runa Wasi**, next door (basic cabins run by the local Kichwa community, US$25 per night with three meals, guiding extra).

Yachana ⓘ *Reina Victoria N24-217 y Roca, Quito, T02-252 3777, www.yachana.com.* Located in the village of Mondaña, two hours downstream from Misahuallí or 2½ hours upstream from Coca. Proceeds go towards supporting community development projects. US$510-760 for four days. Recommended.

LODGES NEAR PUYO

Altos del Pastaza Lodge ⓘ *Leonardo Murialdo E11-04 y los Nardos, Quito, T09-9767 4686, www.altosdelpastazalodge.com.* Access from Km 16 of Puyo–Macas road. Attractive lodge in 65-ha reserve overlooking the Río Pastaza, pool. Don't expect much wildlife, but it's a nice place to relax; one- to four-day packages (**$$$$**).

Las Cascadas Lodge ⓘ *Amazonas N23-87 y Wilson, Quito, T02-250 0530, www.surtrek.com.* First-class lodge 40 km east of Puyo, eight rooms with terraces, includes full board, activities and transport from/to Quito, waterfalls; three- and four-day packages available (**$$$**).

LODGES IN SOUTHERN ORIENTE

ⓘ *Visited from Quito.*

Kapawi ⓘ *Foch E7-38 y Reina Victoria, Quito, T02-600 9333, www.kapawi.com.* A top-of-the-line lodge located on the Río Capahuari near its confluence with the Pastaza, not far from the Peruvian border. Run by the local Achuar community and accessible only by small aircraft and motor canoe. The biodiversity is good, but more emphasis is placed on ethno-tourism here than at other upmarket jungle lodges. US$1265 for four days includes land and air transport from Quito.

MOVING ON
To Baños

The popular resort town of Baños (see page 107) on the eastern slopes of the Andes is part of Dream Trip 2 and is the ideal place to relax in a refreshingly cooler climate after the oppressive heat of the jungle. There are frequent buses from Tena to Baños and on to Quito, Latacunga or Riobamba.

GOING FURTHER
Southern Oriente

Stretching south of the Río Pastaza, the Southern Oriente is made up of the provinces of Morona-Santiago and Zamora-Chinchipe. This is a less-developed region and, although tourism is only just getting started here, it has a great deal to offer.

Macas

The capital of Morona-Santiago province, three hours south of Puyo on a paved road, Macas is situated high above the broad Río Upano valley. It is a pleasant tranquil place, established by missionaries in 1563. **Sangay volcano** (5230 m) can be seen on clear mornings from the plaza, creating an amazing backdrop to the tropical jungle surrounding the town. The modern cathedral, with beautiful stained-glass windows, houses the much-venerated image of La Purísima de Macas. Five blocks north of the cathedral, at Don Bosco y Riobamba in the **Parque Recreacional**, which also affords great views of the Upano Valley, are a butterfly garden and a small orchid collection.

    Ministerio de Turismo ① *Bolívar y 24 de Mayo, T07-270 1480, Mon-Fri 0800-1700.* Macas provides access to **Parque Nacional Sangay** ① *Macas office, Juan de la Cruz y Guamote, T07-270 2368, Mon-Fri 0800-1300, 1400-1700.* The lowland area of the park has interesting walking with many rivers and waterfalls. **Casa Upano** (www.realnaturetravel.com) is a great family-run B&B in Macas, which organizes excellent birdwatching tours. **Fundación Chankuap** ① *Soasti y Bolívar, T07-270 1176, www.chankuap.org,* sells a nice variety of locally produced crafts and food products. There is one flight a week with **TAME** between Quito and Macas, and regular bus services to destinations throughout Oriente and the highlands.

Gualaquiza

Eight hours south of Macas on a mostly paved road, Gualaquiza is a pleasant town with an imposing church on a hilltop. Sadly, the area's pioneer-settlement charm is threatened by large-scale mining projects but tourism offers an alternative. There are lovely waterfalls, good rivers for tubing, caves and undeveloped archaeological sites nearby. Information and tours can be organized by the **Oficina Municipal de Turismo** ① *García Moreno y Gonzalo Pesántez, T07-278 0783, Mon-Fri 0730-1230, 1330-1630,* and by Leonardo Matoche at **Canela y Café,** Gonzalo Pesántez y García Moreno.

Zamora

Further south, is the provincial capital of Zamora-Chinchjpe at the confluence of the Ríos Zamora and Bombuscaro. This former the colonial mission settlement has an increasingly boom-town feel due to more large mining projects. It is reached by paved roads from Gualaquiza in three hours, or from Loja in the Southern Highlands (see Dream Trip 2, page 126), two hours away. The town is hilly, with a pleasant climate. It is the gateway to the lowland portion of **Parque Nacional Podocarpus.** Between town and the park is **Copalinga** (www.copalinga.com), a beautiful bird-rich private reserve with excellent accommodation and meals; highly recommended. Zamora also provides access to the **Alto Nangaritza (**accommodation and tours at **Cabañas Yankuam,** www.lindoecuador tours.com), a beautiful jungle-covered gorge with 200-m-high walls cut by waterfalls.

ON THE ROAD
The high price of petroleum

Coca and Lago Agrio are the two main towns serving the petroleum industry operating in Oriente. The oil companies and their subcontractors have come from various parts of the world: China, the USA, Canada, France, Brazil and Argentina among others, and they are in effect the new conquistadors. Large and powerful, they have turned the Ecuadorean Amazon into a place where barrels of oil mean more than biodiversity or human rights. Neither drawn-out international litigation by indigenous communities nor protests by environmental groups have been able to halt their relentless advance.

Hundreds of thousands of barrels of oil flow out of the jungle every day through two pipelines that snake over the Andes and down to the coast for export. In their wake, feeder pipes crisscross the devastated terrain, toxic waste sumps contaminate watersheds and cancer rates run high among the local population. In 2006, an oil spill contaminated between 24,000 and 35,000 ha in Reserva Faunística Cuyabeno. In 2009 and again in 2013, further spills polluted the Río Coca so badly that they left the city of Coca without drinking water for weeks.

The natural habitat around Lago Agrio was the first to be decimated, followed by that along the Vía Auca, an oil company road running south from Coca into Huaorani territory. The same tragic history is currently being repeated in primary forest south of the Río Napo, between Coca and Misahuallí.

Yet all the direct damage caused by the petroleum industry pales in comparison to that inflicted by the colonists who inevitably follow in its wake. The oil companies build access roads to their wells, and these become corridors of deforestation as settlers take out timber and introduce cattle and crops. Their agricultural practices are unsuited to the poor soils of the rainforest and are not sustainable here. At the same time, the way of life of the native lowland people has been permanently altered.

Although petroleum prices may fluctuate, the ongoing international demand for fossil fuels continues to foster new exploration worldwide. The consequences of this activity are not unique to Ecuador but, since the country's slice of the Amazon is among the smallest and biologically richest in South America, the prospect of catastrophe is all the more imminent.

Oil work has always been actively encouraged by the Quito government, even within protected natural areas. By Ecuadorean law, only the surface of a national park or reserve is protected, while the petroleum and minerals underground remain up for grabs. Now there might be a slim prospect for change. Since 2007 the Ecuadorean authorities have suggested that the latest major petroleum project (Ishpingo-Tiputini-Tambococha, ITT), located in the eastern part of Parque Nacional Yasuní, could be shelved under certain conditions. The innovative proposal would keep the crude underground and the jungle intact, if the international community could compensate Ecuador with one half the revenue it would receive from exploitation of these reserves. This overture has been interpreted by some as genuine, by others as a cynical public relation manoeuvre.

Whatever the outcome, and whatever the future price of a barrel of crude in London or New York, the price paid by the Ecuadorean Amazon has already been too high. For more background and up to date information see www.sosyasuni.org, www.accion ecologica.org and www.yasuni-itt.gob.ec; *Amazon Crude*, and other works by Judith Kimerling; and *Savages*, by Joe Kane.

QUITO TO ORIENTE LISTINGS

WHERE TO STAY

For jungle lodges, tour operators and river cruises, see pages 144-149.

Papallacta

$$$$-$$$ Hotel Termas Papallacta, at the Termas complex (see page 136), comfortable heated rooms and suites, good expensive restaurant, thermal pools set in a lovely garden, nice lounge with fireplace, some rooms with private jacuzzi, also cabins for up to 6, transport from Quito extra. Guests get discounts at the spa. At weekends and holidays expect crowds and book 1 month in advance. Recommended.

$$ La Choza de Don Wilson, at intersection of old unpaved road and road to the Termas, T06-289 5027. Rooms with nice views of the valley, heaters, includes breakfast, good popular restaurant, pools, massage, spa, attentive service.

$$-$ Antizana, on road to the Termas, a short walk from the complex, T06-289 5016. Simple rooms, private or shared bath, includes breakfast, restaurant, pools, a good economy option.

Baeza

$ Gina, Jumandy y Batallón Chimborazo, just off the highway in the old town, T06-232 0471. Hot water, parking, pleasant, good value. Popular restaurant, trout is the speciality

$ La Casa de Rodrigo, in the old town near the highway, T06-232 0467, rodrigobaeza@andinanet.net. Modern and comfortable, hot water, friendly owner offers rafting trips, kayak rentals and birdwatching.

Lago Agrio

$$$ Gran Hotel de Lago, Km 1.5 Vía Quito, T06-283 2415, granhoteldelago@grupodelago.com. Includes breakfast, restaurant, a/c, pool, parking, cabins with nice gardens, quiet. Recommended.

$$ Arazá, Quito 536 y Narváez, T06-283 1287, www.hotel-araza.com. Quiet location away from centre, includes buffet breakfast, restaurant, a/c, pool (US$5 for non-residents), fridge, parking, comfortable. Recommended.

$ Gran Colombia, Quito y Pasaje Gonzanamá, T06-283 1032. Good restaurant, hot water, a/c, cheaper with fan and cold water, more expensive rooms also have fridge, parking, centrally located, modern and good value.

Coca

$$ El Auca, Napo y García Moreno, T06-288 0600, www.hotelelauca.com. Restaurant, disco on weekends, a/c, cheaper with fan, parking, a variety of different rooms and mini-suites. Comfortable, garden with hammocks, English spoken. Popular and centrally located but can get noisy.

$$ Heliconias, Cuenca y Amazonas, T06-288 2010, heliconiaslady@yahoo.com. Includes breakfast, upmarket restaurant, pool (US$5 for non-guests), spotless. Recommended.

$$ La Misión, by riverfront 100 m downriver from the bridge, T06-288 0260, www.hotelamision.com. A larger hotel, restaurant and disco, a/c and fridge, pool (US$2 for non-guests), parking, a bit faded but good location and still adequate.

$ San Fermín, Bolívar y Quito, T06-288 0802. Hot water, a/c (cheaper with fan, shared bath and cold water), ample parking, variety of different rooms, nicely furnished, popular and busy, good value, owner, Roberto Vaca, organizes tours.

Tena

$$ Christian's Palace, JL Mera y Sucre, T06-288 6047. Includes breakfast, restaurant, a/c, cheaper with fan, pool, modern and comfortable.

$$ Los Yutzos, Augusto Rueda 190 y 15 de Noviembre, T09-9567 0160, www.uchutican.com/yutzos. Comfortable rooms and beautiful grounds overlooking the Río Pano, quiet and family-run. Includes breakfast, a/c, cheaper with fan, parking. Recommended.
$ La Casa del Abuelo, JL Mera 628, T09-9900 0914. Nice quiet place, comfortable rooms, small garden, hot water, ceiling fan, parking, tours. Recommended.
$ Limoncocha, Sangay 533, Sector Corazón de Jesús, on a hillside 4 blocks from the bus station, ask for directions, T06-284 6303, http://limoncocha.tripod.com. Concrete house with terrace and hammocks, private or shared bath, hot water, fan, laundry and cooking facilities, breakfast available, parking, German/Ecuadorean-run, enthusiastic owners organize tours. Out of the way in a humble neighbourhood, nice views, pleasant atmosphere, good value.

Archidona
$$$ Hakuna Matata, Vía Shungu Km 3.9, off the road between Tena and Archidona, T06-288 9617, www.hakunamat.com. Comfortable cabins in a lovely setting by the Río Inchillaqui. Includes breakfast and dinner, walks, river bathing and horse riding. Excellent food, Belgian hosts, pleasant atmosphere. Warmly recommended.
$$$ Orchid Paradise, 2 km north of town, T06-288 9232. Cabins in nice secondary forest with lots of birds. Includes full board, owner organizes tours in the area.

$ Regina, Rocafuerte 446, 1 block north of the plaza, T06-288 9144. Private or shared bath, cold water, ample parking, pleasant, family-run.

Misahuallí
Jungle tours (US$25-50 pp per day) can be arranged by most hotels. See also page 147.
$$$$ Hamadryade, behind the Mariposario, 4 km from town, T09-8590 9992, www.hamadryade-lodge.com. Luxury lodge in a 64-ha forest reserve, 5 designer wood cabins, packages include full board and excursions, French chef, pool, lovely views down to the river.
$$$ pp El Jardin Aleman, jungle lodge on shores of Río Mishualli, 3 km from town, T289 0122, www.eljardinaleman.com. Comfortable rooms with bath, hot water. Price includes 3 meals and river tour, set in protected rainforest.
$$-$ Cabañas Río Napo, cross the suspension bridge, then 100 m on the left-hand side, T09-9990 4352. Nice rustic cabins with thatched roof, private bath, hot water, ample grounds along the river, run by a local Kichwa family, enthusiastic and friendly.
$ Shaw, Santander on the Plaza, T06-289 0163, hostalshaw@hotmail.com. Good restaurant, hot water, fan, simple rooms, annex with kitchen facilities and small pool, operate their own tours, English spoken, very knowledgeable. Good value. Recommended.

RESTAURANTS

Coca
$$ Denny's, Alejandro Labaka by the airport. Mon-Sat 0800-2000, Sun 1200-1400. Steaks, ribs and other US-style meals and drinks, friendly.
$ La Casa del Maito, Espejo entre Quito y Napo. Daily 0700-1700. *Maitos* in the morning and other local specialities.

Tena
$$ Chuquitos, García Moreno by the plaza. Mon-Sat 0730-2130, Sun 1100-2130. Good food, à la carte only, seating on a balcony overlooking the river. Pleasant atmosphere, attentive service and nice views. Popular and recommended.
Café Tortuga, Malecón south of the footbridge. Open 0730-2100, closed Sun midday. Juices, snacks and sweets, nice location, spotless, friendly Swiss owner.

GALÁPAGOS ISLANDS
7 to 10 days

GOING FURTHER

GALAPAGOS ISLANDS

A trip to the Galápagos Islands is easily combined with any itinerary on the mainland of Ecuador, and it is well and truly an unforgettable experience. As Charles Darwin put it: "... it seems to be a little world within itself".

The islands are world renowned for their fearless wildlife but no amount of hype can prepare the visitor for such a close encounter with nature. Here you can snorkel with penguins, sea lions and the odd hammerhead shark, watch giant 200-kg tortoises lumbering through cactus forest and enjoy the courtship display of the blue-footed booby and magnificent frigate bird, all in startling close-up.

A visit to the islands doesn't come cheap. The return flight from Quito and national park fee add up to over US$600; plus a bare minimum of US$200 per person per day for sailing on an economy-class boat. There are few such inexpensive vessels and even fewer really good inexpensive ones. Since you are already spending so much money, it is well worth spending a little more to make sure you sign up with a reputable agency on a better cruise, the quality of which is generally excellent.

Land-based island-hopping and independent travel on the populated islands are alternatives to cruises, but there is simply no way to enjoy Galápagos on a shoestring. For those with a passion for nature, the once-in-a-lifetime Galápagos experience merits saving for, and at the same time, high prices might be one way of keeping the number of visitors within sustainable levels. The islands have already suffered the impact of rapidly growing tourism and a viable mechanism is urgently needed to ensure their survival as the world's foremost wildlife.

GETTING THERE

Airports at **Baltra**, across a narrow strait from Santa Cruz, and **Puerto Baquerizo Moreno**, on San Cristóbal, receive flights from mainland Ecuador. The two islands are 96 km apart and on most days there are local flights in light aircraft between them, as well as to **Puerto Villamil** on Isabela. There is also speedboat service between Puerto Ayora (Santa Cruz) and the other populated islands. There are no international flights to Galápagos.

AeroGal, LAN and TAME all fly from Quito and Guayaquil to Baltra or San Cristóbal. Baltra receives more flights but there is at least one daily to each destination. You can arrive at one and return from the other. You can also depart from Quito and return to Guayaquil or vice versa, but you may not buy a one-way ticket. The return airfare varies considerably, starting at about US$500 from Quito, US$450 from Guayaquil (2013 prices). See also Fees and inspections, below.

Airport transfers Two buses meet flights from the mainland at Baltra: one runs to the port or *muelle* (10 minutes, no charge) where the cruise boats wait; the other goes to Canal de Itabaca, the narrow channel which separates Baltra from Santa Cruz. It is 15 minutes to the Canal, free, then you cross on a small ferry (US$0.80). On the other side, buses (US$1.80, may involve a long wait while they fill) and pickup truck taxis (US$18 for up to four passengers) run to Puerto Ayora, 45 minutes. For the return trip to the airport, buses leave the Terminal Terrestre on Avenida Baltra in Puerto Ayora (2 km from the pier, taxi US$1) at 0700, 0730 and 0830 daily.

GETTING AROUND

Emetebe Avionetas ① *Guayaquil at Hotel City Plaza, T04-230 9209; Puerto Baquerizo Moreno at the airport, T05-252 0615; Puerto Villamil, Antonio Gil y Las Fragatas, T05-252 9155; www.emetebe.com;* offers inter-island flights in light aircraft. Two daily flights (except Sunday) travel between **Puerto Baquerizo Moreno** (San Cristóbal), **Baltra** and **Puerto Villamil** (Isabela). Fares US$155-170 one way; baggage allowance 11 kg (25 lbs).

Fibras (fibreglass speedboats for about 20 passengers) operate daily between Puerto Ayora and each of Puerto Baquerizo Moreno, Puerto Villamil and Puerto Velasco Ibarra

(Floreana); US$30-35 one way, two hours or more depending on the weather and sea. Tickets are sold by several agencies in Puerto Baquerizo Moreno, Puerto Ayora and Puerto Villamil. This can be a wild ride in rough seas, life vests should be provided, take drinking water.

INFORMATION AND ADVICE

A recommended bilingual website is www.galapagospark.org. It describes each visitor site and gives details of guides and tourist vessels operating in the islands.

Tourist offices **Puerto Ayora:** iTur ① *Av Charles Darwin y 12 de Febrero, T05-252 6614 ext 22, www.santacruz.gob.ec, Mon-Fri 0730-1230, 1400-1930, Sat-Sun 1600-1930,* has information about Puerto Ayora and Santa Cruz Island; **Ministerio de Turismo** ① *Charles Binford y 12 de Febrero, T05-252 6174, Mon-Fri 0830-1300, 1430-1700,* is mostly an administrative office but also receives complaints about agencies and vessels. **Puerto Baquerizo Moreno: Municipal tourist office** ① *Malecón Charles Darwin y 12 de Febrero, T05-252 0119 ext 120, Mon-Fri 0730-1230, 1400-1800,* is downstairs at the Municipio. Ministerio de Turismo ① *12 de Febrero e Ignacio Hernández, T05-252 0704, Mon-Fri 0830-1230, 1400-1730,* operates as in Santa Cruz, above. **Puerto Villamil: Municipal tourist office** ① *by the park, T05-252 9002, ext 113, Mon-Fri 0730-1230, 1400-1700,* has local information.

Fees and inspections A US$10 fee is collected at Quito or Guayaquil airport, where a registration form must be completed. Some tour operators pre-register their passengers on line. Bags are checked prior to flights to Galápagos, no live animals, meat, dairy products, fresh fruit or vegetables may be taken to the islands. On arrival, every foreign visitor must pay a US$100 national park fee. All fees are cash only. Be sure to have your passport to hand at the airport and keep all fee receipts throughout your stay on the islands. Bags are checked again on departure, as nothing may be taken off the islands. Puerto Villamil charges cruise passengers a US$20 port fee on arrival in Isabela.

Basic rules Do not touch any of the animals, birds or plants. Do not transfer sand, seeds or soil from one island to another. Do not leave litter anywhere; do not take food on to the uninhabited islands, which are also no-smoking zones. There is increasingly close contact between people and sea lions throughout Galápagos. The pups are incredibly cute but never touch them, and keep your distance from the male 'beach-masters'; they have been known to bite. Always take food, plenty of water and a compass or GPS if hiking on your own. There are many crisscrossing animal trails and it is

ON THE ROAD
Difficult choices for Galápagos

As you enjoy your unforgettable Galápagos experience, consider the future of the islands. Their current reality is as complex as their unique natural history but it all boils down to a question of attitude. Are the Galápagos Islands first and foremost a sanctuary, a treasure so unique and precious for all mankind as to merit the strictest conservation in the sovereign custody of Ecuador? Or is Galápagos primarily a province of a developing South American republic, with natural resources to be exploited for the enjoyment of visitors and to satisfy the economic needs of residents? And who decides?.

easy to get lost. Also watch out for the large-spined opuntia cactus; and the poisonwood tree (*manzanillo*) found near beaches; contact with its leaves or bark can cause severe skin reactions.

What to take A remedy for seasickness is recommended. A good supply of sun block and skin cream to prevent windburn and chapped lips is essential, as are a hat and sunglasses. You should be prepared for dry and wet landings, the latter involving wading ashore; keep photo equipment and other delicate items in plastic bags. Take plenty of memory cards with you; the animals are so tame that you will take far more photos than you expected. Snorkelling equipment is particularly useful as much of the sea-life is only visible under water. The cheaper boats may not provide equipment or it may be of poor quality. If in doubt, bring your own. Good sturdy footwear is important, boots and shoes soon wear out on the abrasive lava terrain. Always bring some US dollars cash to Galápagos, there are only a few ATMs and they may be out of order.

Tipping A ship's crew and guides are usually tipped separately. Amounts are often suggested onboard or in agencies' brochures, but these should be considered in light of the quality of service received and your own resources.

If you have problems Raise any issues first with your guide or ship's captain. Serious complaints are rare but may filed with **iTur** or **Ministerio de Turismo** offices in Puerto Ayora or Puerto Baquerizo Moreno, see Tourist offices, above.

Best time to visit The Galápagos climate can be divided into a hot season (December to May), when there is a possibility of heavy showers, and the cool or *garúa* (mist) season (June to November), when the days are generally more cloudy and there is often rain or drizzle. July and August can be windy (force 4 or 5). Daytime clothing should be lightweight. (Clothing generally, even on 'luxury cruises', should be casual and comfortable.) At night, however, particularly at sea and at higher altitudes, temperatures fall below 15°C and warm clothing is required. The sea is cold July to October; underwater visibility is best January to March. Ocean temperatures are usually higher to the east and lower at the western end of the archipelago. Despite all these climatic variations, conditions are generally favourable for visiting Galápagos throughout the year.

High season for tourism is June to August and December and January, when last-minute arrangements are generally not possible. Some boats may be heavily booked throughout the year and you should plan well in advance if you want to travel on a specific vessel at a specific time.

There are a growing number of options for visiting Galápagos but in our opinion the best remains the traditional **live-aboard cruise** (*tour navegable*), where you travel and sleep on a yacht, tour boat or cruise ship. These vessels travel at night, arriving at a new landing site each day. Cruises range from three to 14 nights; seven is recommended. Itineraries are controlled by the national park to distribute cruise boats evenly throughout the islands. All cruises begin with a morning flight from the mainland on the first day and end on the last day with a midday flight back to the mainland. The less expensive boats are normally smaller and less powerful so you see less and spend more time travelling; also

GALAPAGOS ISLANDS

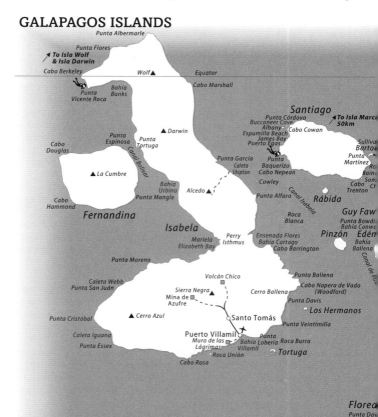

the guiding may be mostly in Spanish. The more expensive boats have air conditioning, hot water and private baths. All boats have to conform to certain minimum safety standards; more expensive boats are better equipped. Boats with over 20 passengers take quite a time to disembark and re-embark people, while the smaller boats have a more lively motion, which is important if you are prone to seasickness. Note also that there may be limitations for vegetarians on the cheaper boats. The least expensive boats (economy class) cost about US$200 per person per day and a few of these vessels are dodgy. For around US$250-350 per day (tourist and tourist superior class) you will be on a better, faster boat which can travel more quickly between visitor sites, leaving more time to spend ashore. Over US$400 per day are the first-class and luxury brackets, with far

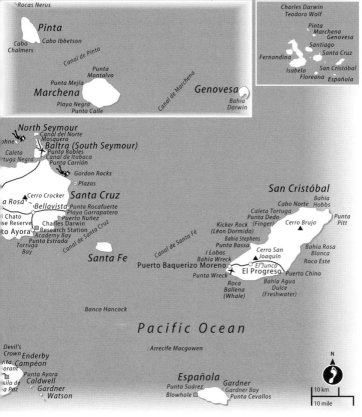

more comfortable and spacious cabins, as well as a superior level of service and cuisine. No boat may sail without a park-trained guide.

Island-hopping is another option for visiting Galápagos, whereby you spend a night or two at hotels on some of the four populated islands, travelling between them in speedboats. You cover less ground than on a cruise, see fewer wildlife sites, and cannot visit the more distant islands. Island-hopping is sold in organized packages but visitors in no rush can also travel between and explore the populated islands independently and at their leisure. **Day tours** (*tour diario*) are yet another alternative, based mostly out of Puerto Ayora. Some take you for day-visits to national park landing sites on nearby unpopulated islands, such as Bartolomé, Seymour, Plazas and Santa Fe, and can be quite good. Others go for the day to the populated islands of Isabela or Floreana, with no stops permitted along the way. The latter require at least four hours of speedboat travel and generally leave insufficient time to enjoy visitor sites; they are not recommended.

None of the above options is cheap, with the flight from the mainland and entry fees alone amounting to about US$600. Galápagos is such a special destination for nature-lovers, however, that most agree it is worth saving for and spending on a quality tour. If nature is not your great passion and you are looking mainly for an exotic cruise or beach holiday, then your money will go further and you will likely have a better experience elsewhere.

BOOKING A CRUISE

You can book a Galápagos cruise in several different ways: 1) over the internet; 2) from either a travel agency or directly though a Galápagos wholesaler in your home country;

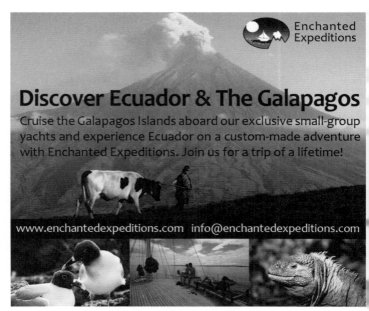

BOOKING A GALAPAGOS CRUISE

Overseas agencies

Galápagos Classic Cruises, 6 Keyes Rd, London NW2 3XA, T020-8933 0613, www.galapagoscruises.co.uk. Specialists in cruises and diving holidays to the islands, as well as tailor-made land tours to Ecuador and additions to Peru and Bolivia on request.

Galápagos Holidays, 14 Prince Arthur Av, Suite 311, Toronto, Ontario M5R 1A9, T416-413 9090, T1-800-661 2512 (toll free), www.galapagosholidays.com.

Galápagos Network, 5805 Blue Lagoon Dr, Suite 160, Miami, FL 33126, T305-2626264, www.ecoventura.com.

INCA, 1311 63rd St, Emeryville, CA 94608, T510-420 1550, www.inca1.com.

International Expeditions, 1 Environs Park, Helena, Alabama, 35080, T205-428 1700, T1-800-633 4734, www.internationalexpeditions.com.

Select Latin America, 3.51 Canterbury Court, 1-3 Brixton Rd, London SW9 6DE, T020-7407 1478, www.selectlatinamerica. co.uk. David Horwell arranges quality tailor-made and small group tours to Ecuador and the Galápagos.

Sol International, PO Box 1738, Kodak, TN 37764, T931-536 4893, T1-800-765 5657, www.solintl.com.

Wilderness Travel, 1102 Ninth St, Berkeley, CA 94710, T510-558 2488, T1-800-368 2794, www.wildernesstravel.com.

3) from one of the very many agencies found throughout Ecuador, especially in Quito but also in other tourist centres and in Guayaquil; or 4) from local agencies, mostly in Puerto Ayora but also in Puerto Baquerizo Moreno. The trade-off is always between time and money: booking from home is most efficient and expensive, last-minute arrangements in Galápagos are cheapest and most time-consuming, while Quito and Guayaquil are intermediate. It is not possible to obtain discounts or make last-minute arrangements in high season (see Best time to visit, page 159). Surcharges may apply when using a credit card to purchase tours on the islands, there are limits to ATM withdrawals and no cash advances at weekends, so bring cash if looking for a last-minute cruise. Also, if looking for a last-minute sailing, it is best to pay your hotel one night at a time since hoteliers may not refund advance payments. Especially on cheaper boats, check carefully what is and is not included (eg drinking water, snorkelling equipment, etc).

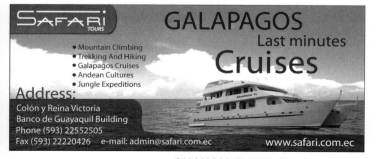

GALAPAGOS TOURIST VESSELS

Name	Description	Capacity	Website
Galápagos Explorer II	cruise ship	100	canodros.com
Galápagos Legend	cruise ship	100	kleintours.com
Xpedition	cruise ship	100	galapagosxpedition.co.uk
Santa Cruz	cruise ship	90	galapagosvoyage.com
Nat Geo Edeavour	cruise ship	80	expeditions.com
Eclipse	cruise ship	48	galapagos-eclipse.com
Nat Geo Islander	cruise ship	48	expeditions.com
Isabela II	cruise ship	40	galapagosvoyage.com
Millenium	cruise ship	40	galasam.com
Coral I	motor yacht	36	kleintours.com
Evolution	cruise ship	32	galapagosexpeditions.com
La Pinta	cruise ship	32	lapintagalapagoscruise.com
Coral II	motor yacht	20	kleintours.com
Eric	motor yacht	20	ecoventura.com
Flamingo I	motor yacht	20	ecoventura.com
Galápagos Adventure	motor yacht	20	various
Letty	motor yacht	20	ecoventura.com
Aída María	motor yacht	16	various
Amigo I	motor vessel	16	various
Anahi	motor catamaran	16	andandotours.com
Angelito I	motor yacht	16	angelitogalapagos.com
Archipel II	motor yacht	16	various
Athala II	motor catamaran	16	various
Beluga	motor yacht	16	enchantedexpeditions.com
Cachalote	2-mast schooner	16	enchantedexpeditions.com
Carina	motor yacht	16	various
Cormorant Evolution	motor catamaran	16	cormorantgalapagos.com
Darwin	motor vessel	16	various
Edén	motor yacht	16	various
Estrella del Mar I	motor yacht	16	galasam.com
Floreana	motor yacht	16	yatefloreana.com
Fragata	motor yacht	16	various
Galap Adventure II	motor yacht	16	various
Galap Journey I	motor catamarans	16	galapagosjourneycruises.com

Name	Description	Capacity	Website
Galapagos Odyssey	motor yatch	16	galapagosodyssey.com
Galapagos Vision I	1-mast catamaran	16	various
Galapagos Voyager	motor yatch	16	galapagos-voyager.com
Galaxy	motor yacht	16	various
Golondrina I	motor vessel	16	various
Grace	motor yatch	16	galapagosexpeditions.com
Gran Monserrat	motor yacht	16	various
Guantanamera	motor yacht	16	various
Integrity	motor yacht	16	various
Liberty	motor yacht	16	various
Mary Anne	3-mast barquentine	16	andandotours.com
Monserrat	motor vessel	16	various
Monserrat II	motor vessel	16	various
Ocean Spray	motor catamaran	16	galapagosoceanspray.com
Pelíkano	motor vessel	16	various
Queen Beatriz	motor catamaran	16	various
Queen of Galap	motor catamaran	16	galasam.com
Reina Silvia	motor yacht	16	reinasilvia.com
Samba	motor yacht	16	various
San José	motor yacht	16	various
San Juan II	motor vessel	16	various
Sea Man II	motor catamaran	16	various
Tip Top II	motor vessel	16	rwittmer.com
Tip Top III	motor yacht	16	rwittmer.com
Tip Top IV	motor yacht	16	rwittmer.com
Treasure of Galap	motor catamaran	16	treasureofgalapagos.com
Xavier III	motor vessel	16	various
Yolita II	motor yacht	16	various
Albatros	motor yacht	14	various
Beagle	2-mast schooner	13	angermeyercruises.com
Amazonía	1-mast catamaran	12	various
Encantada	2-mast schooner	12	scubagalapagos.com
New Flamingo	motor vessel	12	various
Merak	1-mast sailer	8	various

The Galápagos Islands are among the most desirable scuba-diving destinations in the world. At first look you might wonder why, with cold water, strong currents, difficult conditions and limited visibility (15 m or less). So what is the attraction?

There is a profusion and variety of animals here that you won't find anywhere else, and so close up that you won't mind the low visibility; not just reef fish and schooling fish and pelagic fish, but also sea lions, turtles, whalesharks, schools of hammerheads, flocks of several species of ray, diving birds, whales and dolphins – an exuberant diversity including many endemic species. You could be watching a Galápagos marine iguana, the world's only lizard that dives and feeds in the sea, or perhaps meet a glittering man-sized sailfish. Make no mistake, this is no tame theme park: Galápagos is adventure diving, where any moment could surprise you.

There are basically two options for diving in the Galápagos: live-aboard dive cruises and hotel-based day trips. Live-aboard operations usually expect the divers to bring their own equipment, and supply only lead and tanks. The day trip dive operators supply everything. Day-trip diving is mostly offered by boats operating out of Puerto Ayora on Santa Cruz, but there are also a couple of operators in Puerto Baquerizo Moreno on San Cristóbal, and Puerto Villamil on Isabela. Live-aboard dive cruises (typically seven days) can only be done on specialized boats, which are few, expensive and usually reserved far in advance. You cannot dive as part of a standard Galápagos cruise.

Day-trip diving is more economical and spontaneous, often arranged at the dive shop the evening before. The distances between islands limit the range of the day-trip boats to the central islands. Nevertheless, day boats can offer reliable service to superb dive locations including Gordon Rocks, world-famous for schooling hammerheads. The day-trip dive boats cannot take passengers ashore at the usual visitor sites but you can always do some diving day trips before or after a regular Galápagos cruise.

The following vessels offer live-aboard diving tours: **Darwin Buddy** and **Wolf Buddy**, www.buddydive-galapagos.com; **Deep Blue**, www.deepbluegalapagosdiving.com; **Galápagos Agressor I and II**, www.aggressor.com; **Galápagos Sky**, www.ecoventura.com; **Humboldt Explorer**, www.galasam.com. Cruises cost US$4000-5000 for seven days. For a list of day-trip dive operators see Listings, page 178.

Visitors should be aware of some of the special conditions in Galápagos. The national park includes practically all of the land and the surrounding waters. The national park prohibits collecting samples or souvenirs, spear-fishing, touching animals or other environmental disruptions. Guides apply the national park rules, and they can stop your participation if you do not cooperate.

Experienced dive guides can help visitors have the most spectacular opportunities to enjoy the wildlife. Nonetheless, diving requires self reliance and divers are encouraged to refresh their skills and have equipment serviced before the trip. Though the day-trip operators can offer introductory dives and complete certification training, this is not a place for a complete novice to come for a diving vacation. On many dives you could meet any combination of current, surge, cold water, poor visibility, deep bottom and big animals.

Like many exotic dive destinations, medical care is limited. There is a **hyperbaric chamber** in Puerto Ayora at **Centro Médico Integral** (Marchena y Hanny, T05-252 4576, www.sssnetwork.com). Check if your dive operator is affiliated with this facility or arrange your own insurance from home. To avoid the risk of decompression sickness, divers are advised to stay an extra day on the islands after their last dive before flying to the mainland, especially to Quito at 2840 m above sea level.

DIVE SITES

Santa Fe This site offers wall dives, rock reefs, shallow caves, fantastic scenery and usually has clear calm water. You can dive with sea lions, schooling fish, pelagic fish, moray eels, rays and Galápagos sharks. Like everywhere in Galápagos, you should expect the unexpected.

Seymour Norte You can see sea lions, reef fish, hammerhead sharks, giant manta rays and white-tipped reef sharks. Occasionally you'll see whalesharks, humpback whale and dolphins.

Floreana Island The dive sites are offshore islets, each with its own character and scenery. Devil's Crown is a fractured ring of spiked lava around coral reefs. Champion is a little crater with a nesting colony of boobies, sea lion shelves and underwater rocky shelves of coral and reef fish. Enderby is an eroded tuff cone where you often meet large pelagics: rays, turtles, tunas and sharks. Gardner has a huge natural arch like a cathedral's flying buttress. These and other islets offer diving with reef fish, schooling fish, sea lions, invertebrates, rays, moray eels, white-tipped reef sharks, turtles, big fish including amberjack, red snapper, and grouper. Sometimes you can see giant mantas, hammerheads, Galápagos sharks, whales, seahorses, and the bizarre red-lipped batfish.

Gordon Rocks Just north of the Plazas are two large rocks that are all that remains of the rim of a long-extinct volcano. On the inner side of the collapsed caldera rim the seabed is a mass of rocks jumbled over each other, while on the outer wall the sea drops away into thousands of feet of water. Currents here are exceptionally strong and the local name for the dive site is La Lavadora (the washing machine). Here you can see schools of hammerheads, amberjacks and pompano, eagle rays, golden cowrays, whitetips and turtles.

→ THE ISLANDS

UNPOPULATED ISLANDS VISTOR SITES

Baltra Once a US Airforce base, Baltra is now a small military base for Ecuador and also the main airport into the islands. Also known as South Seymour, this is the island most affected by human presence. **Mosquera** is a small sandy bank just north of Baltra, home to a large colony of sea lions.

Bartolomé A small island located in Sullivan Bay off the eastern shore of Santiago, Bartolomé is probably the most easily recognized, the most visited and most photographed of all the islands in the Galápagos, with its distinctive **Pinnacle Rock**. The trail leads steeply up to the summit, taking 30-40 minutes, from where there are panoramic views. At the second visitor site on the island there is a lovely beach from which you can snorkel or swim and see penguins.

Daphne Major West of Baltra, Daphne island has very rich birdlife, in particular the nesting boobies. Because of the problems with erosion, only small boats may land here and are limited in the number of visits per month.

Española This is the southernmost island of the Galápagos and, following a successful programme to remove all the feral species, is now the most pristine of the islands with many migrant, resident and endemic seabirds. **Gardner Bay**, on the northeastern coast, is a beautiful white-sand beach with excellent swimming and snorkelling. **Punta Suárez**, on the western tip of the island, has a trail through a rookery. As well as a wide range of seabirds (including blue-footed and masked boobies) there is a great selection of wildlife including sea lions and the largest and most colourful marine iguanas of the Galápagos plus the original home of the waved albatrosses.

Fernandina The youngest of the islands, at about 700,000 years old, Fernandina is also the most volcanically active. The visitor site of **Punta Espinosa** is on the northeast coast of Fernandina. The trail goes up through a sandy nesting site for huge colonies of marine iguanas. The nests appear as small hollows in the sand. You can also see flightless cormorants drying their atrophied wings in the sun and go snorkelling in the bay.

Genovesa Located at the northeast part of the archipelago, this is an outpost for many sea birds. It is an eight- to ten-hour all-night sail from Puerto Ayora. Like Fernandina, Genovesa is best visited on longer cruises or ships with larger range. One of the most famous sites is **Prince Phillip's Steps**, an amazing walk through a seabird rookery that is full of life. You will see tropic birds, all three boobies, frigates, petrels, swallow-tailed and lava gulls, and many others. There is also good snorkelling at the foot of the steps, with lots of marine iguanas. The entrance to **Darwin Bay**, on the eastern side of the island, is very narrow and shallow and the anchorage in the lagoon is surrounded by mangroves, home to a large breeding colony of frigates and other seabirds.

Plaza Sur One of the closest islands to Puerto Ayora is Plaza Sur. It's an example of a geological uplift and the southern part of the island has formed cliffs with spectacular views. It has a combination of both dry and coastal vegetation zones. Walking along the sea cliffs is a pleasant experience as swallow-tailed gulls, shearwaters and red-billed tropic birds nest here. This is the home of the Men's Club, a rather sad-looking colony of bachelor sea lions who are too old to mate and who get together to console each other. There are also lots of blue-footed boobies and a large population of land iguanas on the island.

Rábida This island is just to the south of Santiago. The trail leads to a salt-water lagoon, occasionally home to flamingos. There is an area of mangroves near the lagoon where brown pelicans nest. This island is said to have the most diversified volcanic rocks of all the islands. You can snorkel and swim from the beach.

Santa Fe This island is located on the southeastern part of Galápagos, between Santa Cruz and San Cristóbal, and was formed by volcanic uplift. The lagoon is home to a large colony of sea lions who are happy to join you for a swim. From the beach the trail goes inland, through a semi-arid landscape of cactus. This little island has its own species of land iguana.

Santiago This large island, also known as James, is to the east of Isla Isabela. It has a volcanic landscape full of cliffs and pinnacles, and is home to several species of marine bird. This island has a large population of goats, one of the four species of animal introduced in the early 1800s.
    James Bay is on the western side of the island, where there is a wet landing on the dark sands of **Puerto Egas**. The trail leads to the remains of an unsuccessful salt mining operation. Fur seals are seen nearby. **Espumilla Beach** is another famous visitor site. After landing on a large beach, walk through a mangrove forest that leads to a lake usually inhabited by flamingos, pintail ducks and stilts. There are nesting and feeding sites for flamingos. Sea turtles dig their nests at the edge of the mangroves. **Buccaneer Cove**, on the northwest part of the island, was a haven for pirates during the 1600s and 1700s. **Sullivan Bay** is on the eastern coast of Santiago, opposite Bartolomé Island. The visitor trail leads across an impressive lunar landscape of lava fields formed during eruptions in 1890.

Seymour Norte Just north of Baltra, Seymour Norte is home to sea lions, marine iguanas, swallow-tailed gulls, magnificent frigate birds and blue-footed boobies. The trail leads through mangroves in one of the main nesting sites for blue-footed boobies and frigates in this part of the archipelago.

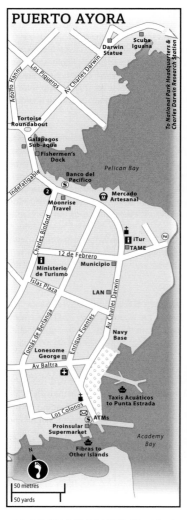

Sombrero Chino This is just off the southeastern tip of Santiago, and its name (Chinese hat) refers to its shape. It is most noted for the volcanic landscape including sharp outcrops, cracked lava formations, lava tubes and volcanic rubble. This site is only accessible to smaller vessels.

SANTA CRUZ: PUERTO AYORA

Santa Cruz is the most central of the Galápagos islands and the main town is Puerto Ayora. About 1.5 km from the pier is the **Charles Darwin Research Station** ① *Academy Bay, www.darwinfoundation. org, office Mon-Fri 0700-1600, visitor areas daily 0600-1800, free.* A visit to the station is a good introduction to the islands. Collections of several of the rare sub-species of giant tortoise are maintained on the station as breeding nuclei, together with tortoise-rearing pens for the young. The **Centro Comunitario de Educación Ambiental** ① *east end of Charles Binford, Mon-Fri 0730-1200, 1400-1700, Sat morning only, free,* has an aquarium and exhibits about the Galápagos Marine Reserve.

There is a beautiful beach at **Tortuga Bay**, 45 minutes' easy walk (2.5 km each way) west from Puerto Ayora on an excellent cobbled path through cactus forest. Start at the west end of Calle Charles Binford; further on there is a gate where you must register, open 0600-1800 daily, free. Make sure you take sun screen, drinking water, and beware of the very strong undertow. Do not walk on the dunes above the beach, which are a marine tortoise nesting area. At the west end of Tortuga Bay is a trail to a lovely mangrove-fringed lagoon, with calmer warmer water, shade and sometimes a kayak for rent.

Las Grietas is a lovely gorge with a natural pool at the bottom which is popular and splendid for bathing. Take a water taxi from the port to the dock at Punta Estrada (five minutes, US$0.50). It is a five-minute walk from here to the **Finch Bay** hotel and 15 minutes further over rough lava boulders to Las Grietas – well worth the trip.

The Puerto Ayora–Baltra road goes through the agricultural zone in the highlands. The community of **Bellavista** is 7 km from the port, and **Santa Rosa** is 15 km beyond. The area has national park visitor sites, walking possibilities and upmarket lodgings. **Los Gemelos** are a pair of large sinkholes, formed by collapse of the ground above empty magma chambers. They straddle the road to Baltra, beyond Santa Rosa. You can take a taxi or airport bus all the way; otherwise take a bus to Santa Rosa, then walk one hour uphill. There are several **lava tubes** (natural tunnels) on the island. Some are at **El Mirador**, 3 km from Puerto Ayora on the road to Bellavista. Two more lava tubes are 1 km from Bellavista. They are on private land. It costs US$1.50 to enter the tunnels (bring a torch) and it takes about 30 minutes to walk through them. Tours to the lava tubes can be arranged in Puerto Ayora.

The highest point on Santa Cruz Island is **Cerro Crocker** at 864 m. You can hike here and to two other nearby 'peaks' called **Media Luna** and **Puntudo**. The trail starts at Bellavista where a rough trail map is painted as a mural on the wall of the school. The round trip from Bellavista takes six to eight hours. A permit and guide are not required, but a guide may be helpful. Always take food, water and a compass or GPS.

Another worthwhile trip is to the **El Chato Tortoise Reserve**, where giant tortoises can be seen in the wild during the dry season (June to February). In the wet season the tortoises are breeding down in the arid zone. Follow the road that goes past the Santa Rosa school to 'La Reserva'. At the end of the road (about 3 km) you reach a faded wooden memorial to an Israeli tourist who got lost here. Take the trail to the right (west) for about 45 minutes. There are many confusing trails in the reserve itself; take food, water and a compass or GPS. If you have no hiking experience, horses can sometimes be hired at Santa Rosa or arrange a tour from Puerto Ayora.

Tortoises can also be seen at **Cerro Mesa** and at several private ranches, some of which have camping facilities; eg **Butterfly Ranch (Hacienda Mariposa)** (entry US$3, camping US$25 per person including breakfast). Access is at Km 16, just before Santa Rosa; walk 1 km from here – make previous arrangements at Moonrise Travel.

SAN CRISTOBAL: PUERTO BAQUERIZO MORENO

Puerto Baquerizo Moreno, on San Cristóbal island, is the capital of the archipelago. Electrical energy here is provided by wind generators in the highlands, see www.eolicsa. com.ec. The town's attractive *malecón* has many shaded seats shared by tourists, residents and sea lions. The **cathedral** ① *Av Northía y Cobos, 0900-1200, 1600-1800*, has interesting artwork combining religious and Galápagos motifs.

To the north of town, opposite **Playa Mann** (suitable for swimming), is the Galápagos National Park Visitor Centre or **Centro de Interpretación** ① *T05-252 0138, ext 123, daily 0700-1700, free*. It has excellent displays of the natural and human history of the islands including contemporary issues; recommended. A good trail goes from the Centro de Interpretación to the northeast through scrub forest to **Cerro Tijeretas**, a hill overlooking town and the ocean, 30 minutes away. From here a rougher trail continues 45 minutes to **Playa Baquerizo**. Frigate birds nest in this area and can be observed gliding overhead;

there are sea lions on the beaches below. To go back from Cerro Tijeretas, if you take the trail which follows the coast, you will end up at **Playa Punta Carola**, a popular surfing beach, too rough for swimming. To the south of Puerto Baquerizo Moreno, 30 minutes' walk past the stadium and high school (ask for directions), is **La Lobería**, a rocky shore with sea lions, marine iguanas, and a rough trail leading to beautiful cliffs with many birds, overlooking the sea.

Five buses a day run the 6 km inland from Puerto Baquerizo Moreno to **El Progreso**, US$0.20, 15 minutes, then it's a 2½-hour walk to **El Junco lake**, the largest body of fresh water in Galápagos. Pickup trucks to El Progreso charge US$2, or you can hire them for touring: US$20 to El Junco (return with wait), US$40 continuing to the beaches at **Puerto Chino** on the other side of the island, past a man-made tortoise reserve. Camping is possible at Puerto Chino with a permit from the national park; take food and drinking water. At El Junco there is a path to walk around the lake in 20 minutes. The views are lovely in clear weather but it is cool and wet in the *garúa* season, so take adequate clothing. Various small roads fan out from El Progreso and make for pleasant walking. **Jatun Sacha** (www.jatunsacha.org) has a volunteer centre on an old hacienda in the highlands beyond El Progreso, working on eradication of invasive species and a native plant nursery; US$15 taxi ride from town, take repellent.

Boats go to **Punta Pitt** in the far north of San Cristóbal where you can see all three species of booby (US$65 for a tour). Off the northwest coast is **Kicker Rock** (León Dormido), the basalt remains of a crater; many seabirds, including Nazca and blue-footed boobies, can be seen around its cliffs (five-hour trip, including snorkelling; recommended, US$40).

ISABELA: PUERTO VILLAMIL

This is the largest island in the archipelago, formed by the coalesced lava flows of six volcanoes. Five are active and each has (or had) its own separate sub-species of giant tortoise. Isabela is also the island which is changing most rapidly, driven by growing land-based tourism. It remains a charming place but is at risk from uncontrolled development. Most residents live in Puerto Villamil. In the highlands, there is a cluster of farms at Santo Tomás. There are several lovely beaches right by town, but mind the strong undertow and ask locally about the best spots for swimming.

It is 8 km west to **Muro de las Lágrimas**, built by convict labour under hideous conditions. It makes a great day-hike or hire a bicycle (always take water); motor vehicles are not permitted. Short side-trails branch off the road to various attractions along the way, and a trail continues from the Muro to nearby hills with lovely views. Along the same road, 30 minutes from town, is the **Centro de Crianza**, a breeding centre for giant tortoises surrounded by lagoons with flamingos and other birds. In the opposite direction, 30 minutes east toward the *embarcadero* (pier) is **Concha de Perla Lagoon**, with a nice access trail through mangroves and a small dock from which you can go swimming with sea lions and other creatures. Tours go to **Las Tintoreras**, a set of small islets in the harbour where white-tipped reef sharks and penguins may be seen in the still crystalline water (US$25 per person). There are also boat tours to **Los Túneles** at Cabo Rosa (US$65 per person, a tricky entrance from the open sea), where fish, rays and turtles can be seen in submerged lava tunnels.

ON THE ROAD
The Galápagos Affair

One of the more bizarre and notorious periods of human life on the islands began in 1929 with the arrival of German doctor and philosopher, Friedrich Ritter, and his mistress, Dore Strauch. Three years later, the Wittmer family, attracted in part by Ritter's writings, also decided to settle on the island. Floreana soon became so fashionable that luxury yachts used to call. One visitor was Baroness von Wagner de Bosquet, an Austrian woman who settled on the island with her two lovers and grandiose plans to build a hotel for millionaires.

Soon after landing in 1932, the Baroness proclaimed herself Empress of Floreana, which was not to the liking of Dr Ritter or the Wittmer family, and tensions rose. There followed several years of mysterious and unsavoury goings-on, during which everyone either died or disappeared, except Dore Strauch and the Wittmer family. The longest survivor of this still unexplained drama was Margret Wittmer, who lived at Black Beach on Floreana until her death in 2000, at age 95. Her account of life there, entitled *Floreana, Poste Restante*, was published in 1961 and became a bestseller, but she took the complete story of what really happened on the island in the 1930s with her to the grave. A more revealing book is *The Galápagos Affair*, by John Treherne.

Sierra Negra volcano has the second-largest basaltic caldera in the world, 9 by 10 km. It is 19 km (30 minutes) by pickup truck to the park entrance (take passport and national park entry receipt), where you start the 1½-hour hike to the crater rim at 1000 m. It is a further 1½ hour's walk along bare brittle lava rock to **Volcán Chico**, with several fumaroles and more stunning views. You can camp on the crater rim but must take all supplies, including water, and obtain a permit the day before from the national park office in Puerto Villamil. A tour including transport and lunch costs about US$50 per person. Highland tours are also available to **La Cueva de Sucre**, a large lava tube with many chambers; be sure to take a torch if visiting on your own. A bus to the highlands leaves the market in Puerto Villamil at 0700 daily, US$0.50; ask the driver for directions to the cave and return times.

Cruise-boat visitor sites on Isabela include **Punta Moreno**, on the southwest part of the island, where penguins and shore birds are usually seen. **Elizabeth Bay**, on the west coast, is home to a small colony of penguins living on a series of rocky islets. **Tagus Cove**, on the west coast across the narrow channel from Fernandina island, is an anchorage that has been used by visiting ships going back to the 1800s, and the ships' names can still be seen painted on the cliffs. A trail leads inland from Tagus Cove past Laguna Darwin, a large saltwater lake, and then further uphill to a ridge with lovely views.

FLOREANA: PUERTO VELASCO IBARRA

Floreana is the island with the richest human history and the fewest inhabitants, most living in Puerto Velasco Ibarra. You can easily reach the island with a day-tour boat from Puerto Ayora, but these do not leave enough time to enjoy the visit. A couple of days' stay is recommended; however, note that there may not always be space on boats returning to Puerto Ayora, so you must be flexible. Services are limited, one shop has basic supplies and, although there are a handful of places to eat and sleep, none is cheap. Margaret

GOING FURTHER
After your cruise

Take a few days after your cruise to relax and get to know one of the inhabited islands: Santa Cruz, San Cristóbal, Isabela or Floreana. **Santa Cruz** has the largest city (Puerto Ayora) with plenty of excellent hotels and restaurants, as well as opportunities for worthwhile excursions within walking distance of town, up in the highlands and offshore for day-trip diving. **San Cristóbal** is home to the provincial capital (Puerto Baquerizo Moreno), with a more relaxed atmosphere complete with urban sea lions, and also offers various interesting excursions. **Isabela** best fits the image of a typically laid-back South Pacific island, with sand-covered streets, many miles of beaches to stroll and the world's largest basaltic volcano. **Floreana**, with fewer than 200 inhabitants, offers delightful solitude and a glimpse of the early human history of Galápagos.

Wittmer, one of the first settlers on Floreana (see The Galápagos Affair, opposite), died in 2000, but you can meet her daughter and granddaughter.

La Lobería is a beautiful little peninsula (which becomes an island at high tide), 15 minutes' walk from town, where sea lions, sea turtles, marine iguanas and various birds can be seen. The climate in the highlands is fresh and comfortable, good for walking and birdwatching. A *ranchera* runs up to **Asilo de La Paz**, with a natural spring and tortoise area (Monday-Saturday 0600 and 1500, returning 0700 and 1600; Sunday 0700 returning 1000). Alternatively, you can walk down in three to four hours, detouring to climb **Cerro Allieri** along the way.

Post Office Bay, on the north side of Floreana, is visited by tour boats. There is a custom (since 1792) for visitors here to place unstamped letters and cards in a barrel and deliver, free of charge, any addressed to their own destinations.

→ BACKGROUND

Lying on the equator, 970 km west of the Ecuadorean coast, the Galápagos consist of six main islands, 12 smaller islands and over 40 islets. The islands have an estimated population of 27,000, but this does not include many temporary inhabitants. Santa Cruz has 16,600 inhabitants and Puerto Ayora is its main city and tourist centre. San Cristóbal has a population of 7900 and the capital of the archipelago, Puerto Baquerizo Moreno. The largest island, Isabela, is 120 km long and forms over half the total land area of the archipelago; some 2500 people live there, mostly in and around Puerto Villamil on the south coast. Floreana, the first island to be settled, has about 160 residents.

The Galápagos have never been connected with the continent. Gradually, over many hundreds of thousands of years, animals and plants from over the sea somehow migrated there and as time went by they adapted themselves to Galápagos conditions and came to differ more and more from their continental ancestors. Unique marine and terrestrial environments, due to the continuing volcanic formation of the islands in the west of the archipelago and its location at the nexus of several major marine currents, have created laboratory-type conditions where only certain species have been allowed access. The formidable barriers which prevent many species from travelling between the islands, has led to a very high level of endemism. A quarter of the species of shore fish, half of the

ON THE ROAD
Charles Darwin and the Galápagos

Without a doubt, the most famous visitor to the islands is Charles Darwin and his brief stay on the archipelago proved hugely significant.

In September 1835, Darwin sailed into Galápagos waters on board the *HMS Beagle*, captained by the aristocratic Robert FitzRoy whose job was to chart lesser-known parts of the world. FitzRoy had wanted on board a companion of his own social status and a naturalist, to study the strange new animals and plants they would find en route. He chose Charles Darwin to fill both roles.

Darwin was only 22 years old when he set sail from England in 1831 and it would be five years before he saw home again. They were to sail around the world, but most of the voyage was devoted to surveying the shores of South America, giving Darwin the chance to explore a great deal of the continent. The visit to the Galápagos was just a short stop on the return journey, by which time Darwin had become an experienced observer.

During the six weeks that the Beagle spent in the Galápagos, Darwin went ashore to collect plants, rocks, insects and birds. The unusual life forms and their adaptations to the harsh surroundings made a deep impression on him and eventually inspired his revolutionary theory on the evolution of species. The Galápagos provided a kind of model of the world in miniature. Darwin realized that these recently created volcanoes were young in comparison with the age of the Earth, and that life on the islands showed special adaptations. Yet the plants and animals also showed similarities to those from the South American mainland, where he guessed they had originally come from.

Darwin concluded that the life on the islands had probably arrived there by chance drifting, swimming or flying from the mainland and had not been created on the spot. Once the plants and animals had arrived, they evolved into forms better suited to the strange environment in which they found themselves. Darwin also noted that the animals were extremely tame, because of the lack of predators. The islands' isolation also meant that the giant tortoises did not face competition from more agile mammals and could survive.

On his return to England, Darwin in effect spent the rest of his life publishing the findings of his voyage and developing the ideas it inspired. It was, however, only when another scientist, named Alfred Russel Wallace, arrived at a similar conclusion to his own that he dared to publish a paper on his theory of evolution.

Then followed his all-embracing *The Origin of Species* by means of natural selection, in 1859. It was to cause a major storm of controversy and to earn Charles Darwin recognition as the man who "provided a foundation for the entire structure of modern biology".

plants and almost all the reptiles are found nowhere else. In many cases different forms have evolved on the different islands. Charles Darwin recognized this speciation within the archipelago when he visited the Galápagos on the *Beagle* in 1835 and his observations played a substantial part in his formulation of the theory of evolution.

This natural experiment has been under threat ever since the arrival of the first whaling ships and even more so since the first permanent human settlement. New species were introduced and spread very rapidly, placing the endemic species at risk. Quarantine programmes have since been implemented in an attempt to prevent the introduction and spread of even more species, but the rules are not easy to enforce. There have also been campaigns to eradicate some of the introduced species on some islands, but this is inevitably a very slow, expensive and difficult process.

Another threat has been the steady growth in tourism: from 11,800 visitors in 1979, to 68,900 in 2000, to 180,800 in 2012. From 2007 to 2010, Galápagos was on the UNESCO list of endangered World Heritage Sites. Although it is now off the list, promoting environmental conservation and sustainable development in the face of growing tourism and population remains a substantial challenge.

GALAPAGOS ISLANDS LISTINGS

WHERE TO STAY

Santa Cruz: Puerto Ayora

$$$$ Angemeyer Waterfront Inn, by the dock at Punta Estrada, T05-252 6561, www.angermeyer-waterfront-inn.com. Gorgeous location overlooking the bay. Includes buffet breakfast, restaurant, very comfortable modern rooms and apartments, a/c, some kitchenettes.

$$$$ Silberstein, Darwin y Piqueros, T05-252 6277, Quito T02-225 0553, www.hotelsilberstein.com. Modern and comfortable with lovely grounds, pool in tropical garden, a/c, buffet breakfast, restaurant, bar, spacious rooms and common areas, offers diving tours.

$$$ Lobo de Mar, 12 de Febrero y Darwin, T05-252 6188, Quito T02-250 2089, www.lobodemar.com.ec. Modern building with balconies and rooftop terrace, great views over the harbour. Includes breakfast, a/c, small pool, fridge, modern and comfortable.

$$ España, Berlanga y 12 de Febrero, T05-252 6108, www.hotelespanagalapagos.com. Pleasant, quiet and spacious rooms, a/c (**$** with fan), small courtyard with hammocks, good value, friendly. Recommended.

Santa Cruz: Highlands

$$$$ Galápagos Safari Camp, T09-9179 4259, www.galapagossafaricamp.com. Luxury resort with a central lodge and accommodation in comfortable, en suite tents. Includes breakfast and dinner, swimming pool, organizes tours.

$$$$ Semilla Verde, T05-301-3079, www.gps.ec. Located on a 5-ha property being reforested with native plants, comfortable rooms and common areas, includes breakfast, other meals available or use of kitchen facilities, British/Ecuadorean-run, family atmosphere.

San Cristóbal: Puerto Baquerizo Moreno

$$$ Casablanca, Mellville y Darwin, T05-252 0392, www.casablancagalapagos.com.

Large white house with lovely terrace and views of harbour. Includes breakfast, each room is individually decorated by the owner who has an art gallery on the premises.

$$ Mar Azul, Northía y Esmeraldas, T05-252 0139. Nice comfortable lodgings, electric shower, a/c (cheaper with fan), fridge, kitchen facilities, pleasant. Same family runs 2 more expensive hotels nearby.

Isabela: Puerto Villamil

$$$$ La Casa de Marita, at east end of beach, T05-252 9238, www.galapagos isabela.com. Tastefully chic, includes breakfast, other meals on request, a/c and fridge, very comfortable, each room is slightly different, some have balconies; **$$$** across the road away from the sea. A recommended little gem.

$$$$-$$$ Albemarle, on the beachfront in town, T05-252 9489, www.hotel albemarle.com. Attractive Mediterranean-style construction, includes breakfast, restaurant, bright comfortable rooms with wonderful ocean views, a/c, small pool, British/Ecuadorean-run, attentive owner. Recommended.

$$ San Vicente, Cormoranes y Pinzón Artesano, T05-252 9140, www.sanvicente galapagos.com. Very popular and well-organized hotel which also offers tours and kayak rentals, includes breakfast, other meals on request or use of cooking facilities, a/c, jacuzzi, rooms a bit small but nice, family-run. Same family runs several other good hotels.

Floreana: Puerto Velasco Ibarra

$$$ Hostal Santa María, opposite the school, T05-252 4904. Modern rooms with private bath, hot water, fan, fridge, screened windows, friendly owner Sr Claudio Cruz.

$$$ Hotel Wittmer, right on Black Beach, T05-252 4873. Lovely location with beautiful sunsets, simple comfortable rooms with private bath, electric shower, fan, very good meals available, family-run,

German spoken, reservations required.

RESTAURANTS

Santa Cruz: Puerto Ayora
$$$ Angermeyer Point, at Punta Estrada across the bay, take a water-taxi, T05-252 7007. Daily 1800-2230. Former home of Galápagos pioneer and artist Carl Angermeyer, with his works on display. Gorgeous setting over the water (take insect repellent). Excellent, innovative and varied menu, attentive service. Reservations advised. Highly recommended.
$$$ Il Giardino, Charles Darwin y Charles Binford, T05-252 6627. Open 0800-2230, closed Tue. Very good international food, service and atmosphere, excellent ice cream, very popular.
$$$ La Dolce Italia, Charles Darwin y 12 de Febrero. Daily 1100-1500, 1800-2200. Italian and seafood, wine list, a/c, pleasant atmosphere, attentive owner.
$$ Kiosks, along Charles Binford between Padre Herrera and Rodríguez Lara. Many kiosks serving local fare, including a variety of seafood, outdoor seating, lively informal atmosphere, busy at night.

San Cristóbal: Puerto Baquerizo Moreno
$$$-$$ Rosita, Ignacio de Hernández y General Villamil. Daily 0930-1430, 1700-2230. Old-time yachtie hangout, good food, large portions, nice atmosphere, à la carte and economical set meals. Recommended.

Isabela: Puerto Villamil
$$$-$$ There are various outdoor restaurants around the plaza, including **Cesar's** and **Los Delfines**.

Floreana: Puerto Velasco Ibarra
$$$-$$ Meals available at hotels or from a couple of restaurants catering to tour groups, all require advance notice.

WHAT TO DO

Santa Cruz: Puerto Ayora
Galápagos Sub-Aqua, Av Charles Darwin e Isla Floreana, T05-252 6350, Guayaquil T04-230 5514, www.galapagos-sub-aqua. com. Instructor Fernando Zambrano offers full certificate courses up to PADI divemaster level. Repeatedly recommended.
Moonrise Travel, Av Charles Darwin y Charles Binford, T05-252 6348, www. galapagosmoonrise.com. Last-minute cruise bookings, day-tours to different islands, bay tours, airline reservations, run guesthouse in Punta Estrada. Owner Jenny Devine is knowledgeable and speaks English.
Scuba Iguana, Charles Darwin near the research station, T05-252 6497, www.scubaiguana.com. Matías Espinoza runs this long-time reliable and recommended dive operator. Courses up to PADI divemaster.

San Cristóbal: Puerto Baquerizo Moreno
Sharksky, Darwin y Española, T05-252 1188, www.sharksky.com. Highlands, snorkelling, island-hopping, last-minute cruise bookings and gear rental. Also has an office on Isabela. Swiss/Ecuadorean-run, English, German and French spoken, helpful.
Wreck Bay Dive Center, Darwin y Wolf, T05-252 1663, www.wreckbay.com. Reportedly friendly and respectful of the environment.

Isabela: Puerto Villamil
Carapachudo Tours, Escalecias y Tero Real, T05-252 9451. Mountain biking downhill from Sierra Negra. Also rents good bikes, snorkelling gear and surf boards.
Isabela Dive Center, Escalecias y Alberto Gil, T05-252 9418, www.isabeladivecenter. com.ec. Diving, land and boat tours.

Galápagos wildlife

Introduction

One striking feature of the islands is the tameness of the animals. The islands were uninhabited when they were discovered in 1535 and the animals still have little instinctive fear of man. Plant and animal species in the Galápagos are grouped into three categories:

Endemic species, which occur only in the Galápagos and nowhere else on the planet. Examples include the marine and land iguana, Galápagos fur seal, flightless cormorant and daisy tree (*Scalesia pedunculata*).

Native species, which make their homes in the Galápagos as well as other parts of the world. Examples include all three species of booby, frigate birds and the various types of mangrove. These native species have been an integral part of the Galápagos ecosystems for a very long time.

Introduced species on the other hand are very recent arrivals, brought by man, and inevitably the cause of much damage. They include cattle, goats, donkeys, pigs, dogs, cats, rats and over 500 species of plants such as elephant grass (for grazing cattle) and fruiting plants such as the raspberry and guava. The unchecked expansion of these introduced species has upset the natural balance of the archipelago.

Title page: Avian courtship in Galápagos: dance of the blue-footed booby.
Above: Display of the frigate bird.

The reptiles found on the Galápagos are represented by five families: iguana, lava lizards, geckos, snakes and, of course, the giant tortoise. Of the 27 species of reptile on the islands, 17 are endemic.

Giant tortoise (*Geochelone elephantopus*)

The Galápagos and the Seychelles are the only island groups in the world that are inhabited by giant tortoises. The name Galápagos derives from the subspecies saddleback tortoise (*galápago* means saddle). Fourteen subspecies of tortoise have been discovered on the islands, although now only 10 survive. No one knows the maximum age of these huge reptiles, but the oldest inhabitant of the Darwin Research Station may be old enough to have met Darwin himself.

Mating takes place during the wet season from January to March. Later, between February and May, the females head down to the coast to search for a suitable nesting area. They dig a nest about 30 cm deep, lay between three and 16 eggs and cover them with a protective layer of urine and excrement. The incubation period is three to eight months.

In the past, the tortoise population on the islands was estimated at 250,000, but during the 17th and 18th centuries thousands were taken aboard whaling ships. Their ability to survive long periods without food and water made them the ideal source of fresh meat on long voyages. Black rats, feral dogs and pigs, introduced to the islands, affected the population by feeding on their eggs and young, until in 1980 only 15,000 remained. The Darwin Research Station is now rearing young in captivity for reintroduction to the wild, giving visitors the opportunity to see them close up. To see them in the wild, you can go to one of the tortoise reserves on Santa Cruz, San Cristóbal or Isabela.

Marine turtle (*Chelonia mydas*)

Of the eight species of marine turtle in the world only one is found on the islands: the Pacific green turtle. Mating turtles are a common sight in December and January, especially in the Caleta Tortuga Negra, at the northern tip of Santa Cruz. Egg laying usually takes place between January and June, when the female comes ashore to dig a hole and deposit 80 to 120 eggs under cover of darkness. La Lobería beach on Floreana is a popular spot. After about two months the hatchlings make the hazardous trip across the beach towards the sea, also after dark, in order to avoid the crabs, herons, frigates and lava gulls on the lookout for a midnight feast.

Top: Giant tortoise.
Above: Marine turtle.

Left: Marine iguana. **Right**: Land iguana.
Opposite page left: Flightless cormorant. **Opposite page right**: Waved albatross.

Marine iguana (*Amblyrhynchus cristatus*)

This prehistoric-looking endemic species is the only sea-going lizard in the world and is, in fact, from another era. It could be as much as nine million years old, making it even older than the islands themselves. Marine iguanas gather in huge herds on the coastal lava rocks. They vary in size, from 60 cm (on Isla Genovesa) up to 1 m (on Isla Isabela). Their black skin acts as camouflage and allows them to absorb heat from the fierce equatorial sun, although those on Española have red and green coloration, earning them the nickname 'Christmas iguanas'. The marine iguana's long flat tail is ideal for swimming but, although they can dive to depths of 20 m and stay underwater for up to an hour at a time, they prefer to feed on the seaweed on exposed rocks at low tide. Their tails also leave tell-tale tracks in the sand, resembling those of bicycle tyres.

Land iguana (*Conolophus subcristatus* and *pallidus*)

There are officially two species of land iguana on the islands: *Conolophus subcristatus* is yellow-orange in colour and inhabits Santa Cruz, Plaza, Isabela and Fernandina islands, while the other, *Conolophus pallidus*, is whitish to chocolate brown and is found only on Santa Fe. The latter is the largest land iguana, with the male weighing 6-7 kg and measuring over 1 m in length. Their numbers have been greatly reduced over the years, as the young often fall prey to rats and feral animals; the chances of survival for a land iguana in the wild is less than 10%. The land iguana remains a friendly chap and can be seen at close quarters. It feeds mainly on the fruits and flowers of the prickly pear cactus.

Birds

Sea birds were probably the first animals to colonize the archipelago. Half of the resident population of birds is endemic to the Galápagos, but only five of the 19 species of sea bird found on the Galápagos are unique to the islands. They are: the Galápagos penguin, the flightless cormorant, the lava gull, the swallow-tailed gull and the waved albatross. The rate of endemism of land birds is much higher, owing to the fact that they are less often migratory. There are 29 species of land bird in the Galápagos, 22 of which are endemic.

Galápagos penguin (*Spheniscus mendiculus*)
This, the most northerly of the world's penguin species, breeds on Islas Fernandina and Isabela, where the Humboldt Current cools the sea. The penguin population is small, only around 1000. They may appear distinctly ungraceful on land, hopping clumsily from rock to rock, but underwater they are fast and agile swimmers and can be seen breaking the surface, like dolphins. The best time to see them in the water is early morning, between 0500 and 0700.

Flightless cormorant (*Phalacrocorax harrisi*)
This is one of the rarest birds in the world. It is found only on Isla Fernandina and the west coast of Isla Isabela, where the nutrient-rich Cromwell Current brings a plentiful supply of fish from the central Pacific. Despite having lost the ability to fly, partly due to the lack of predators, the cormorant still insists on spreading its wings to dry in the wind, proving that old habits die hard.

Waved albatross (*Phoebastria irrorata*)
The largest bird in the Galápagos, with a wingspan of 2.5 m, is a cousin of the petrels and puffins. In Galápagos it breeds only on Isla Española, but is no longer endemic to the archipelago since a few breeding pairs took up residence on Isla de la Plata off the coast of mainland Ecuador. Outside the April-December breeding season, the albatross spends its time gliding majestically across the Pacific Ocean, sometimes as far as Japan. It returns after six months to begin its spectacular courtship display, a cross between an exotic dance and a fencing duel, which is repeated over and over again. Not surprisingly perhaps, given the effort put into this ritual, albatrosses stay faithful to their mate for life.

Frigate bird (*Fregata minor* and *magnificens*)
Both the great frigate bird, *Fregata minor*, and magnificent frigate bird, *Fregata magnificens*, are found on the Galápagos. These 'vultures of the sea' have a wingspan almost as big as that of the albatross and spend much of their time aloft, gliding in circles with their distinctive long forked tail and angled wings. Having lost the waterproofing of its black plumage, the frigate never lands on the sea; instead, it pursues other birds – in particular boobies – and harasses

183

them for food, or catches small fish on the surface of the water with its hooked beak. During the courtship display the males inflate a huge red sac under their throats, like a heart-shaped scarlet balloon, and flutter their spread wings. This seduces and attracts females to the nest, which the males have already prepared for mating. This amazing ritual can be seen in March and April on San Cristóbal and Genovesa, or throughout the year on North Seymour.

Unlike the great frigate bird, the magnificent frigate bird is an 'inshore feeder' and feeds near the islands. It is very similar in appearance, but the male has a purple sheen on its plumage and the female has a black triangle on the white patch on her throat.

Booby (*Sula nebouxii, Sula sula* and *Sula dactylactra*)

These are very common throughout the islands. Three species are found in the Galápagos: the blue-footed, red-footed and masked booby. The name 'booby' is thought to derive from *pájaros bobos* (silly birds), due to their extreme tameness, which sadly led to them being killed for sport in earlier times.

Most common is the blue-footed booby, *Sula nebouxii*. This is the only booby to lay more than one egg at a time (three is not unusual), though if food is insufficient the stronger firstborn will kick its siblings out of the nest. Unlike its red-footed relative, the blue-footed booby fishes inshore, dropping on its prey like an arrow from the sky. It is best known for its comical and complicated courtship dance.

The red-footed booby, *Sula sula,* is the only Galápagos booby to nest in trees, thanks to the fact that its feet are adapted to gripping branches. It is light brown in colour, although there's also a less common white variety. The largest colony of red-footed boobies is found on Isla Genovesa.

The masked booby, *Sula dactylactra*, is the heaviest of the three boobies. Its plumage is white with a distinctive black mask on the eyes. Like its blue-footed cousin, the masked booby nests on the ground and surrounds its nest with excrement. It chooses to fish between the other two boobies, thus providing an excellent illustration of the concept of an ecological niche.

Mammals

The number of native mammals in the archipelago is limited to two species of bat, a few species of rat and, of course, sea lions and seals. This is explained by the fact that the islands were never connected to the mainland. Since the arrival of man, however, goats, dogs, donkeys, horses and the black rat have been introduced and threaten the fragile ecological balance of the islands.

Above left: Sea lion. **Above right:** Fur seal.

184

Sea lion (*Zalophus californianus*)

As its scientific name suggests, the Galápagos sea lion is related to the Californian species, although it is smaller. It is common throughout the archipelago, gathering in large colonies on beaches or on the rocks. The male, distinguished from the female by its huge size and domed forehead, is very territorial, especially at the beginning of the May to January mating season. He patrols a territory of 40 to 100 sq m with a group of up to 30 females, chasing off intruders and keeping an eye on the young, in case they wander too far from the safety of the beach.

The friendly, inquisitive females and pups provide one of the main tourist attractions, especially when cavorting with swimmers, but remember, they are wild animals, so keep a safe distance. Sea lions colonies are found on South Plaza, Santa Fe, Rábida, James Bay (Isla Santiago), Española, San Cristóbal and Isabela.

Fur seal (*Arctocephalus galapagoensis*)

Fur seals and sea lions both belong to the *Otariidae* or eared seal family. The fur seal's dense, luxuriant pelt attracted great interest at the beginning of the 20th century and the creature was hunted almost to extinction by whalers and other skin hunters. Fortunately, these *lobos de dos pelos* (double-fur sea wolves), as they are known locally, survived and can be seen most easily in Puerto Egas on Santiago island, usually hiding from the sun under rocks or lava cracks.

Marine life

The Galápagos Islands are washed by three currents: the cold Humboldt and Cromwell currents, and the warm El Niño. This provides the islands with a diverse and unique underwater fauna. The number of fish species has been estimated at around 400, of which 17% are endemic. Among the huge number of fish found in the islands' waters, there are 18 species of moray, five species of ray and about 12 species of shark. The most common sharks are the white-tipped reef shark, the black-tipped reef shark, two species of hammerhead, the Galápagos shark, the grey reef shark, the tiger shark, the horn shark and the whale shark.

Among the marine mammals, at least 16 species of whale and seven species of dolphin have been identified. The most common dolphins are the bottle-nosed dolphin, *Tursiops truncatus*, and the common dolphin. Whales include the sperm whale, humpback whale, pilot whale, the orca and the false killer whale, sei whale, minke whale, Bryde's whale, Cuvier's beaked whale and the blue whale. These whales can be seen around all the islands, but most easily to the west of Isabela and Fernandina. The waters are also rich in starfish, sea urchins, sea cucumbers and crustaceans, including the ubiquitous and distinctive Sally Lightfoot crab.

Above left: Spotted eagle ray. **Above right:** Whale shark. **Next page:** White-tipped reef shark.

PRACTICALITIES

INS AND OUTS

→ BEST TIME TO VISIT ECUADOR

Ecuador's climate is highly unpredictable. As a general rule, however, in the **Sierra**, there is little variation by day or by season in the temperature; this depends on altitude. The range of shade temperature is from 6-10°C in the morning, to 19-23°C in the afternoon, though it can get considerably hotter in the lower basins. Rainfall patterns depend on whether a particular area is closer to the eastern or western slopes of the Andes. To the west, June to September are dry and October to May are wet (but there is sometimes a short dry spell in December or January). To the east, October to February are dry and March to September are wet. There is also variation in annual rainfall from north to south, with the southern highlands being drier. **Quito** is within 25 km of the equator, but it stands high enough to make its climate much like that of spring in England, the days pleasantly warm and the nights cool. Rainy season is October to May with the heaviest rainfall in April. Rain usually falls in the afternoon. The day length (sunrise to sunset) is almost constant throughout the year.

Along the **Pacific Coast**, rainfall also decreases from north to south, so that it can rain throughout the year in northern Esmeraldas and seldom at all near the Peruvian border. The coast, however, can be enjoyed year-round, although it may be a bit cool from June to November, when mornings are often grey with the *garúa* mists. January to May is the hottest and rainiest time of the year. Like the coast the **Galápagos** may receive *garúa*

from May to December; from January to April the islands are hottest and brief but heavy showers can fall. In the **Oriente**, heavy rain can fall at any time, but it is usually wettest from March to September.

Ecuador's **high season** is from June to early September, which is also the best time for climbing and trekking. There is also a short tourist season in December and January. In resort areas at major fiestas, such as Carnival, Semana Santa (Easter), Finados (2 November) and over New Year, accommodation can be hard to find. Hotels will be full in individual towns during their particular festivals, but Ecuador as a whole is not overcrowded at any time of the year.

→ GETTING TO ECUADOR

AIR

International flights to Ecuador arrive either at Quito (UIO) or Guayaquil (GYE). You can arrive in Quito and depart from Guayaquil or vice versa. There are frequent flights between these two main cities, as well as ample bus services. International airfares from North America and Europe to Ecuador may vary with low and high season. High season is generally July to September and December. International flights to Ecuador from other South or Central American countries, however, usually have one price year-round.

Flights from Europe KLM/Air France, Iberia and **LAN** (Lan Chile/Lan Ecuador) offer direct flights from Europe to Ecuador, the first originating in Amsterdam, the last two in Madrid. Connections on several other European carriers can be made in Bogotá and Caracas. US carriers offer connections from Europe through their respective North American hubs, see below.

Flights from North America Miami's busy international airport is the most important air transport gateway linking Ecuador with North America. American has two daily non-stop flights from Miami to Quito, one daily to Guayaquil. **LAN** flies daily from Miami to Quito and Guayaquil, and from New York City (JFK) to Guayaquil. **United** flies daily from less congested Houston to Quito, and **Delta** flies five times a week from Atlanta to Quito.

Flights from Australia and New Zealand There are three options: 1) To Los Angeles, USA, with **Qantas**, **Air New Zealand** or **United**, continuing to Ecuador via Houston or Miami (see above); 2) From Auckland to Santiago, Chile, continuing to Ecuador, all with **LAN**; 3) To Buenos Aires, Argentina, from Sydney or Auckland with **Aerolíneas Argentinas**, continuing to Ecuador with various South American carriers. These are all expensive long-haul routes, round-the-world and Circle Pacific fares may be convenient alternatives.

Flights from Latin America There are flights to Quito and/or Guayaquil from Santiago, Lima, Bogotá, Cali, Caracas, São Paulo, Mexico City, Panama City and San José (Costa Rica). Connections can easily be made from other South American cities. **Copa** and **TACA** offer convenient connections between Ecuador and various destinations in Central America and the Caribbean.

Airport information For most visitors, the point of arrival will be **Mariscal Sucre** airport in Quito (page 35), which was relocated 30 km from the city in 2013. Road connections between Quito and its new airport are often congested. Guayaquil's **José Joaquín de Olmedo** airport (page 89) is closer to the city centre. This is a sensible alternative if you prefer to avoid the altitude of the highlands or are heading directly to Galápagos or the beaches. For international departures from Ecuador, airlines recommend you arrive at either airport three hours before your flight.

→ TRANSPORT IN ECUADOR

Although there is ample domestic air service between main cities, road travel is the mainstay of transport in Ecuador. Buses are available on all routes but may not always be the most convenient option. For those with limited time, we recommend travelling some segments as part of a tour, arranging private transport with a tour agency, using shared taxis or vans, or hiring a car.

AIR
Airlines operating in Ecuador include: **Aerogal** ① *T1-800-237642 or T02-294 2800, www. aerogal.com.ec*, serving Quito, Guayaquil, Cuenca, Coca, Manta and Galápagos; **LAN** ① *T1-800-101075, www.lan.com*, serving Quito, Guayaquil, Cuenca, Manta and Galápagos; **TAME** ① *T1-800-500800 or 02-397 7100, www.tame.com.ec*, serving Quito, Guayaquil, Cuenca, Tulcán, Latacunga, Loja, Coca, Lago Agrio, Tena, Macas, Esmeraldas, Manta, Santa Rosa (Machala) and Galápagos. Note that TAME only accepts Ecuadorean credit cards for the purchase of tickets on line.

RAIL
Empresa de Ferrocarriles Ecuatorianos ① *T1-800-873637, www.ecuadorbytrain.com*. The spectacular Ecuadorean railway system is being restored. In 2013, the following tourist rides were being offered: from **Alausí to Sibambe** via the Devil's Nose; from **Riobamba to Urbina** and **Colta**; from **Quito to Machachi, El Boliche** (Cotopaxi) and **Latacunga**; from **Ibarra to Salinas**; from **El Tambo to Baños del Inca** near Ingapirca; and from **Durán**, outside Guayaquil, to **Yaguachi**. There are plans to re-open additional segments until the entire line from Quito to Durán (across the river from Guayaquil) is completed. For train buffs, tours of up to four days, including travel in a historical train with steam locomotive, are scheduled to start in 2013.

ROAD
Bus Several companies use comfortable air-conditioned buses on their longer routes; some companies have their own stations, away from the main bus terminals, exclusively for these better buses. Bus company information and itineraries are found at www. ecuadorschedules.com. Throughout Ecuador, travel by bus is safest during the daytime.

Driving A very good network of paved roads runs throughout the country. Maintenance of major highways is franchised to private firms, who charge tolls of US$1. Roads are subject to damage during heavy rainy seasons. Always check about road conditions before setting out. Excessive speed and reckless driving are common hazards and some bus drivers are among the worst offenders. Driving at night is not recommended.

To hire (rent) a car you must be 21 or older and have an international credit card. Surcharges may apply to clients aged 21-25. You may pay cash, which is cheaper and may allow you to bargain, but they want a credit card for security. You may be asked to sign two blank credit card vouchers, one for the rental fee itself and the other as a security deposit, and authorization for a charge of as much as US$5000 may be requested against your credit card account. The uncashed vouchers will be returned to you when you return the vehicle. Make sure the car is parked securely at all times. A small car suitable for city driving costs around US$550 per week including unlimited milage, tax and full insurance. A 4WD or pickup truck costs about US$950 a week.

There are two grades of petrol (gasoline): 'Extra' (82 octane, US$1.48 per US gallon) and 'Super' (92 octane, US$1.98-2.30). Both are unleaded. Extra is available everywhere, while Super may not be available in more remote areas. Diesel fuel (US$1.03) is dirty and available everywhere.

Hitchhiking Public transport in Ecuador is so abundant that there is seldom any need to hitchhike along the major highways. On small out-of-the-way country roads, however, the situation can be quite the opposite, and giving passers-by a ride is common practice and safe, especially in the back of a pickup or truck. A small fee is usually charged, ask in advance.

Vans and shared taxis These operate between major cities and offer a faster, more comfortable and more expensive alternative to buses. They may provide pickup and drop-off at your hotel. Details of these services change frequently so make local enquiries.

MAPS
The Instituto Geográfico Militar (IGM) ⓘ *Senierges y Telmo Paz y Miño, east of Parque El Ejido, Quito, T02-397 5100, ext 2502, www.geoportaligm.gob.ec, Mon-Thu 0800-1630, Fri 0700-1430, take ID*, sells country and topographic maps in a variety of paper and digital formats. Prices range from US$3 to US$7. Maps of border and sensitive areas are '*reservado*' (classified) and not available for sale without a permit. Buy your maps here, they are rarely available outside Quito.

PRICE CODES

WHERE TO STAY

$$$$ over US$150   **$$$** US$66-149
$$ US$30-65   **$** under US$30
Prices refer to the cost of a double room including tax and service charges.

RESTAURANTS

$$$ over US$12   **$$** US$7-12   **$** under US$7
Prices refer to the cost of a two-course meal for one person, excluding alcoholic drinks.

→ WHERE TO STAY IN ECUADOR

HOTELS

Outside the provincial capitals and a few resorts, there are few higher-class hotels, although a number of *haciendas* have opened their doors to paying guests. A few are in the **Exclusive Hotels & Haciendas of Ecuador** group (T02-222 4271, www.ehhec.com), but there are many other independent haciendas of good quality. Some are mentioned in the text. Larger towns and tourist centres have many more hotels than we can list. The hotels that are included are among the best in each category, selected to provide a variety of locations and styles. Additional hotels are found at www.hotelesecuador.com, www.ecuadorboutiquehotels.com,www.infohotel.ecandwww.guiahotelesecuador.com. Not all hotels include breakfast. Service of 10% and tax of 12% are added to better hotel bills. Some cheaper hotels apply only the 12% tax, but check if it is included. Some hotel rooms have very low wattage bulbs, keen readers are advised to take a head torch. All but the most basic establishments have Wi-Fi in their rooms or common areas.

CAMPING

Camping in natural areas can be one of the most satisfying experiences during a visit to Ecuador. Organized campsites, car or trailer camping on the other hand are virtually unheard-of. Because of the abundance of inexpensive hotels you should never *have to* camp in Ecuador, except for cyclists who may be stuck between towns. In this case the best strategy is to ask permission to camp on someone's private land, preferably within sight of their home for safety. It is not safe to pitch your tent at random near villages and even less so on beaches. **Bluet Camping Gas** is easily obtainable, but white gas, like US Coleman fuel, is not.

→ FOOD AND DRINK IN ECUADOR

DINING OUT

The cuisine varies with region, you can learn about it at www.ecuador.travel. The following are some typical dishes.

In the highlands *Locro de papas* (potato and cheese soup); *mote* (white hominy, a staple in the region around Cuenca, but used in a variety of dishes in the Sierra); *caldo de patas* (cowheel soup with *mote*); *llapingachos* (fried potato and cheese patties);

FOOD AND DRINK
Fruit salad

Treat your palate to some of Ecuador's exquisite and exotic fruits. They are great on their own as *ensalada de frutas*, or make delicious juices (*jugos*), smoothies (*batidos*) and ice creams (*helados*). Always make sure these are prepared with purified water and pasteurized milk.

Babaco, mountain papaya. Makes great juice.

Chirimoya, custard apple. A very special treat, soft when ripe but check for tiny holes in the skin which usually mean worms inside.

Granadilla, golden passion fruit. Slurp it straight from the shell without chewing the seeds.

Guanábana, soursop. Makes excellent juice and ice cream.

Guava, ice cream bean. Large pod with sweet white pulp around hard black seeds. Not to be confused with *guayaba*, below.

Guayaba, guava. Good plain or in syrup, also makes nice jam and juice.

Mango, the season is short: December and January. Try the little *mangos de chupar*, for sucking rather than slicing.

Maracuyá, yellow passion fruit. Makes a very refreshing juice and ice cream.

Mora, raspberry or blackberry. Not all that exotic but makes an excellent and popular juice and ice cream.

Naranjilla, very popular juice, often cooked with a dash of oatmeal to make it less tart.

Orito, baby banana. Thumb-sized banana, thin skinned and very sweet.

Papaya, great plain or as juice.

Piña, pineapple. A popular juice.

Taxo, banana passion fruit. Peel open the thin skin and slurp the fruit without chewing the seeds.

Tomate de árbol, tamarillo or tree tomato. Popular as juice but also good plain or in syrup.

Tuna, prickly pear. Sweet and tasty but never pick them yourself. Tiny blond spines hurt your hands and mouth unless they are carefully removed first.

Zapote or sapote. Fleshy and sweet, get some dental floss for the fibres that get stuck between your teeth.

---

empanadas de morocho (a fried ground corn shell filled with meat); *sancocho de yuca* (vegetable soup with manioc root); roast *cuy* (guinea pig); *fritada* (fried pork); *hornado* (roast pork); *humitas* (tender ground corn steamed in corn leaves); and *quimbolitos* (similar to *humitas* but prepared with wheat flour and steamed in *achira* lily leaves). *Humitas* and *quimbolitos* come in both sweet and savoury varieties.

On the coast *Empanadas de verde* (a ground plantain shell filled with cheese, meat or shrimp); *sopa de bola de verde* (plantain dumpling soup); *ceviche* (marinaded fish or seafood, popular everywhere, see below); *encocados* (dishes prepared with coconut milk, such as shrimp, fish, etc, very popular in the province of Esmeraldas); *cocadas* (sweets made with coconut); *viche* (fish or seafood soup made with ground peanuts); and *patacones* (thick fried plantain chips served as a side dish).

In Oriente Dishes prepared with *yuca* (manioc or cassava root) and river fish. *Maitos* (in Northern Oriente) and *ayampacos* (in the south) are spiced meat, chicken or palm hearts wrapped in leaves and roasted over the coals.

Throughout the country Upmarket restaurants add 22% to the bill, 12% tax plus 10% service. If economizing ask for the set meal in restaurants, *almuerzo* at lunch time, *merienda* in the evening – cheap and wholesome; it costs US$2.50-5. *Fanesca*, a fish soup with many grains, ground peanuts and more, sold in Easter Week, is very filling (it is so popular that in Quito and main tourist spots it is sold throughout Lent). *Ceviche*, marinated fish or seafood which is usually served with popcorn and roasted maize (*tostado*), is very popular throughout Ecuador. Only *ceviche de pescado* (fish) and *ceviche de concha* (clams), which are marinated raw, potentially pose a health hazard. The other varieties of *ceviche* such as *camarón* (shrimp/prawn) and *langostino* (jumbo shrimp/king prawn) all of which are cooked before being marinated, are generally safe (but check the cleanliness of the establishment). *Langosta* (lobster) is an increasingly endangered species but continues to be illegally caught; please be conscientious. Ecuadorean food is not particularly spicy. However, in most homes and restaurants, the meal is accompanied by a small bowl of *ají* (hot pepper sauce) which may vary in potency. In addition to the prepared foods mentioned above, Ecuador offers a large variety of delicious fruits, some of which are unique to South America (see above).

DRINK

There are many excellent fruit juices (*jugos*) and smoothies (*batidos*), see box, page 193. Remember to ask if they are prepared with purified water. The main beers are *Pilsener* and *Club*. Argentine and Chilean wines are widely available. *Aguardiente* (unmatured rum, many brands) is popular and is also known as *puntas, trago de caña* or just *trago*. The usual soft drinks, known as *colas*, are available. In tourist centres and many upscale hotels and restaurants, good cappuccino and espresso can be found.

→ FESTIVALS IN ECUADOR

Festivals are an intrinsic part of Ecuadorean life. In pre-Hispanic times they were organized around the solar cycle and agricultural calendar. After the conquest, the church integrated the indigenous festivals with their own feast days and so today's festivals are a complex mixture of Roman Catholicism and indigenous traditions. Every community in every part of the country celebrates its own particular festival in honour of the local patron saint and there are many more that are celebrated in common up and down the country, particularly in the Sierra. The exact dates of many fiestas vary from year to year, either with the ecclesiastic calendar or for other reasons; enquire locally to confirm current dates.

Outsiders are usually welcome at all but the most intimate and spiritual of celebrations and, as a gringo, you might even be a guest of honour. Ecuadoreans can be very sensitive, however, and you should make every effort not to offend (for example by not taking a ceremony seriously or by refusing food, drink or an invitation to dance). At the same time, you should keep in mind that most fiestas are accompanied by heavy drinking. It is best to enjoy the usually solemn beginning of most celebrations as well as the liveliness which follows, but politely depart before things get totally out of control.

MAJOR FIESTAS

February-March Carnaval is held during the week before Lent and ends on Ash Wednesday. While the Ecuadorean version can't rival that of Brazil for fame or colour,

Ecuador has its own carnival speciality: throwing balloons filled with water or, less frequently, bags of flour and any other missile guaranteed to make a mess. Water pistols are sold on every street corner at this time of year and even the odd bucket gets put to use. It can take visitors aback at first, but if you can keep your composure or – better still, join in the mayhem – it can all be good fun. For the more sensitive tourist, there is the option of heading to Ambato, south of Quito, where water-throwing is banned and flour is replaced by flowers at the city's **Fiesta de las Frutas y las Flores**.

March-April Semana Santa (Holy Week) is held the week before Easter and begins on Palm Sunday (Domingo de Ramos). This is celebrated throughout the country, but is especially dramatic in Quito, with a spectacularly solemn procession through the streets on Good Friday; also in Riobamba on the Tuesday. A particularly important part of Holy Week is the tradition of eating *fanesca* with family and friends. *Fanesca* is a soup made with salt fish and many different grains, and a good example of the syncretism of Catholic and earlier beliefs. In this case the Catholic component is the lack of meat, which was not consumed during Lent, while the many grains came from native traditions to celebrate the beginning of the harvest at this time of year. The original native version might have been made with *cuy*.

May-June Corpus Cristi is a feast held on the Thursday after Trinity Sunday, usually in mid-June. This is a major event in the Central Highlands, especially in the provinces of Cotopaxi and Tungurahua, but also in Chimborazo province and in Saraguro and Loja. In Salasaca (Tungurahua) the festival is celebrated with music, dance and elaborate costumes, while in Pujilí (Cotopaxi) groups of masked *danzantes* make their way through the streets and the valiant climb *palos encebados*, 20-m-high greased poles, in order to obtain prizes, including live sheep.

21-24 June Inti Raymi, the solstice, 21 June, has enjoyed something of a revival in recent years. Ceremonies are held at archaeological sites such as Ingapirca and Cochasquí, as well as in native communities, including Otavalo and Cotacachi. Inti Raymi often blends with San Juan, 24 June, the main festival of the Otavalo valley. For an entire week, the local men dress up in a variety of costumes and dance constantly, moving from house to house. At one point, they head to the chapel of San Juan and start throwing rocks at each other as different groups vie for control of the plaza; best keep your distance.

29 June San Pedro y San Pablo is another major fiesta in Imbabura province. On the night before, bonfires are lit in the streets and young women who want to have children are supposed to jump over the fires. This festival is particularly important in Cotacachi and Cayambe, and is also celebrated in southern Chimborazo, in Alausí and Achupallas.

23-25 September Mama Negra is a big festival in Latacunga, where a man dressed as a black woman parades through the streets on horseback. It is repeated on the weekend before 11 November.

2 November Día de los Difuntos or Finados (Day of the Dead) is an important holiday nationwide. This tradition has been practised since time immemorial. In the Incaic calendar, November was the eighth month and represented Ayamarca, or land of the dead. The celebration is another example of religious adaptation in which the ancient beliefs of native cultures are mixed with the rites of the Catholic Church. *Colada morada*, a sweet drink made from various fruits and purple corn is prepared, as are *guaguas de pan* (bread dolls). In a few places, native families may build a special altar in their homes or take their departed relatives' favourite food and drink to the cemetery. Most Ecuadoreans commemorate Día de los Difuntos in more prosaic fashion, by placing flowers at the graveside of their deceased relatives.

December Navidad (Christmas) is an intimate family celebration, starting with *Misa del Gallo* (Midnight Mass) followed by a festive meal. *Pases del Niño* (processions of the Christ child), take place through the country on various dates around Christmas time. Families who possess a statue of the baby Jesus carry them in procession to the local church, where they are blessed during a special Mass. The most famous *Pase del Niño* is in Cuenca on the morning of 24 December. Other notable celebrations take place in Saraguro, in Loja province, in Pujilí and Tanicuchí in Cotopaxi province and throughout the province of Cañar.

31 December Año Viejo (New Year's Eve) has a typically Ecuadorean aspect in the life-size effigies or puppets which are constructed and displayed throughout the country on the last day of the year. These puppets, called *años viejos*, usually depict politicians or other prominent local, national or international personalities and important events of the year gone by. Children dressed in black are the old year's widows, and beg for alms (candy or coins). Just before midnight the *años viejos'* will is read, full of satire, and at the stroke of midnight the effigies are doused with gasoline and burned, wiping out the old year and all that it had brought with it. In addition to sawdust, the *años viejos* usually contain a few firecrackers making for an exciting finale; best keep your distance.

→ SHOPPING IN ECUADOR

Almost everyone who visits Ecuador will end up buying a souvenir of some sort from the vast array of arts and crafts (*artesanías*) on offer. The most colourful places to shop for souvenirs, and pretty much anything else in Ecuador, are the street markets which can be found absolutely everywhere. The country also has its share of shiny, modern shopping centres, but remember that the high overheads are reflected in the prices.

Otavalo's massive market is the best-known place for buying wall hangings and sweaters. Another market, at Saquisilí, south of Quito, is renowned for shawls, blankets and embroidered garments. Fewer handicrafts can be found on the coast, but this is where you can buy an authentic Panama hat. The best, called *superfinos*, are reputed to be made in the little town of Montecristi, but the villages around Cuenca also produce excellent models. Cuenca is a good place to buy Panama hats, and other types of hats can be bought throughout the highlands. Ecuador also produces fine silver jewellery, ceramics and brightly painted carvings. Particularly good buys are the many beautiful items fashioned from tagua, or vegetable ivory. By purchasing these you are promoting valuable conservation of the rainforests where the tagua palm grows.

All manner of *artesanías* can be bought in Quito, either at the Mercado Artesanal La Mariscal or in any of the many craft shops. An advantage of buying your souvenirs in a shop is that they'll usually package your gifts well enough to prevent damage on the flight home. Craft cooperatives are also a good place to shop, since there is a better chance that a fair share of the price will go to the artisan.

Stall holders in markets expect you to bargain, so don't disappoint them. Many tourists enjoy the satisfaction of beating down the seller's original price and finding a real 'bargain', but don't take it too far. Always remain good natured, even if things are not going your way (remember that you're on vacation and they're working). And don't make a fool of yourself by arguing for hours over a few cents. The item you're bargaining for may have taken weeks to make and you're probably spending more on a night's hotel than the market seller earns all week.

→ RESPONSIBLE TRAVEL IN ECUADOR

Ecuador is your dream trip, a beautiful and fascinating country, but it is also a living, working place. The natural environment is under especially great pressure here because of the high population density (by South American standards) and a growing demand for resources. Tourism can either accentuate or offset these pressures. You can help by using common sense and observing the guidelines outlined below.

· Where possible choose a destination, tour operator or hotel with a proven ethical and environmental commitment – if in doubt, ask.
· Spend money on locally produced (rather than imported) goods and services, buy directly from the producer or from a fair trade shop, and use common sense when bargaining – the few dollars you save may be a week's salary to others.
· Use water and electricity sensibly – travellers may receive preferential supply while the needs of local communities are overlooked.
· Learn about local etiquette and culture – consider local norms and behaviour and dress appropriately for local cultures and situations.
· Protect wildlife and other natural resources – don't buy souvenirs or goods unless they are clearly sustainably produced and are not protected under CITES legislation.
· Always ask before taking photographs or videos of people.
· Consider staying in local accommodation rather than foreign hotel chains; the economic benefits for host communities are far greater, and there are more opportunities to learn about local culture.
· Do not give money, sweets or other items to begging children. Consider contributing to a local NGO instead. For advice, see www.responsibletravel.org and www.travelers philanthropy.org.

PROTECTED NATURAL AREAS IN ECUADOR

Ecuador has an outstanding array of protected natural areas. National parks and other government reserves cover almost five million hectares of land plus another 14 million hectares of marine reserves. These are distributed throughout the country and include many unique tracts of wilderness. But the term 'protected' may not mean what it does in other parts of the world; native communities, settlements, haciendas, and even oil drilling camps can be found in the heart of some Ecuadorean national parks. Park boundaries are seldom clearly defined, and less often respected. What park facilities exist, along with most park rangers, are concentrated at the access points to a very few frequently visited areas. Elsewhere, infrastructure ranges from very basic to non-existent. Entry to all Ecuadorean national parks except Galápagos is free of charge but there may be fees for camping or use of shelters. Park rangers are usually friendly and helpful.

National parks are administered by the **Ministerio del Ambiente** (Madrid 11-59 y Andalucía, T02-255 3611, ext 1420, Quito, www.ambiente.gob.ec). This administrative head office might provide some limited information but you are better off contacting their local office in the city nearest the park you wish to visit, for example the Loja office for Parque Nacional Podocarpus, Puerto López for Machalilla, and so on.

In addition to national parks, there are many private or NGO-run nature reserves throughout Ecuador. Most cater to birdwatchers but are also of interest to day-hikers, trekkers or anyone with an interest in nature. In healthy forest where birds abound, chances are that you can also find beautiful orchids, bromeliads, frogs, beetles, butterflies and many other fascinating plants and animals.

ECUADOR'S MOST VULNERABLE PLACES

The **Galápagos Islands** are becoming a victim of their own success as a tourist destination. The islands offer a once-in-a-lifetime experience for nature lovers but will rapidly be destroyed if they are used as an ocean-side resort for general recreation. Think carefully about why you want to visit Galápagos and how you choose to travel there.

The **Oriente Jungle** is changing rapidly under the pressures of petroleum development and colonization. Sustainable ecotourism offers an economic alternative that could help conserve the region, but not all tour operators are equally respectful of the jungle or its indigenous people. Choose your jungle tour judiciously and remember that the cheapest is not the best.

ESSENTIALS A-Z

Accident and emergency
Emergency telephone numbers: T911 in Quito and Cuenca, T112 in Guayaquil, T101 for police everywhere.

Electricity
110 volts, 60 cycles. Sockets are for twin flat blades, sometimes with a round earth pin.

Embassies and consulates
For all Ecuadorean embassies and consulates abroad and for all foreign embassies and consulates in Ecuador, see http://embassy.goabroad.com.

Health
See your GP or travel clinic at least 6 weeks before departure for general advice on travel risks and vaccinations. Try phoning a specialist travel clinic if your own doctor is unfamiliar with health in the region. Make sure you have sufficient medical travel insurance, get a dental check, know your own blood group and, if you suffer a long-term condition such as diabetes or epilepsy, obtain a Medic Alert bracelet (www.medicalalert.co.uk).

Vaccinations and anti-malarials
Confirm that your primary courses and boosters are up to date. It is advisable to vaccinate against polio, tetanus, typhoid, hepatitis A and, for more remote rural areas, rabies.

Yellow fever vaccination and malaria precautions are important for the Oriente Jungle and far northern Pacific Coast (below 1500 m) all year round. Specialist advice should be taken before you leave on the best antimalarials to use.

Health risks
Flying into Quito (2850 m) from sea level is likely to leave you affected by mild **altitude sickness** for the first few days, so give yourself a chance to acclimatize before heading off on trips and treks.

Because you are so close to the equator, **sun protection** is vital throughout Ecuador, especially on the beach and in the highlands, regardless of how cool it may feel; always use sun block and a hat. Mountaineers should always use glasses that provide 100% UV protection, and a good pair of sunglasses is recommended to all travellers in Ecuador.

The major health risks on the coast and in the jungle are those diseases carried by insects such as mosquitoes and sandflies. These include **malaria, dengue fever** and, much more rarely, **Chagas disease** and **leishmaniasis**. Because different insects bite at different times of day, repellent application and covered limbs are a 24-hr issue. Long trousers, a long-sleeved shirt and insect repellent all offer protection. Mosquito nets dipped in permethrin provide a good physical and chemical barrier at night.

Some form of **diarrhoea** or intestinal upset is common, the standard advice is always to wash your hands before eating and to be careful with drinking water and ice; bottled water is available everywhere in Ecuador. In a restaurant, ask where the water to make juices has come from. Food can also pose a problem: be wary of raw salads if you don't know how thoroughly they have been washed. Food from street vendors is best avoided.

Road accidents are an often overlooked threat to travellers' health. You can reduce the likelihood of accidents by not travelling at night, avoiding overcrowded buses, not drinking and driving, wearing a seatbelt in cars and a helmet on motorbikes (even if most Ecuadoreans do not).

If you go diving make sure that you are fit do so. The **British Sub-Aqua Club (BSAC)**, Telford's Quay, South Pier Rd,

Ellesmere Port, Cheshire CH65 4FL, UK, T01513-506200, www.bsac.com, can put you in touch with doctors who do medical examinations. Protect your feet and keep an eye out for secondary infection. Check that the dive company have appropriate certification from **BSAC** or **PADI**, Unit 7, St Philips Central, Albert Rd, Bristol BS2 0TD, T0117-300 7234, www.padi.com, and that the equipment is well maintained.

There is a **hyperbaric chamber** in Puerto Ayora, Galápagos and another with the navy in Guayaquil.

Useful websites

www.cdc.gov Centres for Disease Control and Prevention (USA).
www.fitfortravel.scot.nhs.uk Fit for Travel (UK).
www.itg.be Prince Leopold Institute for Tropical Medicine.
www.nathnac.org National Travel Health Network and Centre (NaTHNaC).
www.nhs.uk/nhsengland/Healthcare abroad/pages/Healthcareabroad.aspx Department of Health advice for travellers (UK).
www.who.int World Health Organisation.

Insurance

Travel insurance is a must for all visitors to Ecuador. Always take out insurance that covers both medical expenses and baggage loss. Check that all the activities you may end up doing are covered. Mountaineering and scuba diving, for example, as well as the adrenalin sports practised in Baños and elsewhere, are excluded from many policies. Also check if medical coverage includes air ambulance and emergency flights back home. Mind the payment protocol, in Ecuador you are likely to have to pay out of pocket and later request reimbursement from the insurance company. Have the receipts for expensive personal effects such as cameras and laptops on file, take photos of these items and note the serial numbers.

Internet

Most hotels in Ecuador have free Wi-Fi in their rooms or common areas. In addition, cybercafés are everywhere. They usually charge under US$1 per hr.

Language

The official languages of Ecuador are Spanish and Quichua. English and a few other European languages may be spoken in some establishments catering to tourists in Quito and the most popular tourist destinations. Away from these places, knowledge of Spanish is essential. So it's a good idea to learn some Spanish before you come to Ecuador or begin your travels in Ecuador with a period of language study.

Money

The US dollar (US$) is the official currency of Ecuador. Only US$ bills circulate. US coins are used alongside the equivalent size and value Ecuadorean coins. Ecuadorean coins have no value outside the country. Many establishments are reluctant to accept bills larger than US$20 because of counterfeit notes or lack of change. There is no substitute for cash-in-hand when travelling in Ecuador; US$ cash in small denominations is by far the simplest and the only universally accepted option. Other currencies are difficult to exchange outside large cities and fetch a poor rate.

Money exchange

ATMs Internationally linked ATMs are common, although they cannot always be relied on. Credit cards are easier to use in ATMs than debit cards. ATMs are a focus for scams and robberies, use them judiciously.
Credit cards The most commonly accepted credit cards are Visa, MasterCard, Diners and, to a lesser extent, American Express. Cash advances on credit cards can be obtained through many ATMs (only Banco de Guayaquil for Amex), but daily limits apply. Larger advances on Visa and MasterCard are available from the main

branches of the following banks: **Banco Bolivariano**, **Banco de Guayaquil** (Visa only), **Banco del Austro** and **Banco del Pacífico**. Paying by credit card may incur a surcharge of at least 10%.

Traveller's cheques (TCs) are not accepted by most merchants, hotels or tour agencies in Ecuador. They can be exchanged for cash at **Banco del Pacífico** (main branches; US$5 commission, maximum US$200 a day) and some *casas de cambio*, including **Vaz Corp** (in Quito, Otavalo, Cuenca and Loja; 1.8% commission). A passport is always required to exchange TCs. **American Express** is the only widely accepted brand, but they are no longer replaced in Ecuador; if they are lost or stolen, you must file a claim from home. A police report is required if TCs are stolen.

Cost of travelling

Despite the US-dollar economy, prices remain modest by international standards and Ecuador is affordable for the budget traveller. A very basic daily travel budget in 2013 was about US$20 pp based on 2 travelling together. For US$60 a day you can enjoy a good deal more comfort. Allow for much higher costs in Galápagos, at jungle lodges, in upmarket hotels in main cities and at resorts. Bus travel is cheap, about US$1 per hr, flights cost 5 to 10 times as much as buses for the same route.

An **International Student Identity Card** (ISIC) may help you obtain discounts when travelling. ISIC cards are sold in Quito by **Idiomas Travel**, Roca 130 y 12 de Octubre, p 2, T02-250 0264. They need proof of full-time enrolment in Ecuador or abroad (minimum 20 hrs per week), 2 photos, passport and US$20.

Opening hours

Banks open Mon-Fri 0900-1600. **Government offices** variable hours Mon-Fri, but many close for lunch. **Other offices** 0900-1230, 1430-1800. **Shops** 0900-1900; close at midday in smaller towns, open till 2100 on the coast.

Public holidays

There is no hard and fast rule for public holidays which fall on a weekday. They are sometimes moved – often at the last moment – to make a long weekend (*un puente*); ask around in advance.

1 Jan New Year's Day;
Feb/Mar Carnival: Mon and Tue before Lent.
Mar/Apr Easter (Holy Thu, Good Fri, Holy Sat).
1 May: Labour Day.
24 May: Battle of Pichincha, Independence.
10 Aug: first attempt to gain the Independence of Quito.
9 Oct: Independence of Guayaquil.
2 Nov: All Souls' Day.
3 Nov: Independence of Cuenca.
6 Dec: Foundation of Quito.
25 Dec: Christmas Day.

Safety

Public safety is an important concern throughout mainland Ecuador; Galápagos is generally safe. Armed robbery, bag snatching and slashing, and holdups along the country's highways are among the most significant hazards. 'Express kidnapping', whereby victims are taken from ATM to ATM and forced to withdraw money, is a threat in major cities, and fake taxis (sometimes yellow official-looking ones, sometimes unmarked *taxis ejecutivos*) are often involved. Radio taxis are usually safer.

Secure your belongings at all times, be wary of con tricks, avoid crowds and congested urban transport, and travel only during the daytime. It is the larger cities which call for the greatest care. Small towns and the countryside in the highlands are generally safer than the coast or the jungle. Enquire about the current public safety situation before travelling to Lago Agrio or the Cuyabeno Wildlife Reserve.

Drug use or purchase in Ecuador is punishable by up to 16 years' imprisonment.

Ecuador's active volcanoes are spectacular, but have occasionally threatened nearby communities. The **National Geophysics Institute** provides daily updates at **www.igepn.edu.ec**.

Tax
Airport taxes Departure tax is included in the ticket price: Quito, US$17 for domestic flights, US$60 for international; Guayaquil, US$5 for domestic, US$30 for international.
VAT/IVA 12%, may be reclaimed on departure if you show official invoices with your name and passport number. High surtaxes apply to imported luxury items.

Telephone
International phone code: +593. Calling within Ecuador dial the area code plus 7 digits when calling land lines, 09 plus 8 digits when calling mobiles. For local calls from a land line omit the area code. Calling from abroad, omit the 0 from the area code. Public phone offices are called *cabinas*. Roaming may not work with foreign mobile phones; for local use it is best to buy an Ecuadorean chip (US$6).

Time
Official time is GMT -5 (Galápagos, -6).

Tipping
In better restaurants 10% service may be included in the bill. In cheaper restaurants, tipping is uncommon but welcome. Taxi drivers do not expect a tip. Airport porters, US$1-2, depending on the number of cases they carry.

Tourist information
Ministerio de Turismo, El Telégrafo E7-58 y Los Shyris, Quito, T1-800-887476, www.ecuador.travel. Local offices are given throughout the book. The ministry has a Public Prosecutors Office where serious complaints should be reported.

Useful websites
www.ecuador.travel A good introduction.
www.ecuador.com; **www.quitoadventure. com** and **www.explored.com.ec** General guides with information about activities and national parks.
www.ecuadorexplorer.com; **www.ecuador-travel-guide.org**; **www.ecuaworld.com** and **www.the bestofecuador.com** Travel guides; the last one includes volunteering options.
www.journeylatinamerica.co.uk.
www.southamericaadventuretours.com.
www.saexplorers.org South American Explorers, has information about volunteering.
www.paginasamarillas.info.ec, **www. edina.com.ec** and **www.guiatelefonica. com.ec** Telephone directories.

Visas and immigration

All visitors to Ecuador must have a passport valid for at least 6 months and an onward or return ticket, but the latter is seldom asked for. Citizens of some Middle Eastern, Asian and African countries require a visa to visit Ecuador, other tourists do not require a visa unless they wish to stay more than 90 days. Upon entry all visitors must complete an international embarkation/disembarkation card. Keep your copy, you will be asked for it when you leave.

Note You are required by Ecuadorean law to carry your passport at all times. Whether or not a photocopy is an acceptable substitute is at the discretion of the individual police officer. Tourists are not permitted to work under any circumstances.

Length of stay Tourists are granted 90 days upon arrival and there are no extensions except for citizens of the Andean Community of Nations. Visitors are not allowed back in the country if they have already stayed 90 days during the past 12 months. If you want to spend more time studying, volunteering, etc, you can get a purpose-specific visa (category '12-IX', about US$200 and paperwork) at the end of your 90 days as a tourist. There is no fine at present (subject to change) for overstaying but you will have difficulties

on departure and may be barred from returning to Ecuador. **Policía Nacional de Migración** (immigration police) have offices in all provincial capitals. Visas for longer stays are issued by the **Ministerio de Relaciones Exteriores** (Foreign Office), through their diplomatic representatives abroad and administered in Quito by the **Dirección General de Asuntos Migratorios** and the **Dirección Nacional de Extranjería**. Visa information is found at www.mmrree.gob.ec.

Weights and measures

Mostly metric, US gallons for petrol, some English measures for hardware and weights and some Spanish measures for produce.

INDEX